The ABC's of FISHING

by Bob Zwirz

Digest Books, Inc., Northfield, Illinois

EDITORIAL DIRECTOR
JACK LEWIS

PRODUCTION EDITOR
BOB SPRINGER

RESEARCH EDITOR
MARK THIFFAULT

ART DIRECTOR
ANDY GRENNELL

STAFF ARTISTS
PAT HOPPER
AL MORA
KATHERINE MALONE

PRODUCTION COORDINATOR
JUDY K. RADER

PRODUCTION ASSISTANT
WENDY L. WISEHART

ASSOCIATE PUBLISHER
SHELDON FACTOR

Produced by

Charger Productions

CONTENTS

INTRODUCTION

It is near inconceivable to many foreigners that we in the United States have such an interesting variety of fishing — most of it free.

One of the greatest assets of our democratic ideology lies in the fact that thousands of miles of rivers and streams are kept open to public angling. The same is essentially true of the majority of our lakes and impoundments. In a nation such as ours, where recreation claims such a large segment of each family's free time, it is not surprising that fishing has become the number one participation sport.

According to a national survey made by the United States Fish and Wildlife Service, more than 30,000,000 Americans are interested in this great outdoor pastime.

This book has been written to give this vast audience an overall view of the opportunities that await the more informed and versatile outdoorsman and his family. However, as in any sport, it will be the skilled performer that will reap the greatest rewards and, in so doing, find the most enjoyment.

Each chapter deals with a segment of fishing, from its beginnings in America to the more complex subject of tackle and its usage. Most important, we discuss the more sought-after species of fish and the most productive methods for catching them. As an extra bonus, you will read about a number of famous fishing areas, worldwide, that we can personally recommend, having spent enjoyable times in all hot spots mentioned in the various chapters.

It is our profound hope that when you have finished reading this book you will have gained some knowledge, and the desire to experience it all yourself. For it is in the doing that we are able to build experience, and experience, you will find, is the all-important key to skill.

Bob Zwirz

Chapter 1

Fishing In These United States Began
As A Need, Later Becoming A Sport

HOW IT BEGAN

FORTUNATELY FOR CONSERVATION, an appreciable number of people have come to think of fishing as a sport. But it wasn't always that way in America — back in the days of our country's first settlers, fish were considered a survival item and an aid to soil fertilization.

Records show that as far back as the Third Century A.D. some imaginative spirit had the ingenuity to fashion an artificial fly made of feathers and hook that produced the desired result. It caught fish! Methods of casting a line, by hand, were far from unknown in the days of the Pharaohs of Egypt.

Books have been passed down to us from the England of the 1600s that have made it quite clear angling in the British Isles reached a stage of development far more advanced than most of us might imagine.

But it was not until the mid-1800s that angling became anything near the sport as we think of it these days. Credit goes to a small group of dedicated individuals of that era, rather than to an industry or to any coordinated mass-thinking on the subject. It is interesting to examine documents of that period and to be able to trace the evolution of fishing, especially in America, first as a means toward an end, then slowly but surely, as a sport to look forward to in our leisure moments.

The first strides in the field of American sport fishing took place in the field of bait-casting, for the most part down South. Back around 1809, in the state of Kentucky, there lived a clever, dedicated bass angler by the name of George Snyder. While fishing with other members of the famous old Bourbon Angling Club, of which he was president, he wished to have a more practical way of working the line — both when casting the bait and while playing the fish. Being a watchmaker by trade, he was just the man to devise the first workable multiplying reel.

By 1840, others had seen the new invention, perfected it and started the first manufacturing of fishing reels in America. The factory was operated by two brothers, B. F. and J. F. Meek of Frankfort, Kentucky.

Through the years, changes have occurred that have made the bait-casting reel a joy to use and practically free of the old problem of back lash, at least while in reasonably skilled hands. The design is still basically the same.

While America was becoming aware of fishing as relaxation and as a sport, there were great strides being made in England by the advocates of the fly rod. More has been learned and recorded by the fly-fishing fraternity than some are willing to admit. In many ways, the dyed-in-the-wool fly fisherman is the statistician of fresh water angling! Part

Florida tarpon are eager feeders, a fact reflected in the fact that this one has hooked up on author's bait.

entomology, part ichthyology and most assuredly equal parts of wisdom, curiosity and patience go into the general make-up of the skilled angler who fishes with the fly and the fly alone.

Probably the greatest arguments concerning tackle of the mid-1800s took place over the merits of various woods to be used in the making of fly rods. For years there were preferences for greenheart wood, or sometimes lancewood or Bethabora as a substance for making up the long, parabolic sticks of that day. However, William Mitchell, a tackle pioneer of that era reported in "The American Angler" that a man by the name of William Blacker of Soho, London, England, made up a split bamboo fly rod for an American, James Stevens, back around 1851. It seems that Mr. Stevens then was the first man to cast to American waters with a bamboo fly rod.

Within a few years, there were several excellent makers of fly rods here on our shores. They were soon involved with various numbers of strips of bamboo, which when assembled and glued had the desired action; a slow, soft action by our modern standards.

Great names in the history of American tackle had their start in those days — names like Charles Orvis, E. A. Green and Charles Murphy. The Orvis company is still one of America's fine prestige houses and continues to turn out excellent bamboo fly rods that require the skill and patience of dedicated know-how. Large general tackle companies such as Horrocks-Ibbotson of Utica, New York, have been on the American scene for well over one hundred years. By 1870, H. L. Leonard of Bangor, Maine, was producing his still famous line of six-strip bamboo rods for the angling public.

From here on, it was one development after another, both in rod making and in reel and line improvements. Bait-casting made great strides, again due to better tackle and a continual gain in interest on the part of our sportsmen. But, no matter how you evaluate it, there were still just two types of tackle available — fly rod or bait-casting. The spinning rig, on our shores, was still a long way off!

It would seem that the best outdoor writers of the period before World War I, at least in the field of angling, were researchers, historians and, in several cases, prophets. They were prophets most certainly, when we evaluate the works of men such as Emlyn Gill, George LaBranche and Edward R. Hewitt. Their observations and theories, compiled at a time when few were in agreement with them, live on as a monument to their love of angling.

There are many names that reappear through the mists

An indisputable virtue of fishing is that it gives one an excuse to spend time in places of vast scenic grandeur.

of time — names that are a part of a heritage dear to the serious fly fisherman of today. Theodore Gordon cast the first dry-fly on the waters of New York's Beaverkill — the result of Gordon's correspondence with H. M. Halford and G. E. M. Skues, of England, on this subject of the dry-fly. When you consider how few anglers even knew of the dry-fly in the early 1900s, it is wonderful indeed that individual dedication was solely responsible for pertinent research on our American waters.

It has been the tedious, patient entomological studies of men like Gordon, Gill, Hewitt, LaBranche, Jennings and Wetzel that have brought fly fishing to its present degree of acceptance. Without their devotion to the sport, most of us would still be groping in the dark!

Prior to World War II, I spent most of my free time, away from school, wading the streams and rivers of New York, New Hampshire and Maine — and occasionally Pennsylvania. It was a time of life when Spring meant trout and late Summer meant off to the shore for salt water fishing, based at our Summer home on the Jersey coast.

Largemouth bass beckoned while bluefish were starting to move close to the jetties and stripers were feeding along the surf, especially during the early hours before dawn. The decisions that had to be made were, I was certain, earth-shattering: The lily-pad ponds and ol' Funnelmouth on a bait-casting rig, or stripers before dawn.

Occasionally, my great love of the Beaverkill and the East and West Branch of the Delaware would trouble me and I'd make the long haul up to the mountains again to see if that old brown trout was still feeding at the jaws of the Beaverkill and East Branch. World War II solved all my problems of indecision! Sharks on a hand line — barracuda in the South Pacific — these were the best we could manage for quite a long spell.

Bright sun, clean air, booming surf and voracious finny clients. How could you possibly ask for more?

If this angler had ever complained about too many fisherman along the river before the war, he had quite a shock coming within a few years of war's end.

Things were afoot in Europe that were to have quite an effect on the number of anglers that were to look to fishing as a new and exciting recreation. It was the spinning reel. "Lancer leger" means light casting, in the language of the French. Call it what you wish, threadline or fixed-spool — it's all spinning in one form or another, here in America!

To say that spinning enjoys popularity in this country today is like saying that children generally like ice cream. Most of our nation's anglers own a spinning outfit, fish with one and wouldn't be without it. When first introduced in the late Forties, it caught on like wildfire among those new to the world of fishing.

It was found that almost anyone could learn to cast with a spinning reel and rod in about thirty minutes. At least, well enough to be able to go out on a piece of water — tie on a shiny lure, cast and be hooked to a startled fish that was as surprised as most of the inexperienced anglers. By 1956 it looked as though the coffee grinders, as they were often called, would take over completely. Fortunately they have not — and will not.

Like any method of fishing, spinning has a definite place in the scheme of things. A place where ease of handling, fine light line and delicate lures must be used and manipu-

Time spent in surroundings such as these is nutritious to the soul. If you catch fish, that's purely a bonus!

lated with finesse. The vast majority of anglers own and use a spinning outfit, but it is a certainty that the more advanced, knowledgeable group has swung back to a realization that it is no more than a valuable tool among other valuable tools.

The larger bass plugs used in the backwaters of the South, the heavier jigs used in the Tennessee Valley Authority or heavy white water areas and the weed-choked maze of many muskie lakes call for a bait-casting outfit. Bass-bugging with a fly rod is still the wonderful sport it was before the advent of spinning. Trout and salmon will always be traditional fly rod fish, not because someone insists on this usage, but simply because it is more fun on a fly rod and more satisfying sport.

Each type of tackle, each lure, has a place in the vast network of modern angling as it exists today in both fresh and salt water.

The wise outdoorsman will study the use of all methods and then, with practice, come to use each with skill at the correct time and in the proper place.

The world of fishing is a fascinating one! It is a world of never-ending surprises, of never completely learned lessons, and, most of all, it is a never-ending phantasmagoria of excitement, beauty and nature at its very best.

One last word — look forward to your hours on the water as moments well spent in a world that has become a little too frantic, a little too preoccupied with oft-times dangerous philosophies. Stand knee deep along the swirling boulder-strewn course of a favorite river, or along the shore of some deserted oceanside beach, and close your eyes for just a moment! Relax, unwind and think back to the days of Gordon, of the camaraderie of such men as Hewitt, LaBranche and Heilner, the contentment it brought to their lives.

Remember them, nod to the past and take up where they and so many other greats left off.

Skimming down a limpid Canadian river amid the lusty growth of a Northern Spring: Getting there's half the fun.

Chapter 2

FUNDAMENTALS OF FISHING

A Great Deal Of Angling Success Depends On Knowledge Of Fishing Equipment And Its Proper Usage!

FOR THE UNINITIATED, that individual who never has fished before, he soon will learn that the sport is largely a matter of semantics. Terms change in meaning from one geographical area to another, or a term that explains some facet in angling in one area may be an unknown quantity in another.

Such lack of standardization creates problems in writing a book such as this, but we have done our best to cover such probabilities, attempting to explain the various name changes and meanings in broad terms.

One of the best answers to this, of course, is to find yourself a tackle shop with an experienced, knowledgeable proprietor or manager. He can answer most of your questions of a semantics nature, as well as advising on the technicalities, helping to choose tackle that will suit you best in the area in which you intend to fish.

In writing the book, I have attempted to make each chapter self-inclusive, yet the truth of the matter is that each chapter could, in itself, be expanded into a full-length book...and many of these subjects have been developed into books. When you learn the direction in which you choose to go angling-wise, I would suggest you learn more about your chosen facet by checking that tackle shop for more information on the specific subject. Again, the manager or proprietor can be of great help in getting you started with

the best, not to mention the correct, information on any specific type of fishing.

If you are new to the sport of fishing, one of the problems you face is what to buy in the way of tackle. Depending upon whom you've been talking to, you've learned that there are three or four basic forms of fishing — fly-casting, spinning, spin-casting (which many consider just a variation of spinning), and bait or plug-casting.

You'll notice that each of these fishing styles has its advocates and the advice you've been receiving in regards to tackle often seems contradictory and confusing. So, let's just try and work our way through the twin mazes of advice and tackle available to you and see if we can help you make an intelligent selection of both.

Tackle is simply the equipment — rod, reel, line, lures, et al. — that you will need to successfully hook, play and land fish. The type of tackle you purchase will depend on two things: the type of fishing you plan to do and the amount of money you have to invest in tackle. One word of caution, though: With fishing tackle, as with anything else in life, what you get is what you pay for. Get the most for your money, but shop wisely.

All four types of tackle are used in both fresh water and salt water angling. What we are trying to do here is take a brief look at each so you can decide which type of tackle is

Fly fishing is the most difficult of all methods to master, but in some areas it's the only presentation that lawfully can be used. In some Nova Scotia waters, anglers not using fly tackle can be fined when taking sea trout like this one.

going to best suit your own needs.

Let's start with fly fishing tackle. In fly fishing, practically weightless lures such as artificial flies, bass bugs, streamers and a few natural insects are used. These are made from feathers, bucktails — made from the tail hairs of a buck or doe deer — furs, et al., and tied onto various-size hooks according to intended usage.

Since these lures aren't heavy enough to be cast by their own weight, the line used in fly-casting supplies the needed weight. In fly-casting, unlike the other methods we'll be discussing, you cast the line, not the lure.

The rod used in fly fishing is long and light with a fast or wavy — parabolic or semi-parabolic — action. The term, action, refers to the degree of flexibility in the rod blank. You impart the power for your cast by flexing the action of the rod with a motion closely akin to a parabolic arc.

Fly rods generally run between seven to ten feet in length, but for a newcomer to fly fishing I would suggest a rod between 7½ and eight feet. You'll notice that fly rods are made from split bamboo, tubular glass fibers or graphite shafts. All of these rod types do their job well so the choice is a matter of your personal taste. Notice, when you are looking at fly rods, that the line guides are close together and there are more of them on the rod than on a spinning or casting rod. This is to keep your line close to the rod so

that when a strike is made and the rod flexes, the bend is under equal pressure along the entire rod length. The close guides also allow the line to cast freely.

Perhaps the most important piece of equipment in your fly fishing tackle is the line. This is because you literally cast the line in fly fishing and it must have the necessary weight to carry your cast. The line also must bring out the action of your rod. As you flex your rod back and forth, the weight of the line beyond the rod tip is working the rod and producing the power needed to cast the line.

I suggest starting your fly fishing career by using a double taper line. It is just what its name implies. Throughout its length, a double taper line goes from thin to thick to thin, to balance with the action of your rod.

While all line comes marked (AFTMA) so you can match it to your rod — the result being matched or balanced tackle — I personally feel that most anglers use too light a fly line. The recommendations of the manufacturers are made for ideal casting conditions, which somehow rarely seem to occur in the field. If you feel that your rod and line aren't balanced, go to the next heavier weight of line; chances are, your problems will be solved. Remember: For every angler using too heavy a fly line, a hundred others are using too light a line.

If you're going to be fishing mostly wet flies and

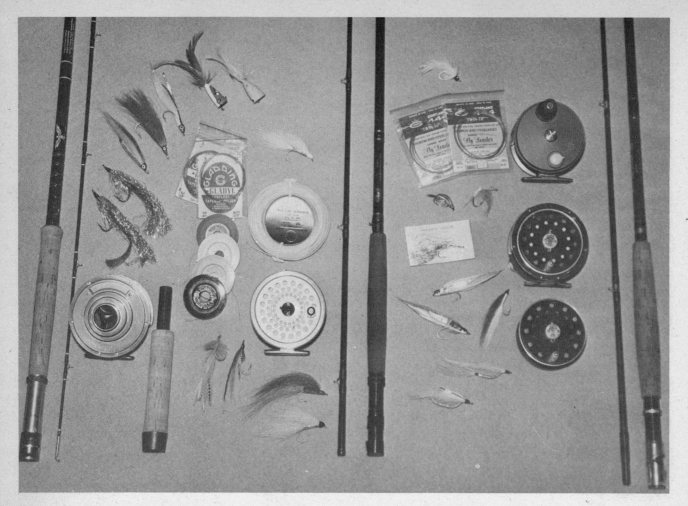

These three fly fishing outfits which the author has assembled can cover a variety of fishing conditions and targets. Primarily geared toward salt water or large fresh water gamefish, these outfits have proved capable of standing the gaff. Each fly fishing advocate must assess his own particular fishing situation, then use tackle matched to that area.

nymphs, it's worth your while to purchase a sinking fly line, or one which has a sinking tip. Conversely, if you're fishing dries, then a floating fly line should be your pick. No matter which you choose or your particular style of fly-casting, there are going to be times when you'll pull your hair: like when you're fishing dries and the fish are down deep. Or when you're fishing wet flies way down and the lunkers are frothing the surface, feeding on dropping insects.

An important consideration the novice fly-caster should note is that fly lines won't always act as they're supposed to. Such things as water temperature and condition play a big part on the actions of your line. If the water is roily, your floating fly line won't float. It's the same story when the water temperature rises into the mid-seventies or higher, often found when tempting a mess of bluegills, crappie or inshore salt water rogues.

Regardless of the type you desire, purchase the best you can afford. It tends to get expensive but, if treated with respect and occasional cleaning and dressing, it will last a long time.

On the end of your line you'll require a leader. The leader, which will take most of the wear and tear when you're fishing, is made of monofilament nylon and should also be tapered. At the terminal end of the leader you can tie an additional tip of even lighter weight and then tie your fly to this; or tie your fly directly on your leader. This technique allows you some additional flexibility as to terminal-pound test.

Probably the least important piece of equipment in your fly fishing tackle is your reel. I don't mean to imply that you can get by with a piece of junk, just that in fly-casting the line and rod are more important. The reel, in fly-casting, primarily is used to store the line, which is stripped

WEIGHT FORWARD (WF)

LEVEL LINE (L)

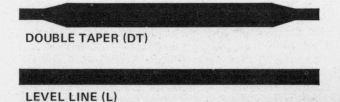

DOUBLE TAPER (DT)

14

The wide variety of fly rods currently on the market is shown by this sampling from the Browning Company. Varying in lengths, weights and materials, the angler must match his rod with his flies and fly line.

Many fly-casters prefer the hollow fiberglass rods to bamboo, and both work well. Note the reel seat.

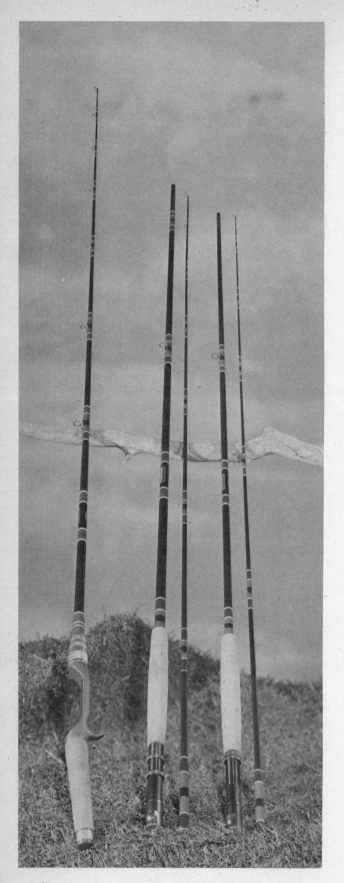

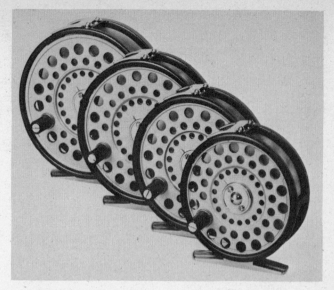

Fly reels, like rods, are sized to the gamefish sought and, while author feels this is least important piece of tackle, care should be taken in its selection. He favors single-action fly reels, as do most other anglers.

This Fly'r-4 reel from Browning is a good example of a lightweight specimen used when after the lighter panfish and small bass found in the nation's lakes and rivers.

off when needed for casting and retrieved when not needed. Exceptions to this statement are when fishing for some of the heftier species of salt water gamefish, like the tarpon, bonefish or Atlantic salmon. These situations do require a top quality reel — with a reliable drag system — since these fish are played off the reel!

There are three types of fly reels: automatic, semi-automatic and single-action reel. Most fly fishermen I know will recommend the single-action reel. It is simple to operate and dependable. It weighs about half as much as the average automatic reel and has a greater line capacity. Again, the choice is up to you.

Fly-casting tackle gives the angler a tremendous range of lures to choose from, again depending on the type fish he is after. It is ideal for small wet flies, dry flies, artificial nymphs, streamers or bucktails. You also can handle small

The difference between a one-piece bait-casting rod (left) and the two-piece fly rods is easily seen in the above photo. Both have their particular uses in angling.

This close-up of a Daiwa Model 254 gives a good image of a fly fishing reel. Note knob for click mechanism.

The Air Cel line of fly lines from Scientific Anglers has been used by many for years. As noted on packet, this will fit all rods shorter than 8½ feet and it should be matched to the rod. See text for details.

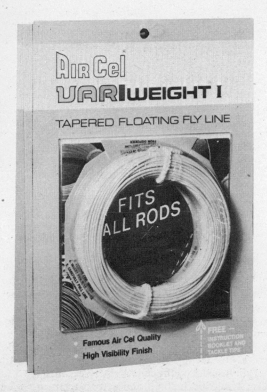

bass-bugs, including the slightly bulky but light ones dressed with cork or hair bodies, as well as such light baits as very small worms, minnows, crickets, grasshoppers, grubs, salamanders, very small frogs, small strip baits, small dough balls and other such lures which have very little bulk or weight. You even can try the tiny wobbling spoons and spinners, along with very light spinner and fly or spinner and bait combinations.

Just remember, however, the heavier the lure, the less suitable it's going to be for fly-casting. Anytime you get to lures weighing 1/32 of an ounce you are getting out of the fly-casting range. I should mention that a fly-casting rig is great for special trolling situations, even if you are using lures somewhat heavier than those we've mentioned.

While fly-casting originally was used just to take trout or salmon, it's now considered the most sporting method for taking any fresh water or salt water fish that will strike an artificial lure. Salt water fly fishing has been around for nearly a century, but it's only during the past ten or fifteen years that the sport zoomed into its present popularity. During the 1880s, Julian and A. W. Dimock hooked, fought and boated tarpon on fly rods from Fort Myers to the Homosassa River on Florida's west coast, but except for

This large variety of rubber insect imitations shows what's available in the line of baits, although not all are suitable for fly-casting. Presentation of lightweight, small bugs is a proven method of taking sluggish bass and other gamefish.

brief flurries of interest from time to time, salt water fly fishing remained dormant until recent years.

Salt water fly fishing requires no new equipment except a salt water type fly line and possibly more rods. I would suggest a torpedo-head fly line since it is easier to cast into the wind. Most salt water fly fishermen I know prefer nylon lines of the type produced by such outfits as Scientific Anglers or 3M.

Due to the larger size and greater energy of salt water gamefish, as compared to fresh water black bass and trout, it's a good idea to back your fly line with some other line, such as one hundred yards of braided nylon or dacron line. No matter what type of line you use or how you back it, don't forget to clean it in fresh water and dress it with a good fly line dressing and cleaner each time you use it in salt water.

For lures, try streamer flies and bass bugs made of balsa and bucktail for southern waters. A small spinner will be a helpful addition if you're fishing between Virginia and Maine. If you're going for shad in the tidal waters of Chesapeake Bay's tributaries, try a black-and-white fly tied on a long shank hook with a hackle at both ends. Generally speaking, however, black, brown, yellow or white streamer

flies — sometimes with a touch of red — will do the job in most localities.

Flies used by the angler fall into three basic categories: Wets, dries and nymphs. Streamer flies are the largest and heaviest, and are tied from chicken-neck hackle feathers. Bucktails are constructed of the tail hairs of the buck or doe deer and are somewhat lighter than streamer flies.

Wet flies should be small, about the size of an underwater insect that either is drowned or hatching. Sparsely tied so they sink readily, the wet flies imitate the aquatic stages of mayflies, stone flies and the caddis fly, these being a major food source for nearly all types of gamefish.

Wet flies should be presented in across-stream casts. They then drift downstream slightly and are retrieved in short jumps and hops across or near the surface when the water is slightly off-color. When the water is clear, wet flies should be allowed to drift with the current.

Dry flies are imitations of aquatic insects in their flying stages, and also terrestrial critters which haplessly get caught on the waters. It is an absolute must to match the size and color of your dry fly with the insect it is meant to imitate, or you'll spend a long, fruitless day casting.

Dry flies should be cast up and across-stream in most

This assortment of salt water flies, streamers and bucktails has been used with tremendous results by Zwirz. Note shrimp imitations (bottom row).

Dry flies imitate flying insects that alight on waters, and usually are employed when after trout in fresh water. They fool some big fish!

A bushy, buggy appearance has been the medicine needed to lure finicky fish into striking, especially after they've been bombarded with offerings from anglers.

cases, and their presentation should be gentle; like real insects alighting on the surface. Most gamefish spook at sudden movements, such as a fly hitting the surface like a rock. Occasionally, a downstream cast, letting the fly wend its way unfettered or unhindered, takes fish.

To keep the fly floating, it should be treated with one of the commercially available fly dope solutions on the market. If you want the fly to sink, use a wet fly or a nymph.

Nymphs are pretty much the same as wet flies, except they are tied to represent an underwater nymph. Sometimes they imitate the aquatic stage of a flying insect, on which fish feed. Sparsely tied to sink quickly and deeply, they are

fished in much the same manner as the wet flies mentioned previously.

Any streamer flies and bucktails you procure should resemble baitfish, the most common size being a small minnow. Trout are partial to streamer flies at nearly any time, and big bass just can't seem to let such an easy meal escape. And, bass show a real liking for the big, bushy bass bugs, when presented in a lifelike manner, especially if they've been deluged with other offerings from anglers.

In making the decision of whether or not to purchase fly fishing tackle, the prospective angler should give some consideration to the area he intends using such gear. For

These wet flies are some of the deadliest of all when it comes to taking Atlantic salmon in Nova Scotia. Fished early in the season, the bits of tinsel aid in attraction in the roily, often muddy waters. They sink quickly to reach feeders.

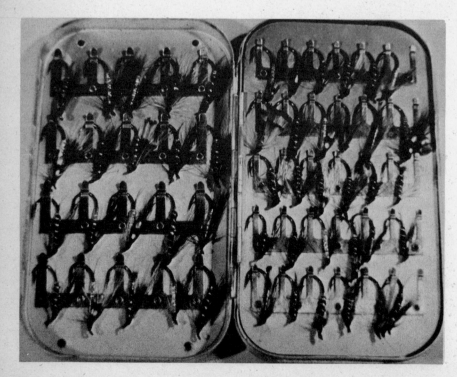

Clip-type pouches are fine for the transporting of wet flies, but they play hob with dries as they flatten the hackles. Pouch fits in pocket.

As the fly-caster actually casts his line instead of fly, he must whip the line out to appropriate distance. This is done by stripping line from reel with left hand and feeding it to the tip by whipping action of rod, as shown at left and below. Note the position of casting elbow: close in by the trunk throughout casting.

Picking fly up off water is done as shown below, with a hoisting of rod arm to get the line moving upwards.

LINE ILLUSTRATIONS COURTESY OF GARCIA

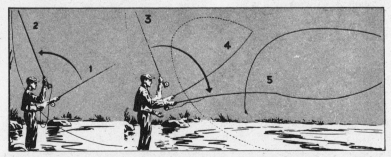

The roll cast, as shown at left, is used by most anglers. As rod is raised, line rolls off to one side and its weight, plus speed of rod descending toward water, flips it out.

example, if the novice is limited to brushy, narrow streams around his home, perhaps one of the other fishing combinations would be of better use. Unless the fly-caster is skilled, his back-cast will become entangled in the brush at streamside repeatedly, and he'll end up spending more time retrieving flies from the trees and bushes than fishing. This also tends to dampen his enthusiasm for fly fishing.

Wind is another problem for the prospective fly fisher-

man. Casting the lightweight flies during a healthy blow is next to impossible for the beginner, and necessitates usage of different fly lines. Consequently, if you reside in an area where dust-devils kick up the sod with some degree of regularity and forcefulness, perhaps another type of tackle will fit your needs.

Fly fishing in the purest sense requires a great deal from the sport's practitioners. Besides using somewhat more

Zwirz, a master of the fly fishing arts, demonstrates the proper usage of a roll cast while after tarpon feeding near the banks of this cove. Great casting distance can be attained without disturbing fish. Check the leader frequently for wear.

complicated tackle, a more in-depth knowledge of the fish sought is required, if one is to score with any amount of regularity. And, the way a newcomer is going to learn about diet, holding water, peak fishing periods, barometric and solunar influence, and the myriad other little details that go into the makeup of a successful fly fisherman is through reading — lots of it.

Knowledge, coupled with experience in learning the basics of handling the ofttimes unwieldly tackle, are requirements. If you don't see yourself as ready to devote the necessary time to this end, try one of the other fishing combinations listed in this chapter. While all require proficiency with the chosen tackle, much of the gamefish knowledge already is on hand.

Now let's jump to the opposite extreme of fly-casting and take a look at bait/plug-casting tackle. Bait tackle differs from fly-casting in that the bait or lures are heavy enough to be cast by their own weight and do not require a heavy line. Bait-casting line is relatively light and, when cast, is drawn off the reel spool by the weight of the bait or plug.

Bait-casting rods range from 4½ to seven feet in length. The rods can be made of bamboo, fiberglass or graphite and the reel has a revolving spool which is controlled by the angler. You'll notice, too, that the reel is mounted on top of the reel seat, opposite of fly or open face spinning gear which hangs downward. The rod handle on a bait-casting rod can be either straight or off-set. The choice is yours as to which handles easiest.

For bait-casting you should have fifty yards of mono or nylon line with a tensile strength of nine to eighteen pounds, depending on what type of fish you are after, along with an assortment of artificial lures with one or more hooks attached.

Ideally, you should have two bait-casting reels. One would be for open-water use for fish from two to ten pounds. With a rig like this, you should be able to cast lures from 1/8 ounce up to 5/8 ounce. The second reel would take care of really big fish and for those times when you are casting outsized lures. This second reel also would be used when you are trolling or fishing for salt water gamefish.

Bait-casting plugs come in a dizzying array of shapes and perform in a wide variety of actions. Some dive, wobble, make noise, disturb the surface, run fast or a combination of these, all of which have taken their share of both fresh and salt water gamefish. Most plugs average around one-half ounce, are made of plastic or wood and painted to resemble some food type fish are fond of.

While the fact is disputed, I personally feel that color plays an important part in whether a fish strikes a plug or

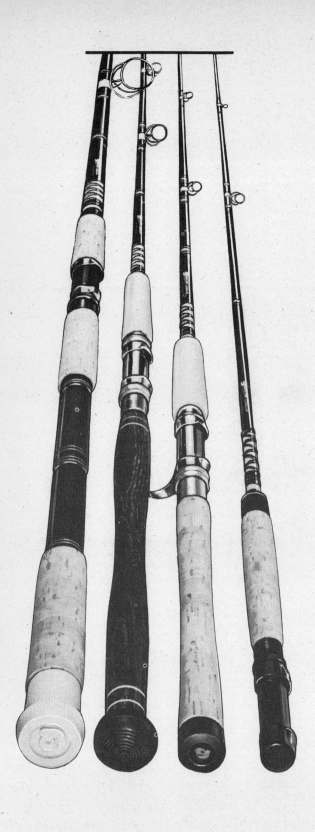
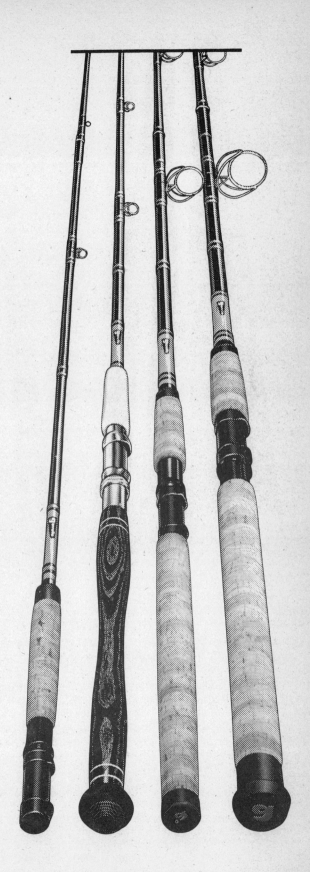

The assortment of heavy-duty salt water rods from Garcia
(above and right) have found wide angling application.
They of necessity are constructed of heavy materials
to cope with the punishment only big fish can dispense.

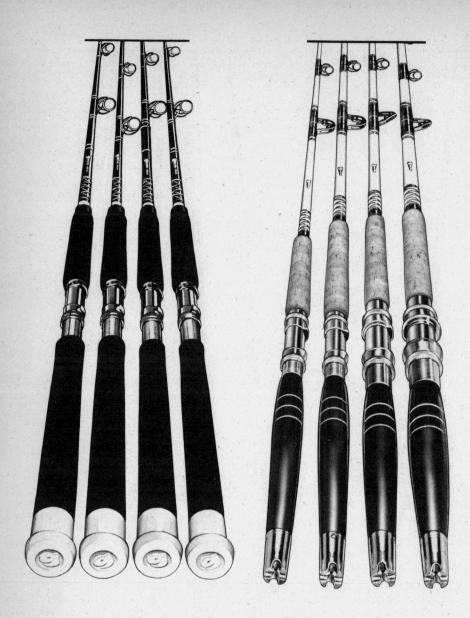

As can be seen, Garcia recognizes individual preferences in angling equipment. Some like fatter handle or close-to-butt guides, while some salt water buffs don't.

watches it pass in disgust. It is known that fish see contrast, so plugs with contrasting coloration should look like a wounded food source.

Plugs are divided into two categories: those with and without weedless hooks. When fishing in shallow waters, or where there is an abundance of underwater obstacles which could tend to hang up the lure, the weedless hook is in its element.

It really is simple in construction, with just a piece of wire from the body of the plug over the barb of the hook, sheltering it from the snags waiting below. When a fish strikes, the wire is moved out of the way, so the barb is free to bury itself in the mouth of the attacker.

Plugs without weedless hooks usually are the surface disturbers or deep-diving models. The former are constructed to attract fish through the noise and disturbance they make on the top of the water, resembling wounded baitfish, terrestrial critters like mice or frogs, or even bats. The deep-diving plugs float on the surface when not retrieved. When the angler starts cranking, under they go; the harder he reels, the deeper the plug dives. Should it hang up, putting some slack in the line usually enables it to float free.

Spoons also have taken a great toll on gamefish. This wobbling metal creation often is adorned with a feather or strip of pork rind which, when combined with the flash from the metal, attracts fish.

Spinners, on the other hand, attract fish from the action of either a single or twin propellers, located near the head and at the tail. Sometimes the wires holding the propellers are adorned with bright colored beads. Both spinners and spoons must be retrieved the instant they hit the water, or they will sink and become entangled in the bottom growth. Their height in the water is regulated by the speed of the retrieve, plus rod tip action.

Undoubtedly, the biggest single drawback of the bait-casting rig — and the one that led to the popularity of spinning and spin-casting tackle — is its proneness to backlash, often called "professional overrun" by fishing experts. Bait-casting requires the most angling skill of any method next to fly fishing, because of the level-wind reel design.

The thumb is used to control the amount of line removed during a cast. As the plug shoots through the air, the spool gets to revolving rapidly as the line peels off and, if the angler doesn't stop the spool with his thumb when the

Some of the guesswork has been alleviated for novice anglers, as some makers package balanced outfits.

Bait-casting reels run from what is termed conventional (far left) to heavier salt water and finally to big game reels (right). Components also increase in strength.

plug reaches its destination, the spool continues to whirl and the result is a magnificent snarl. But, as you become more proficient with the use of this tackle, it happens less frequently.

Newcomers to the world of plug-casting often have difficulty with the erratic rod action necessary for the alternate fast and slow reeling, and the energetic popping and manipulation of the plugs for a lifelike presentation. But, the sore muscles will subside and, if you persevere, you soon will master the art of bait-casting.

One of its best uses lies in the trolling method. On most level-wind reels there is a small lever or push button which activates a click mechanism. After you've stripped off the proper amount of line, the click is activated, which keeps just enough pressure on the line to keep more from slipping off the spool. It allows you to rest the rod in the boat while paddling, and also acts as a drag when a fish is hooked.

In between fly and bait-casting is spinning. A relatively new innovation in the United States — it became popular after World War II — spinning dates back to the early 1900s, when the first stationary-spool spinning reel for public use was designed by Holden Illingworth in England.

The idea behind spinning tackle is that monofilament or light braided line can be cast off a fixed or non-revolving, open face spool easier and to longer distances with weighted lures than with any other type of tackle. This is because all possible friction is eliminated.

You can test this by holding a spool of thread by one end and pulling the thread of the other end. It will come off in a spiral with much less friction than if the spool were to revolve as the thread comes off it. This is the reason spinning tackle can cast small, compact, weighted lures with ease and for greater distances.

Spinning tackle basically is intermediate equipment — between the lightweight fly and heavier bait-casting tackle. You use it primarily for casting light lures. If you should decide on spinning tackle, for average-type situations, your rod should be between six and 7½ feet in length. Spinning rods of split bamboo will weigh between 3½ and five ounces, while the weights of rods made of fiberglass or graphite will vary according to the wall thickness and the length of the rod.

You can identify a spinning rod by the long cork handle. Some of these run up to twenty-six inches in length. The

When after tuna or other super-sized creatures, the series of Garcia's Ambassadeur reels (top) come into play and have aided in wrestling monsters to boatside. The center and bottom rows feature bait and spin-casting reels available to anglers, and note the differences in design. Depending upon your preference, there is something here for any angler.

rod has two sliding rings that hold the reel on the handle and large guides. The first guide, nearest the grip, is particularly large, since it must gather the line as it comes off of the reel when you cast. The rest of the guides will taper down in size toward the tip of the rod. This minimizes friction when you cast.

The open face reel allows the line to flow from the spool without the spool rotating, which practically eliminates backlashes when you're casting. However, if you don't keep the line tight on the reel spool at all times you can get snarls. When the line on the reel is loose, a tight coil will pull off loose coils in a bunch. These will catch and knot together as they pass through the rod guides, resulting in snarls. If you keep your line tight on the spool, and if your spool isn't overloaded with line, you shouldn't have any problems. If it does happen to you, it means you've been careless or, in a rare instance, you have a faulty reel.

You retrieve line onto a spinning reel with a pickup arm, bailer or roller. The line is wound on the spool of the reel as it moves in and out of the reel shell while the pickup arm revolves around the spool.

Spinning line is made of nylon, either braided or, preferably, monofilament. Its breaking strength runs from 1½ to twenty pounds for fresh water fishing and twelve to forty pounds for use in salt water fishing.

What type of lures should you use with your spinning tackle? Well, as an example, for fresh water, fishing lures in the one-quarter ounce range are ideal for use with lines testing from four to eight pounds in strength. You can get lighter lures and ultralight spinning tackle, but I suggest you stay away from these until you get some experience under your belt. These fresh water lures will include spinners, spoons, plugs and bugs. The heavier lures of one-half ounce or more require heavy spinning tackle. With such lures,

These are just three samples of the line often used by bait-casters, depending upon location and gamefish sought. The IGFA line at right is used when after record fish.

spin-casting or bait-casting tackle might serve your purpose better. Heavy lures and spinning tackle are best confined to salt water fishing or for such fresh water whoppers as muskellunge and big pike.

You also can use dry flies with spinning gear by using a plastic float for additional weight. Generally speaking, though, you can use light spinning tackle for trout, bass and panfish in both lakes and streams. Medium tackle is for heavy bass, steelhead and salmon fishing. Heavy tackle normally should be reserved for salt water fish in the heavier/stronger categories.

This brings us to spin-casting. It's a development of the spinning method and many anglers consider it a form of spinning rather than a separate fishing method. While the two are alike in many ways, they are in many other ways quite different. A spin-casting reel is a fixed-spool reel, as is the spinning reel. The spin-casting reel, however, is not open face, but closed face. A small cover or hood covers the front of the reel, concealing the line.

The line emerges from the reel through a small hole or eyelet in the center of the cover. This causes the spin-

Salt water lures that are favorites of the author include this eel rig and baitfish imitation rig. Silver tubes of latter imitate baitfish, while eel is sought always.

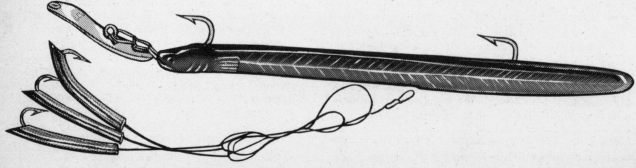

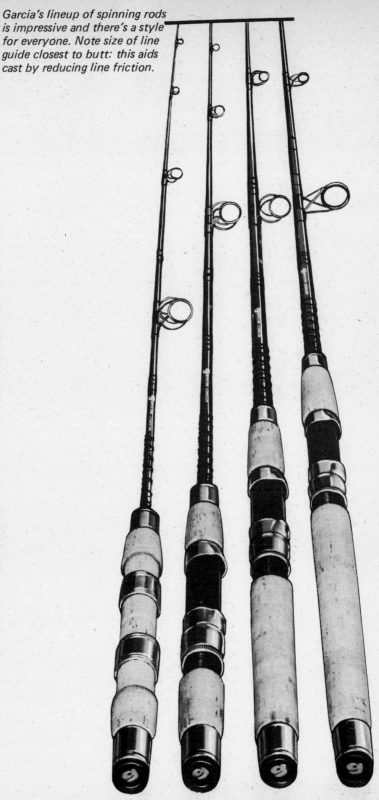

Garcia's lineup of spinning rods is impressive and there's a style for everyone. Note size of line guide closest to butt: this aids cast by reducing line friction.

Spinning outfits are favored by many anglers because of presentation ease. Rods like this Browning work well.

casting reel to cast with more friction than a spinning reel. This makes it somewhat less suitable for casting very light lures. When you cast, the line is released by a thumb trigger and is retrieved by a device that revolves as you turn the handle. Personally, I feel that for the most accurate casting, an open face unit is superior.

While the line used for spin-casting is the same as is used for straight spinning, you do have a choice when it comes to picking a rod. Spin-casting reels work equally well with either a spinning rod or a bait-casting rod. One big advantage of spin-casting is that you can use the heavier lures usually reserved for plug-casters without worrying about backlash. However, as is the case with spinning gear, you have to watch for snarls, although spin-casting tackle is less apt to do this.

You can use spin-casting gear in the light and medium

Recognizing the problem of transportation, Browning has developed a rod system for spinning enthusiasts that breaks down to just over butt size (left). As noted by the above photo, that company also presents a wide selection for spinners. Hollow glass costs more money.

class for every species of fish in America with the exception of Atlantic salmon, where it isn't allowed. Your fresh water medium-size outfit will serve for most of your light salt water spin-casting fishing as well.

Since we are discussing your first selection of tackle, perhaps a word or two is in order here on how to take care of it.

If you decide on a fiberglass rod, you'll discover they need little care. All you really have to do is clean them with a wet, soapy cloth. Before you assemble the rod, rub the male ferrule in your hair or against your nose to oil it slightly. Don't, I repeat, don't use machine oil: if you use too much or too heavy an oil, it will increase the suction and make the ferrules difficult, if not next to impossible, to pull apart.

If you can't seat the male ferrule properly, the cause is either dirt or corrosion. Use a pipe cleaner and some lighter

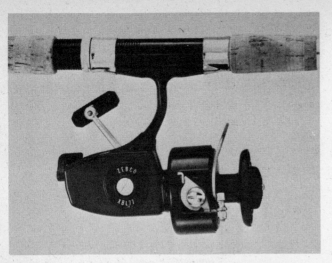

Most spinning reels are similar in design, with minor differences of the maker's preference. This is Zebco's Model XBL77 open face spinning reel in black finish.

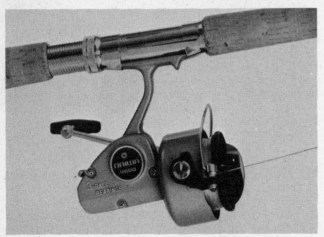

Daiwa's 8600 Model spinning reel features three-ball bearing operation for trouble-free casting. Most will spool more than 100 yards of nylon or monofilament line.

As with most Daiwa reels, the lever at rear of reel is moved to activate click mechanism, heard during retrieve. In this case, it's on a black-finished Model 4300 reel.

The Japanese have a way of taking American ideas and streamlining them into a better and cheaper-costing item and reels are no exception. This Model 8100 is sturdy!

Daiwa's Model 8300 features two-ball bearings, anodized gears and rigid construction. With care, a reel like this will outlast most anglers and be used by grandchildren!

fluid to swab out the inside of the female ferrule and polish the male ferrule.

Check your rod windings to make sure they aren't starting to fray. If they are fraying, a drop of lacquer on your finger, rubbed lightly onto the winding to coat it should do the trick. In some cases, two or three applications of lacquer may be called for.

When you disassemble your rod, always use a pulling motion rather than a twisting one. If the ferrules stick badly, clean them.

Dirt and fish slime on your rod grips harm nothing except the rod's appearance. Use a soapy scrub brush or fine wire soap pad to clean them.

Reels should give you little trouble unless you manage to damage them, but you do have to clean and oil them once in a while. If you choose a fly reel, just remove the spool

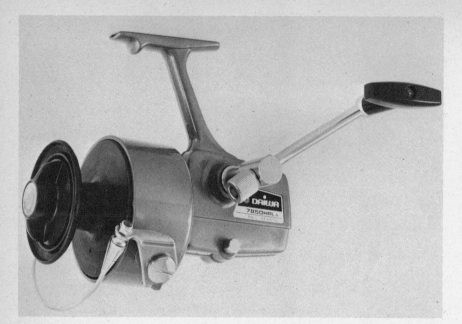

Note the difference in the reel handles between this Daiwa (left) and Penn (above). Pick your favorite.

from the reel housing and clean the inside with a slightly oily cloth or a small brush. Put a dab of Vaseline or reel grease on the gears. The more complicated reels should be handled according to the instructions that come with them, so hang onto the instruction folders.

While spinning and plug-casting lines can be left on reel spools indefinitely, fly lines are another matter. You should remove them at the end of the fishing season, coil loosely and hang them in a plastic bag in a cool, dark closet. If your fly lines become sticky, rub them with talcum powder. You also should rub them with line dressing as often as necessary to keep them pliant and capable of fast-shooting.

The monofilament spinning and plug-casting lines which you leave on the reel spools may be stiff and wiry after being stored for a while. To make them limp again, tie a

fishhook to the forward end and hook it to a stump or branch. Then walk backwards until you have all your castable line off of the reel. A couple of pulls will remove the stiffness and also help test your line for weak spots.

You should hang onto any broken lures, since they can be repaired or new ones fashioned from them. If the blades of your unpainted spoons or spinners become corroded, polish them with mud, metal polish or crocus cloth, which is like extremely fine sandpaper. You can varnish polished lures to prevent tarnish. A dull lure may be better on bright days or when the water is low, so polish them only when it's necessary and don't lacquer them.

Check the sharpness of your hooks frequently, remove any rust and touch up the barbs and points. Damaged hooks should be disposed of carefully where bare feet and

Spin-casting equipment resulted in a 20-pound muskie for this happy Canadian angler (left). Muskies also have been boated with spinning tackle, like Daiwa at top.

animals can't come in contact with them.

Since you've invested good money in your tackle, an ounce of prevention is worth a pound of cure in its maintenance and will add years to its life.

While we have discussed fly-casting, spinning, spin-casting and bait-casting tackle, let's not overlook a few of the other ways of catching fish that might interest you, also. The nice thing is that, in a couple of instances, you can use some of the same tackle already mentioned in those other four methods. The first of these is still-fishing.

Still-fishing probably is the oldest and most common, as well as the simplest method of fishing. Still-fishing tackle consists of a long rod, a line somewhat longer than the rod, a bobber or floater adjusted to keep your baited hook the desired distance from the bottom of a lake or stream, a weighted lead to take the bait down, and one or two hooks baited to entice the greatest variety of fish.

For still-fishing in the ocean, a bay or in a deep lake, you can forget the rod and use a long hand-line with a sinker and baited hook. Fishermen along river banks often refer to these hand-lines as throw-lines, since the weighted and baited end is given about three circular swings and then thrown far out into the river, while the other end is held in the left hand or tied to a bush.

You can rig your fly or bait-casting outfit for still-fishing. The reel will allow you to cast the bait farther out from the boat than the ordinary rod will. Most still-fishing is done from an anchored boat, a bridge, a pier or a stream bank.

You can catch most fish by still-fishing. For fresh water fish, try night crawlers, earthworms and minnows. For salt water fishing give bloodworms, sandworms, shrimp, pieces of soft-shell crabs, pealer crabs, squid, clams and sea mussels a try.

Ice fishing provides the angler's solution to the problems of Winter and decreased fishing activity. While he may have

The above and below photos show the wide range of application there is for spinning tackle, from the Spin'r-15 salt water specimen to the Spin'r-18 ultra-light reel. Both models are from Browning Company.

The Garcia salt water spinning reels (below center, right) spool large quantities of line often needed when gamefish run. Spinner (below left) has a 5:1 retrieve ratio.

One of the top producers on spinning tackle is the simple red and white spoon, this model a Shdevil Jr., from the Worth Company. It must resemble baitfish or something a gamefish finds attractive. Treble hooks should be sharp.

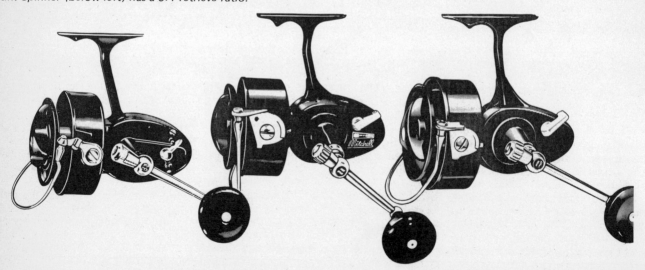

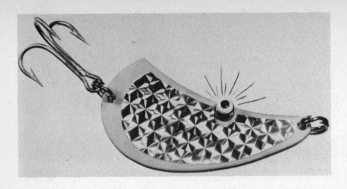

The weird-looking creation at left is termed the Flecto-lite Cyclops lure, made by Glen L. Evans. It presents plenty of flash in the water and is a good tackle box addition. Volumes have been written about the effective performance of the Rebel minnow imitations, like the one below. Colored dark on top and silver on the sides, it gets down deep where lunkers hang out and is deadly.

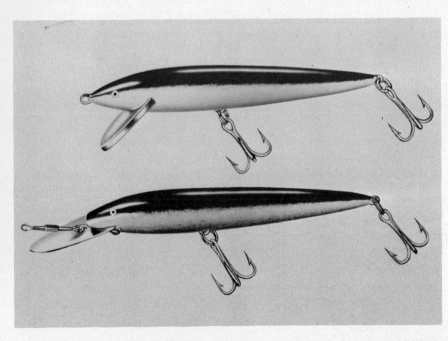

Rapala's Magnum lures are others favored by nearly everyone for spinning at some time of the season. The floating model (top) and the sinking variety combine for a high/low combo that's hard to beat for results on waters.

the proper equipment for ice fishing already purchased, it surely pays to invest in warm clothing for those cold days on the ice.

Basically there are three universally accepted combinations for use in ice fishing: short, ice fishing rods; conventional rods saddled with inexpensive level-wind reels; and tip-ups and traps — the latter ofttimes called tilts.

An ice angler using the tilts actually is still-fishing for his quarry, while the rod-wielding sect usually jigs his presentation. Either method yields good rewards, although the rod-holder limits himself to fishing only one hole — unless he is fast enough on his feet to watch his rod tip and reel in fish taken with tip-ups at the same time!

If using a conventional rod, make sure that the level-wind reel is capable of storing adequate quantities of the proper test line. Line choice for ice fishing is either braided nylon or dacron, with a forward section of the more invisible monofilament.

Tip-ups are favored by the majority of ice fishermen, for the simple reason that, once set, they can be watched from

The bucktail and fly combinations pictured above are nothing short of deadly for lunker-size Northern pike and muskie. With the flash of the single propeller, plus leader wire decorated with colored beads and skirting, they're hard to beat.

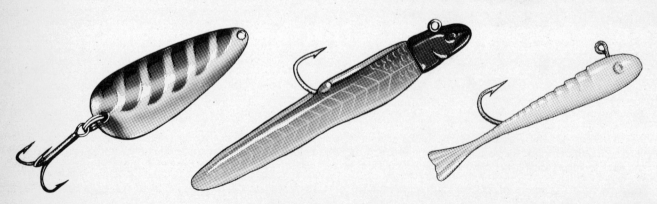

Garcia's Sierra Spoon (left), Bait Tail (center) and Shrimp Bait Tail (right) are finding growing acceptance from both salt and fresh water anglers. Spoon represents baitfish, Bait Tail a worm or eel and shrimp, naturally, its namesake. The latter has fooled plenty of big bonefish when cast in their line of feeding without startling them. Try 'em out!

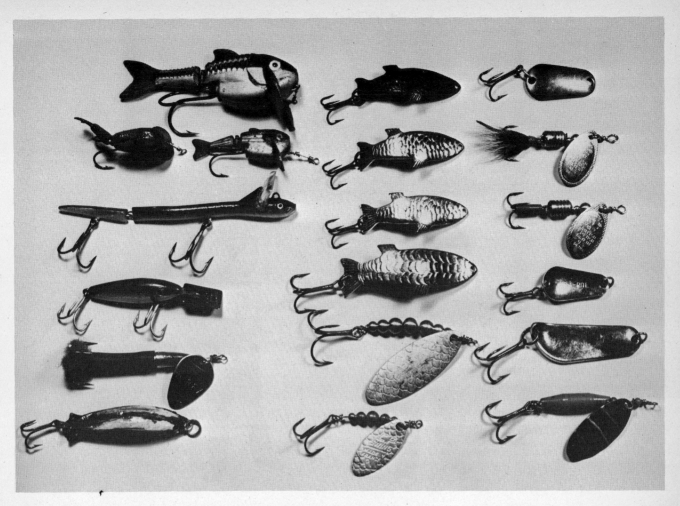

Zwirz' personal selection for "lures of all time" honors include these designs (above). There's one for every fishing situation.

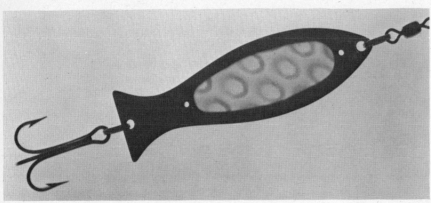

As seen from a fish's perspective, it's easy to understand why the Worth Company's Chroma-Glo takes a good number of fish. Its glow attracts fish when used properly.

inside a protective shelter. They are so designed that, when a fish strikes, a flag pops up, a hunk of wood tilts or a flag drops, signaling the attentive angler that he's got some action on the hook end of his rig. Most have a spool attached to the framework, so the angler simply reels in his fish. Using tilts allows the angler to watch several baits, usually fished at different levels in the impoundment, river or lake.

Live bait, artificial lures and preserved baits are the usual fish attractors when ice fishing. Shiners, or one of the Dace family of baitfish, make up the overwhelming choice of live bait fishermen, and should range from two to three inches if angling for the panfish species of bluegill and perch. Slightly larger offerings should be made when pickerel, walleye, lake trout and Northern pike are the sought game-fish.

These fish also are agreeable to — if you can find them — worms or night crawlers, white grubs, corn borers and even the smallest of the manure worms.

For the sportsman who doesn't relish waiting for flags to pop up, jigging is the answer. For the smaller fish, many anglers like what's termed an ice fly, which is of a single color and weighted. In the water, it looks and acts like a small baitfish's head. Other proven fish-getters are shiny metal jigs and lures.

If you are planning on doing a lot of salt water fishing, you might also want to try your hand at surf-casting. While you can use spinning and spin-casting gear, you might want to check out what's available in conventional surf-casting tackle.

Conventional surf-casting rods usually have a tip weight

Prior to making cast with spinning gear, index finger must grip line and bailer cocked out of way (below).

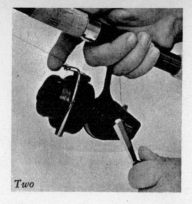

One

Two

After cast has been executed, start reeling and bailer will flop back into position. Monitor line with a finger to glean unwanted matter.

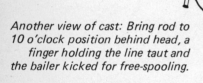

Another view of cast: Bring rod to 10 o'clock position behind head, a finger holding the line taut and the bailer kicked for free-spooling.

Taking aim, whip the rod forward and release the index finger at about the 2 o'clock position. Then reel with left hand to take up any slack on the water.

Sometimes the overhand cast isn't possible. In such a case, holding the line, whip the rod tip downwards. It will bend and as it starts to whip upwards, release the line. It will shoot out to the appointed destination.

Sometimes a sidearm or backhand cast are necessary for proper presentation of the lure. In such case, swing the rod back, keeping it parallel with the water and whip it forward, releasing the line out to the spot. A backhand cast calls for whipping the rod across the chest and, as it flies forward, releasing the line. It's a matter of timing and release, like bait-casting.

LINE ILLUSTRATIONS COURTESY OF GARCIA

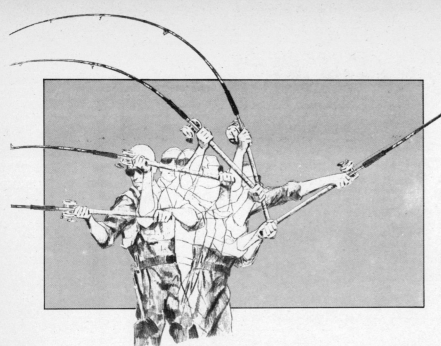

Surf-casting is performed as outlined here. A thumb remains on the spool until rod hits about 2 o'clock. Rod also is turned over in the hand.

of fourteen ounces, with the tip measuring about seven feet. The rod butt will measure about thirty-one to thirty-five inches and most surf-casters like to have the rod butt just long enough to pass easily under the armpit when the rod is held correctly and the thumb is on the reel spool.

The conventional reels used for surf-casting are of the free-spool type, similar in design to the smaller bait-casting reels. The free-spooling design, as with bait-casting reels, allows the angler to cast heavy lures way out where the big ones lie or, if accuracy is a necessary quality to take powerful gamefish, this can be almost guaranteed. The angler regulates the distance of the cast with his thumb.

The free-spooling is achieved by means of a throw-off lever that allows the reel spool to run freely while the

handle remains stationary. Twisted linen lines of twelve or fifteen-thread are used by some surf-casters, but twisted and braided nylon lines are by far the most popular.

Surf fishermen have turned to spinning and spin-casting rigs in a big way. The gear is less cumbersome than standard surf-casting tackle and easier to cast. It also minimizes line trouble such as backlashing, which always has been a problem for surf-casters. Simplification of the terminal tackle — leaders, swivels and sinkers — has been especially beneficial in surf-casting.

Baits used in surf-casting will vary according to the fish being sought and the locality being fished. Along the North Atlantic Coast, such natural baits as mossbunker and crab are favored, while Pacific Coast surf-casters go for sardines

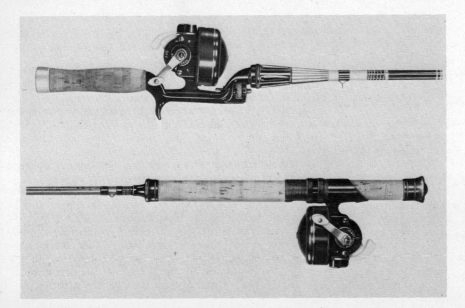

Spin-casting reels offer the angler some versatility in his choice of rods, as seen by this Johnson specimen mounted on bait-casting and spinning rods.

Some spin-cast reels come outfitted with a practice plug, usually made of rubber. Use it and learn how the equipment functions before fishing!

Spin-casting reels find favor with anglers who don't want to worry about backlash. Daiwa's model at left is typical of spin-cast designs.

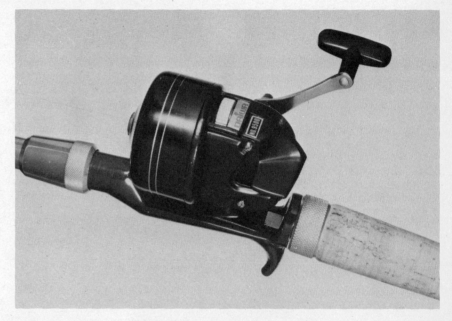

Manufacturers change the push-button free-spooling levers only after lots of testing. Note the difference between button at right and above, both from the same maker: Daiwa.

and anchovies. In the South, pilchards, mullet and shrimp are favored.

Among the artificial lures used by surf-casters are squid, bone squid, metal spoons and plugs.

The accessories available to the modern angler are altogether too numerous to list here, but I will mention a few comfort items which, based on thirty years of angling experience, you wouldn't catch me without.

I always pack along a pair of sunglasses, even if the weatherman says showers are inevitable. I favor those with Polarized lenses, which aid in viewing the action, even when there is glare on the water. These come in clip-on design for anglers who wear prescription-ground glasses and are relatively inexpensive. A salt water sportsman never should be without them.

Another comfort item I emphatically recommend is a hat of some sort. I personally favor the type with a bill, much like a baseball cap, which saves sunburn on my face or, when the sun's behind me, on the back of my neck by wearing the cap backwards. Again, a must for salt water anglers.

While on the subject of sunburn, that painful dilemma millions suffer from yearly, I strongly advise carrying a tube or can of suntan lotion in your creel or stowage box at all times. Apply it liberally when on the waters and your mind won't be on anything but the fish you're after. And, you won't lose any precious fishing time with a burn that forces you to bed.

Another item that you won't find me without at any time, except when ice fishing, is a good insect repellent. It's mighty hard to concentrate on your fishing when mosquitos are feasting on your exposed flesh! Apply it once at the fishing hole and repeat the application as needed.

Once you get out on the waters in your specific areas of the nation, you'll discover numerous other accessories which are indispensible to the serious fisherman. These items normally are needed throughout the country at some time of the year. Expand upon them as the situation demands.

Each year, I see disaster strike fly fishermen when out on their favorite streams; something that results in guffaws of laughter from onlookers. In selecting a fly, he pulls more

While they rarely are seen on the majority of the nation's waterways, cane poles still are used and with good results. This hefty stringer of crappie provided great sport for this couple, using their super-long cane specimens in Kentucky.

than one from his fly box and, in an effort to scoop up the dropped flies, often upsets the entire box.

Usually, this happens when the angler is waist-deep in fast moving water. He scrambles after the flies, slipping on the underwater rocks, precariously balancing his fly rod in one hand. If luck is truly against him, he'll lose his flies and take a dousing when he falls in the water; the latter malady inconsequential when compared to the loss of his flies.

While the fishing hat adorned with flies is pretty on television or in pictures, I don't recommend it as a way of transporting your flies. For one thing, they're buggers to get out when needed, as the barb clings like mad in the cloth fabric. It also takes a lot of time to ease the fly out of the hat — time which could be better spent casting for trophy fish.

By far the best arrangement for wet flies and nymphs is a box which holds the flies by clips. The best method of preserving dry flies when not in use is in a compartment

41

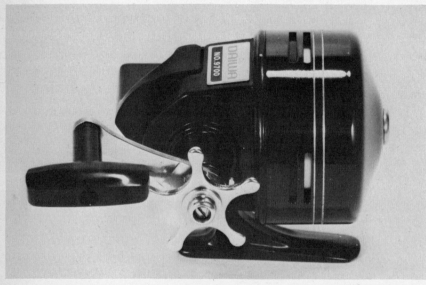

Perhaps smacking his lips in eager anticipation of eating his monster rockfish — or maybe just straining to hoist critter into boat — this Tennessee angler shows the results of properly used spinning gear (above). Match a sturdy bait-casting rod with a good spin-casting reel (left) and you're set for fun. This combination is from Browning.

box, one with hinged covers over each compartment.

Why one system for wets and nymphs and another for dries? As wets and nymphs are tied to represent underwater insects or flying insects in their aquatic stages — sparsely tied because perfection in appearance is not as critical as with dries — they can be retained in a clip-type box. These clips have a tendency to flatten some of the materials used in construction, but the effect isn't noted underwater.

To clip a dry fly, however, would crush some of the materials and make the appearance on the water something other than lifelike. Fish are smart critters (the ones that aren't don't reach trophy-size) and know exactly what that insect is supposed to look like. If it doesn't appear like a real insect on the water, he'll pass it by.

Once you get involved in the world of fishing, you'll be amazed by the amount of lures, terminal tackle and other paraphernalia you'll accumulate. The logical place to store this gear is in a roomy tackle box, of which there are many designs on the market, one of them surely to fill your needs. While you generally won't tote the bigger specimens

Crayfish (left), often called crawdads, and the hellgrammite are top baits for nearly all gamefish (above). Hook both as shallow as possible under collars.

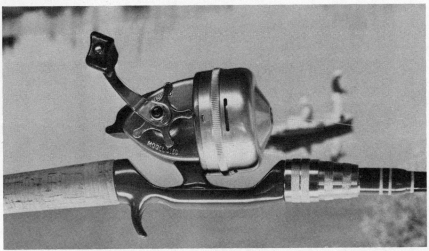

Note the convenient location of the star drag on this Daiwa spin-cast reel (left). It is easily manipulated with index finger during a tussle.

along on the waters, a small one is ideal for keeping your equipment safe and protected.

I favor a tackle box with many compartments, into which individual lures can be placed for safe-keeping. Putting more than one lure — especially when outfitted with treble hooks — in any compartment is asking for trouble, as they will tangle and cost you precious fishing time trying to unfoul the mess and rig up.

Depending upon your fishing method and area, you will find use for such items as scissors, knives, hook sharpeners, disgorgers, pliers, et al. Once you've made a couple of outings, you'll discover which of the time-savers you'll need and add them to your equipment.

When you're out on the waters, you'll need some way of getting your hooked fish from the water and onto the bank or into the bottom of the boat. Pictures in this book show various ways of accomplishing this feat: tailing, lipping and gaffing, for example. These are all fine but, for the new angler, I'd seriously recommend purchasing a net of some sort. Once you've really gotten the hang of what to do with

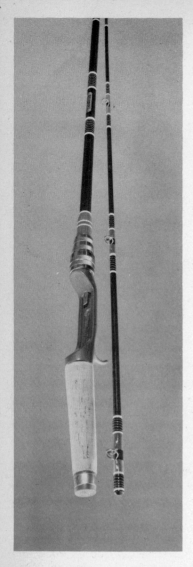

This two-piece bait-casting rod from Browning shows the reel seat well. It tightens on a screw/shoe system.

While Garcia's fly rod (above left) and salt water spinning rod (above right) are conventional, the pair of bait/spin-casting rods in center are anything but! The moulded handle grip lends to more casting stability.

The massive size of this Browning rod and reel combination tells that it's to be used for trolling (left). Built strong to fight monsters to boatside, it primarily is used in salt waters.

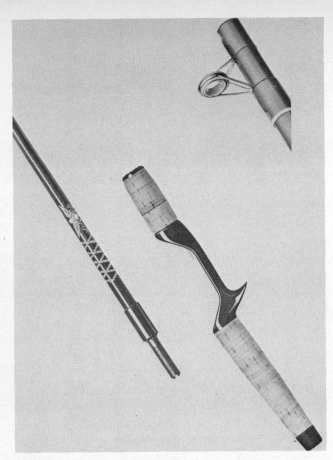

Sevenstrand, makers of the Fenwick line of rods, has designed this Lunkerstik 1400 with transportation ease in mind. It breaks down to a small package, capable of fitting inside an airplane's coat storage compartment.

those played-out fish, then you can discard the net, if you wish.

There are numerous styles of nets on the market, some better than others, but personal preference is the dictating factor on which type you should purchase. For streamside angling, many fishermen I know wouldn't use anything but a net with an elastic cord which is slipped around the shoulder. Others favor a net with a ring and snap, which is hooked to a belt or belt loop until needed. In plenty of cases, either is better than none at all!

Boaters should get hold of a net with a long handle and one that has a good capacity. Fish coming from lakes and similar impoundments tend to run larger than their streamside counterparts, so the need for a larger net is real.

What are you going to do with your fish once you've gotten him on the bank or in the boat? If you don't have the right equipment and follow proper procedure, that delicious-looking fish is going to be anything but, once it's on the table!

The best way of ensuring your fish will be tasty is to keep it alive after netting. If you're in a boat which has a live well, this is no problem, as the aerator supplies the fish with enough oxygen to survive. For the streamside angler, a lip stringer will keep the caught fish alive, although it is a

While some bait-casting rods come in two pieces, the vast majority are single hunks of fiberglass, like the Browning model at right, beside a pair of fly rods.

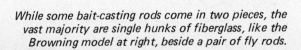

45

This strange-looking Worth Company creation, dubbed the Flutter-Fin, has succeeded in winning anglers' hearts by taking fish. If it works, who cares what it looks like?

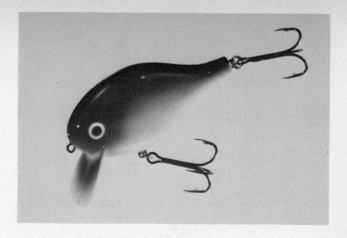

Doll Lures' "Top Secret" is a subsurface lure that imitates a food source (above). The Rebel Jig Spin (below) is unique in that blade is affixed to hook.

bother when you get to moving around out of the water.

If you can't keep the fish alive, the best thing to do is kill it and clean its entrails out of the body at once. If you keep a dead fish in the water, the flesh will become soft. And that doesn't lead to gourmet dining!

Probably the best and most-used method of carrying fish is in a wicker creel. It should be stuffed with leaves and grass or moss before the fish is placed on this bed. It will remain several degrees cooler than the outside temperature and ensure tasty table fare.

Don't be bamboozled into purchasing one of the less expensive canvas creels during the Summer months. While these are all right for Winter fishing expeditions, they don't keep the fish as cool during the Summer as does the wicker creel.

What if you've banked a wallboard fish, one that's too large to fit in the creel or live well? Chances are, your fishing day is over, anyway, as you'll want to share your triumph with friends, so quick transport home will keep it fine. But if you're going to stay on the waters and try for another, a good way of keeping the fish is to lay it in the shade and cover well with leafy branches or grass. This also will keep flies off your trophy, although it limits your scope of operations to the immediate area.

One of the most frequently asked questions, whenever I get around anglers new to the sport, is how to set a hook. On the surface, this seems an easy enough question to answer. But, when you take into consideration all the types of riggings that are used in fishing, the thousands of possible lure/rod combinations, it becomes something less than simple.

To know how to hook a fish, you first must learn what a

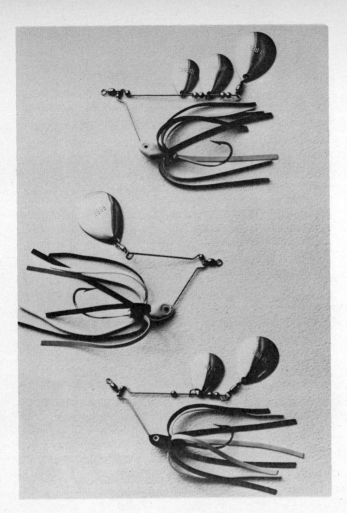

bite is. And, the difference between a strong hit and a gentle nibble must be learned, or setting the hook never will happen. Rather, if you're lucky and the fish is hungry, he might swallow your live or preserved bait, but almost never will a fish get a metal lure or fly as far as his gullet before spitting it out.

Learning to distinguish between a nibble and a strong hit is pretty easy. Many of the tough-fighting gamefish like tarpon, bonefish, sailfish and fresh water species like lake trout, muskie and Northern pike, often hit a bait with utter savagery. When they hit your lure, there's no doubt about what's taking place on the other end of your rig.

But the nibble is different, and oftentimes almost indiscernible. It may come as a fish plays with your bait preparatory to gobbling it down, and often results in just the lightest of taps or tugs on your line. Chances are, if you tried to set the hook right now, you'd end up without a fish — you'd be pulling the lure away before he had enveloped it with his mouth.

How can you learn what a hit is? The best teacher is waiting for you in the lakes and streams around your locale — the fish. Naturally, you're going to miss a great number of fish because you're learning the ropes, and you'll try to set the hook on a lot of taps and tugs which are, in reality, your setup bouncing on rocks or other submerged obstacles. But, by paying close attention, you'll learn to distinguish the difference between rock-caused taps and those from your quarry.

And that's what fishing's all about. To have flags pop up or skyrockets go off when you get a hit would take much out of the challenge of the sport. And remember: You're

This trio of Rebel spinnerbaits in single, double and triple-spin designs with vari-colored skirting and epoxy-painted heads tempt lunkers in shallow waters.

Buzzing one of the Rebel spinnerbaits past stickups is an effective way to take bass. It appears that bass are somewhat territorial in nature and will strike at something they feel is entering their zone. Also, they will strike out of reflex action: a spinnerbait swishing past them disturbs the water and makes noise, which leads them to attack the invader.

never going to hook each and every fish that hits your presentation. But it wouldn't be any fun if you did, would it?

The best way I've found to hook fish, on any type of tackle except deep-sea fishing or surf-casting, is to jam the rod-holding wrist downward — just the wrist, not the whole arm — and at the same time pull the rod arm up sharply. When your wrist snaps downward, the tip of your rod actually raises quickly and, when this is combined with the force of your entire arm, a hooked fish will result — if you're fast enough. If that fish feels any metal in his mouth, he'll spit the bait out faster than you can sock it to 'em.

Now that you've snared your first fish, just how do you go about applying a firm hold on this infernally slippery critter so that you can get him onto the bank or into the boat? I've often seen fishermen juggling their wiggling catch on the stream banks to the extent that they resemble witch doctors doing primitive dances, trying to keep their prized trophies from returning to whence they came.

Usually, about the easiest hold to apply to a fish is a simple finger thrust through one of his gills, into his mouth cavity. In this manner, you can lug just about any fish from the water, except heavyweight salt water species, which are gaffed. By holding a fish in this manner, you avoid both sharp teeth or stinging spines, like those found on the dorsal fins and whiskers of catfish.

Many bass anglers I've known prefer a lip-lock to this gill method, and it surely does work for hoisting ol' funnel-mouth into the boat. Once you've reeled the fish close to your station, simply reach down as his head is held up and grab the tip of his lower jaw with your thumb and forefinger. This expands his jaws wide open and you can hoist him over the side of the boat.

In the chapter on Atlantic salmon fishing in Nova Scotia, you'll note shots of my guide tailing one of the monsters I nailed while fly fishing in the area. This tailing procedure is more complicated than simply netting a salmon, and calls for a true eye and strong hand.

When the fish was played out and near the shoreline, my guide signalled me to be ready and then reached down, grasped the fish just ahead of the tail and lifted straight up. He then caught the fish with his other hand and, while it isn't shown in the photos, hot-footed it for the bank. This practice of tailing is one I'd suggest leaving for the more experienced anglers, or until you've seen it done a few times.

And, while I'm on the subject of removing fish from the waters, let me emphatically recommend that you don't net, tail or lip another angler's fish unless he has asked you to. I

Casting to hefty rainbows like these with fly tackle is great sport. Advocates of the other fishing methods outlined in this chapter are just as loyal to theirs. Each is just another method of taking fish, Zwirz feels, not the only way.

don't know how many times I've seen well-meaning anglers attempt to net another's fish and, in the process, either missed or fouled the line so that the trophy escapes. This has resulted in hot-tempered exchanges and even fights, in some instances.

If a man asks your assistance with his fish, and you're a newcomer, don't hesitate to let the angler know of your status. He may give you instructions or prefer to go it alone, but at least you won't have made a bad situation worse by losing his fish for him.

Okay, you've hooked a fish, gotten him landed and have him firmly in your clutches. How do you go about getting the hook out?

Now, this might sound overly basic. But, each year, I see anglers put out of commission by using their hands instead of their heads: They attempt to remove the hook from inside a big fish with their fingers.

By glancing at the photos of some gamefish in this book, it's readily apparent that doing this is asking for a painful bite or deep scratch. Look at the jaws of a big muskie, lake trout, Atlantic salmon, brown trout, dolphin, weakfish or most of our prized species, and you'll note that they all have long, sharp teeth. In fact, some of the South American varieties I've encountered, like the dorado, actually have severed completely the fingers of careless anglers.

So, the best method of getting a hook out of a fish, as far as I'm concerned, is with a hook disgorger. These are to be found in most any sporting goods store for little money, and can save you lost fishing time confined to your den with a badly torn finger. If you do use fingers, as we all must upon occasion, use caution and slip the barb out when holding the hook's shank. Don't stab yourself with a sharp barb!

So, now that we've covered all the possibilities, it's time for you to choose the type of tackle you want to buy. Hopefully, you now have a little better idea of just what each type of gear can do and what you think will best serve your fishing purposes.

And, while you're buying that new tackle, don't forget to pick up a fishing license if the type of fishing you plan on doing requires it. Don't get out of the sporting goods store without a copy of the current fishing regulations booklet, either. Not only will you find established limits and length of seasons, but also types of baits or lure presentations which aren't allowed. The booklet is free for the asking.

With this gear slung over your shoulder, you'll be fully prepared to join the other twenty-five million Americans who spend about 425 million man-days a year fishing, while spending $3 billion to do it.

This tidy pile of striped bass were nailed with bait-casting tackle. Ol' Linesides is just one of the many varieties of hard-fighting gamefish that are awaiting the angler's presentation. Pick your equipment, rig up and get after them!

BASICS OF SPIN-FISHING

Chapter 3

With The Equipment Available Today, This Sport Can Make The Novice Look Good — But There Still Are Tricks To Be Learned!

To MANY PEOPLE fishing is a simple matter. All you need is a pole, some string, a hook and a worm.

But, as the song says, "it ain't necessarily so," and if you're a newcomer to the sport of fishing, that first trip to the sporting goods store to buy gear can be something of an eye-opener.

The array of rods, reels, lures and other assorted fishing paraphernalia available to a budding Izaak Walton is enough to make him wish he never had left the comforting arms of televised football. If our would-be fisherman hasn't got an old hand to advise him and if he, himself, hasn't stopped to consider just what type of fishing he plans on doing, that first flush of panic arrives as the salesman approaches. Our would-be angler is a fish out of water.

This needn't be the case, though. Having been bitten by the fishing bug, the wise would-be angler would do well first to sit down and analyze the seriousness of that bite.

How often do you plan to go fishing? How serious are you about the sport? Is it just going to be a vacation-time diversion or have you made a strong, reasoned decision that fishing is your thing?

In the first instance, you probably won't do any reading about the sport, will seldom if ever practice and — believe it or not — rarely take care of your tackle. If you've decided to become a fisherman through careful consideration, the opposite will be true. You'll read volumes of books and magazines on the sport, gleaning all possible information from them. You'll angle for tips from more experienced fellow fishing fanatics on techniques, equipment and the best spots to land the big ones.

You'll also practice knot-tying and casting like a golfer practices putting and you'll become a regular Daniel Boone in learning to read the waters you're planning on fishing. Once a certain skill or tackle is mastered and added to your

51

Jigging a plastic worm with his spin-casting outfit brought this big bass up. The open face reel is easy to use, even for the novice!

A wide variety of lures and live baits (below) can be fished with spin-cast outfit. Spare spools with different test line makes for easy switching after a new quarry!

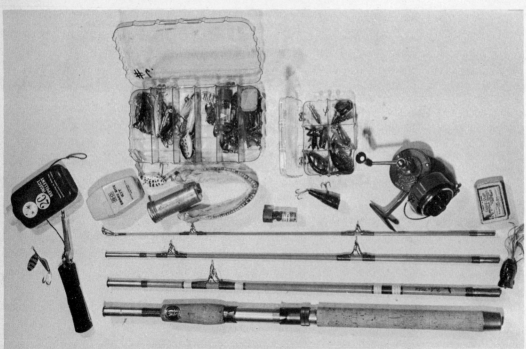

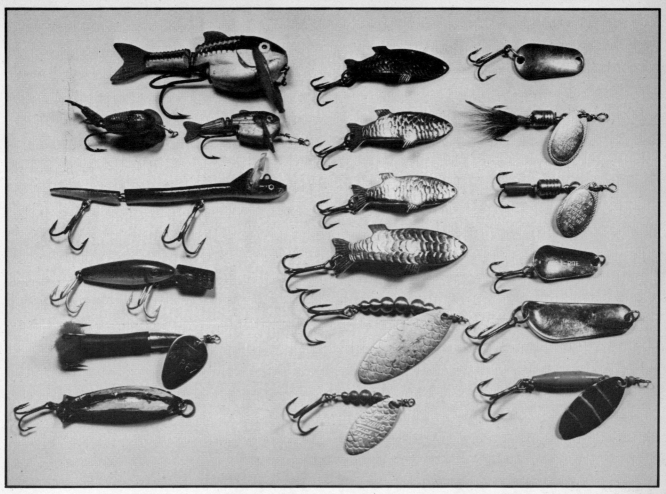

A number of the better spinning lures closely imitate the appearance of common baitfish, eels and other fish foods. Their flash and action add to their effectiveness. They're easy to cast, too.

repertoire, you'll move on, until you have learned them all and newcomers to the sport start picking your brain for fishing tips the way you once did and still do, from other more experienced fishermen.

The chances are that, if you take your fishing seriously from the beginning — if you started with fresh water angling — it's only a matter of time before you are ready to add salt water skills to your bag of tricks. If you were weaned on salt water fishing, the reverse is true. It's only a matter of time before you just have to try the fresh water challenge of the sport.

Now I'm not knocking the occasional linewetter. This section has plenty of tips for him, but it is the serious student of fishing that will benefit most. As we discuss the basics of spinning, I'll be talking about tackle, its uses in fresh and salt water, the differences between the two types of spinning equipment and what you'll need to know and have depending on what kind of fish you're trying to land.

Now, let me emphasize that, for the brand new fisherman, the easiest casting method will require spinning tackle. We do have a choice of reels. There are two types. If you aren't going to do much practicing and the old fishing rod makes it to the back of the garage once you're home from vacation, then pick the gear that can be the least frustrating to learn and use. This is important, because if you don't enjoy your fishing experiences, you're not going to want to fish and your interest will wane rapidly.

The majority of experienced fishermen will agree that a closed face spin-casting outfit is best for a novice or occasional angler. In fact, it's so similar to the open face spinning reel that fishing publications tend to lump the two together in general fresh water fishing articles. Most of these articles are written under the assumption that the reader already knows the differences between the two and the differences between lines, rods and casting techniques.

But, there are differences. Perhaps the most basic one is in the naming of the two reels — closed and open face.

I'm not going to go into any great detail on the inner workings of the two. Both types release the line from the reel without too much help from you, the caster. With the closed face, spin-cast reel, a simple release button lets the line off the spool as you cast. As you cast, a pick-up mechanism inside the cone-shaped face begins to operate. When you begin reeling in your line, this pick-up engages it and winds it back on the spool.

With an open face reel, a bail-arm has to be opened before you cast. When you're ready to rewind, the bail-arm shuts and winds the line onto the non-rotating spool.

Now, with a closed face reel, you can be all thumbs and still make a good cast. Everything just sort of works automatically once you press that release button I mentioned. The line is fairly well protected from coming off the spool and from the other bugaboos that can plague an angler.

The open face reel, though, takes a little more skill and

This lunker lake trout fell to a West Coast fisherwoman, using an Alcedo 2 C/S spin-cast outfit, stout rod.

you have to concentrate a lot more on what you're doing. I should point out that an open face reel will allow you a little more distance on your cast and gives somewhat better control off the lip of the spool. It also permits you to make an easy check of your line, if you need to know how many feet you have out. This can be important when trolling.

Most closed face reels are mounted on top of your rod, while the opposite is true of open face reels. There are exceptions to this. A few closed face reels are made that are designed to go under the rod, but like I said, these are exceptions to the general rule.

Now let's check out rods for a minute. Special spin-casting rods are manufactured to match the wide range of popular closed face reels available. Most of these are designed to handle spinning lures and weights up to three-eighths ounce. Again there are those exceptions. Spin-cast rods, reels and lines can be found that will handle lures and baits up to five-eighths ounce. The only trouble with these is that they are a bit too heavy for the lighter and more common spinning lures.

Your reel, depending on the type of fishing you plan to do, should spool line that tests from 6 to 12-pound mono-filament.

A word here to salt water buffs. It is only in recent years that satisfactory heavy-duty closed face reels for salt water fishing have been developed. A few seasons ago, I noticed two of these first made their appearance in tackle shops. They spooled a minimum of two hundred yards of 15-pound test monofilament which should be sufficient for most needs, including fresh water fishing for large muskie in weed-choked water if, and that's a big if, the reel is skill-fully handled.

Now the question is bound to come up when talking with your sporting goods dealer as to just what pound test you should use. Most spin-cast reels come with a general, all-purpose line pre-wound on the spool. If you intend to do most of your fishing in open fresh water, a 6 or 8-pound test should do the trick. It's heavy enough to handle any-thing you're liable to hook and it's still light enough to cast most of the popular spinning lures with relative ease.

54

With open face reels you'll undoubtedly find it easier to handle the light monofilament lines. With the right touch, these will allow you to make those better casts with light and ultra-light spinning lures. This type of reel and line combination is probably the best one for casting and working a typical worm and split-shot sinker, when you are bait fishing for trout or smaller panfish. It's also a lot more fun.

But to get down to the nitty-gritty of equipment buying, you have to realize that there is no such thing as an all-purpose fishing outfit. It's true that some outfits will handle more fishing situations than others, but one outfit can't handle both fresh and salt water.

You are going to have to have some idea in mind of the kind of fishing you are apt to do so you can ask questions when that sporting goods salesman says, "May I help you?"

What he recommends as an all-around fresh water rig is not going to be what he recommends for an all-around salt water outfit. For fresh water, he might recommend either a closed or open face reel, but if salt water is your bag, he'll point to an open face reel.

Let me assume first that you intend to try fresh water. Here are some general recommendations in regard to lines, rods and lures for some given circumstances. In a spinning rod, my choice is dictated by the fact that I like an open face reel. On the other hand, if you opt for a closed face reel, tell your dealer what type of fishing you're most likely to be doing. For example, if you are going after trout in lakes and streams with only an occasional try for large-mouth or smallmouth bass, walleyes or other popular panfish, the dealer most likely will show you a medium-action rod with which you can cast, troll or baitfish.

With one weight line on your reel and a second weight on your extra spool, you'll be set to handle a wide variety of lures and baits while at the same time you're ready for still-fishing or trolling. As I mentioned, each spool would

All types of spinning lures are available, which will reach fish at any depth when skillfully used by angler.

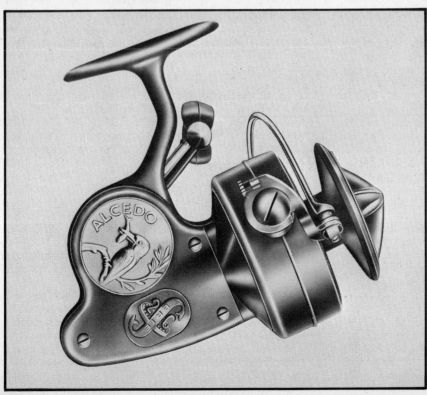

The Alcedo 2 C/S spinning reel is heavy-duty model for fresh or salt water gamefish. With care, it will last for years. See text for hints.

Closed face reels have been perfected in recent years, so that now they are virtually trouble-free. A good example is this Model 200 spin-cast reel from Martin.

have different weight line. A spool of light line will serve for trout and similar type fishing, while the heavier weight would serve for trolling walleyes, largemouths, landlocked salmon and other big, aggressive fish.

Where you are going to fish can also be a deciding factor in your dealer's recommendation. If you are from Georgia, Louisiana or Florida and plan to go after largemouth bass, then the dealer will recommend a fairly stiff, short spin-cast rod and a reel with at least a 12-pound test line, since most of the fishing spots in those areas are known for heavy growth. It's wise to be as specific as you can, when asking for advice about the best gear for your particular needs.

If you decide to go with the open face type of reel and a conventional rod, here are a few tips about rods, actions, lure weights and line test.

My own basic rig for what you could call average fresh water situations is a hollow, 6½-foot fiberglass rod with a medium-light action. With a little care on my part, I can use anything from a 4 to 10-pound test monofilament. This allows me to fish worms or lures ranging from one-fourth to five-eighths ounce, depending on the situation.

I do want to point out, though, that while this combination can handle a great variety of fishing it is not the ideal choice for my lighter requirements. Nor is it the answer for heavier lures and any heavier fish I might run into. Its big advantage is that it's a pretty good all-purpose outfit and would be a good choice for someone who's limited to one rod.

Many rod manufacturers classify their rods according to length and action. To give you some idea of the differences between rods of different length and action, check this table.

ROD LENGTH	ACTION	LINE TEST	LURE WEIGHT
5-6'	ultra-light/light	2-4 lb.	under 1/4 oz.
6-6½'	light	4-6 lb.	3/16 to 1/4 oz.
6-6½'	light/medium	6-8 lb.	1/4 to 1/2 oz.
6½-7'	medium	6-10 lb.	3/8 to 3/4 oz.

Now, if all you wanted to do with your spinning rig was to baitfish, you could save a lot of money on tackle and lures. Almost any normal fishing job can be done with spinning gear. But it really is made to order for casting light lures with minimum effort on your part. If you add the

bonus of being able to cast the live, and lighter, baits, presenting them to your hoped-for catch in a natural manner, the obvious advantages of lightweight tackle are manifest.

Most game fish — fresh or salt water — are candidates for spinning tackle. There is no popular, fresh water game fish that you can't cast to, troll or still fish for — if your rod has the backbone and the line is matched to the job.

Modern spinning tackle, when its automatic drags are correctly set, make the playing of larger fish almost a child's game. Using the proper lines and reels, even the largest muskies have been landed. The record books are filled with all species of trout caught with spinning tackle and the same holds for almost any other game fish.

Moving over into salt water, these are guys who often come up against really big fish. Any number of records have been made with the use of spinning tackle. A 150-pound marlin has been taken, using an open face spinning reel spooled with eight-pound test monofilament. Or how about the fellow who landed a 261-pound mako shark on 12-pound mono? Tarpon, striped bass, salmon and sailfish have all fallen, and continue to fall, to anglers who have confidence in their spinning tackle and handle it with skill.

A word of warning for you salt water buffs. That word is corrosion. As any sailor can tell you, the fight against corrosion is a continuing one. Just because your reel is designed for salt water doesn't mean that it, or any reel for that matter, won't fall prey to corrosion. All reels should be rinsed in lukewarm fresh water after each use. This will remove any salt or grains of sand that may have become lodged in the working parts of the reel. A little care along these lines will give you many extra years of trouble-free casting.

Successful fishing with spinning tackle will depend on your knowledge of how to fish with it. A spin rig is just a casting method. A fish is not guaranteed each time you cast.

All the other aspects of the sport of fishing still apply and are important to the spin fisherman. You have to study the habits of the fish, both fresh and salt water, before you can expect to start reeling them in with any degree of regularity. The how-to of fishing is just as important to the spin fisherman as it is to the bait-caster and the fly fisherman.

Let us now move over and take a look at the kinds of lures and baits available to the light-tackle angler. I'm going to concentrate on salt water tips here for a couple of reasons. First, I'm going to cover poppers separately, because while these very effective surface disturbers are used usually on lakes and streams, they are effective with certain salt water species. Secondly, most of you probably have some familiarity with at least the basic spoons, spinners, plugs and jigs popular in fresh water angling, but at the same time, one may not realize that the same kinds of lures have an important place in several types of salt water fishing.

One of the great attractions of a closed or open face spinning rig is that it can be used to cast surprising distances accurately, even if you are using a light lure. As I mentioned earlier, you can learn to cast well with spinning gear with more ease than if you used a fly or bait-casting outfit. Let me add here that spinning also gives you more flexibility when it comes to choosing plugs. Also, it allows you to use lighter ones that are not practical with a bait-casting rig.

But, even though those are good reasons, it wouldn't be sensible to choose your light tackle on the basis of weight alone. The best way to decide on what type of artificial lure

Using a Mepps spinner, Jeanne Branson waylaid this lunker — almost as big as she is! — while fishing with the author. Her open face spinning reel and strong rod combo proved its durability.

to use is to familiarize yourself with how and where the fish feed.

For instance, if you learn the fish eats mullet and sardines rather than bottom shellfish, you can be sure that metal squids would be effective as would be plugs that ape the appearance and action of baitfish.

These days, you can select from an amazing array of metal spoons, wobblers and squids that have the flash and lifelike motion of the actual baits they are designed to imitate. Some, of thick flat design, act like mullet or herring. These often have a swinging rear hook that can be wrapped with bucktail, used with pork rind or even used undressed. The depth of metal squids can be controlled by the speed at which you reel them in or the speed of a trolling boat. The angle of your rod tip and the flick you give your lure will cause it to work at different depths and with varying action. A little experimentation will show what a lure can and will do under a given set of circumstances.

While some fish prefer a fast-moving lure, others will turn it down. Blues, bonito, albacore, barracuda and mackerel are just a few that respond to the challenge of a fast-moving bait. The smaller striper also will move to intercept a fast retrieve, while larger bass will seldom go for it.

Now you realize that there's no substitute for experience and why a skilled companion can be worth his weight in fish, while you build up that experience.

Where the light tackle angler is concerned, plugs can play a big role. Many plugs are just larger editions of famous fresh water bass models with heavier construction and better hooks. For inshore casting and trolling, successful fresh water plugs can be equally effective on tarpon, snook, stripers, and other fish that like baitfish imitations. The same holds true for rivers, inland bays and backwaters.

Surface and sub-surface darters are tops in my book. White, green, blue, red and yellow and combinations of these, seem to be the best colors. Because they look so much like scurrying bait, the flash of plugs such as the Rebel have had great success the past few years.

The weights of metal lures, including bucktail jigs and highly effective plugs, run from a half-ounce up through weights you can readily handle with either spinning or baitcasting tackle. The selection of truly great lures available is incredible. A visit to a well-stocked tackle store will give you an appreciation as to what is available to you.

Certain areas seem to develop favorite lures; those which work best for local fishermen. It pays to ask questions and listen to the advice of local experts — if you can get them to share their secrets.

While we're talking about artificial lures, we shouldn't forget to mention the bucktail jig as well as those related jigs that are dressed with feathers, rubber skirts — you name it. I'm referring now to the American jigs, not the Japanese and I'm talking about those weighing from one-eighth ounce to less than two ounces.

I can't tell you why they are as effective as they are, but these hunks of painted lead can be deadly when trolled, cast and especially when bounced and jiggled along the bottom. When fished back in regular jerks, these are liable to get a strike at any time. There is hardly a salt water fish that won't show an interest. I've taken blues out of the chum line along with albacore and bonito. The jig appeals to cod, stripers, blacks and even school tuna.

It's up to you to give the lure its fascinating motion when casting a jig. There's nothing in the lure itself to do it. A jig works easily at most inshore depths and can be trolled deep or shallow when you vary the amount and type of line or the speed of the boat.

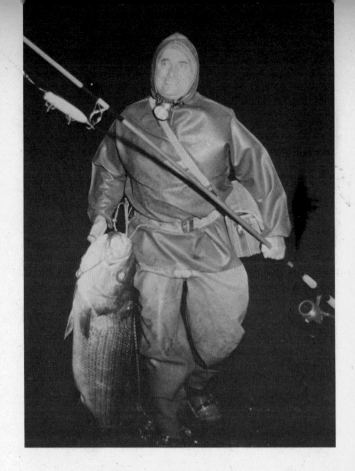

During a Southern fishing trip one week, the usual butterfish failed to produce albacore, so I changed to a bucktail jig and had a ball. Don't ask why. I can't tell you — but never argue with success. But this doesn't mean jigs will work all the time. They often do, but often doesn't mean always. There are times when you'd best know what's what in the world of live bait.

While most fishermen who favor light tackle in salt water prefer to use artificials when practical, they aren't always practical. There are times — and fish — that require a different approach. When that happens, an angler who insists on artificials will go home with a nice sunburn, but no fish. Many times both the smallest and largest salt water fish can be taken with nothing but bait — the real thing.

As when choosing lures, it's again up to you to do a little research on the type fish you're after. Then you can pick the right bait. To give you a listing of which fish likes what bait is impossible. A wise fisherman inquires at local tackle shops and bait stations as to what the local fish are feeding on, their likes, dislikes and where they like to feed.

All of the so-called sea worms make excellent bait. Sand and bloodworms constitute a large proportion of menu for many of the top game fish on both the Atlantic and Pacific Coasts. During the early season especially stripers are partial to any of the worms. Many salt water fish such as flounder, weakfish, porgies, tautog, corbina, yellowfin, croaker and surf perch will go for a trolled worm and spinner or even take it off the bottom, unless a blowfish or crab beats them to it.

Natural food for coastal fish includes shrimp, sandbugs, crabs, clams, squid and a long list of baitfish such as killies, mullet, menhaden, spearing, sardines and the extra-special sand eels. As an angler, these are also important to you. Never turn your nose up at the man using bait. The chances are he knows more about the feeding habits and peculiarities of a given species of fish than those who limit themselves to a single fishing method.

One of the best ways of using artificials or live bait with

Author's wife, Glad, prefers salt water spin-cast hardware when after dolphin, wahoo and similar species. Here, with rod and reel from Daiwa, she holds a Bahama's bull dolphin.

light tackle is to move into areas that hold concentrations of feeding fish. This calls for skillful boat handling on your part.

Last Summer, some friends and I were working the edges of the surf, shoals and rock jetties. Our casts were made right into the turbulent spots where bait is stirred up. Whenever our lures or bait hit the bullseye, stripers, blues and pollack were our reward.

Earlier I said I was going to treat poppers separately. The first thing to remember when casting surface plugs — and this holds for both fresh and salt water — is simply that it must resemble something that interests the game fish you're after. With any surface disturber the secret lies in creating the performance a game fish would expect to see a crippled baitfish display.

Depending on the fish you're after, as well as the type of baitfish found in the area, you will be imitating herring, sardines, spearing and menhaden in salt water.

Surface plugs can be classified in several rough subdivisions. First, there are the traditional poppers. A second group is worked as swimmers; and the third, the torpedo or cigar-shaped variety, usually comes with a tail propeller or head and tail propellers.

Worked properly, each causes a surface disturbance that attracts fish by sound and motion. Along with the plugs that you use to imitate baitfish, there also are many that resemble frogs, mice, large bugs, birds and other tasty things that fish find appetizing. These latter usually are used most successfully in fresh water for such aggressive fish as bass, pike and muskie. But, I have used them to get my share of salt water fish when I used them in canals, backwaters and close along shorelines. Snook and tarpon especially find the lifelike commotion of these tempting and can be egged into a strike by a popper.

One thing I'm always amazed by is the number of opinions I hear on the best way to fish such lures. Many experts will swear that a fast routine is most effective with a popper. First, a fast jerk that makes a plopping kind of noise — a pause — then a skipping across the surface of the

water for a few feet. The performance is repeated until the lure is back near the rod tip.

But I've also had amazing success with a near reverse of the above method. The basic action is the same, but I leave long pauses between each splash and noise, giving the lure but an occasional quiver as it rests on the surface.

I've found that this latter method works best when I'm after a wise old trophy fish in fresh water. And it works in direct proportion to how long I play the waiting game. Nine times out of ten, I get a strike when the lure has been dead in the water for a long time and I give it just an occasional quiver. My largest bass have come to the surface popper, when I've done this.

Accuracy is probably the most important factor when it comes to having success with a surface plug. You have to cast it where it will bring you results. This holds true for salt water as well as fresh water. Big bass, pike or muskie often will go for a popper landing inches short of its station, but ignore your lure completely if it's a foot or two away.

Stories you hear about sliding that plug right in under overhanging branches at the edge of some tangled roots or a rotting stump are true. Mohammed has to go to the mountain. There are times when a big fish will chase a plug, but why gamble? With a little patience and practice you can drop your plug through a knothole at a hundred paces. Not only will you sharpen your casting skills, but the fish you take home will increase in direct proportion to the accuracy of your casts.

In salt water, cruising fish often will ignore the plug that lands to their left or right, much like a bass. They just refuse to go after it. Put that plug a foot or two in front of their faces and you've got an almost certain strike whether they're hungry or not.

I've seen this quite often when after snook or tarpon and, to a lesser degree, with stripers and channel bass. Practice is the key to successful casting.

You'll be rewarded with fishing trips that are far more enjoyable, because they are successful.

Basics of
Modern
Bait-Casting

Chapter 4

This Technique May Seem Old-Fashioned To Those Who Don't Know How To Use It!

DESPITE THE GREAT number of fishermen who have become spinning, spin-casting and fly-rod fans, there still exists a great number of knowledgeable anglers, both fresh and salt water, who depend upon the original and conventional method of tossing plugs, trolling or presenting natural baits.

Even when open face spinning seemed to have replaced bait-casting tackle, as television seemed to have replaced radio, there still was that small, hard core of anglers who would only consider spinning as a refinement. Another worthwhile way to fish, yes, but an answer to everything, no.

While we touched upon the world of bait-casting in the preceding chapter, let's take a closer look at exactly what's available in the way of tackle and exactly how it should be used.

Because bait-casting is used primarily to present larger, heavier lures to gamefish, and have the power to fight those fish to boatside — even through vegetable gardens of underwater growth — it only stands to reason that bait-casting tackle is more rugged and stout than its spinning counterparts.

Bait-casting rods are shorter than those used for spinning, and range between 4½ and seven feet in length at both extremes, the more usually employed varieties scaling between 5½ and six feet. Some are made of solid glass, others of tubular glass fibers with a hollow middle, some even of bamboo.

Both glass types have their advantages, and I personally like the rods of tubular glass construction. They are light in weight, yet exceptionally strong. They don't warp and are unaffected by extremes in temperature. But perhaps their main drawing point, as I see it, is the great variety of actions and tapers that can be engineered into their design. Their main drawback, which leads many anglers to choosing the solid glass models, is their price: Because of their unique features and options open to the fisherman, prices generally are quite a bit higher than for solid glass designs.

Just like some baseball players like a bat with more heft, some anglers prefer the heavier, solid glass rods. They aren't any stronger than their hollow counterparts, and don't have as many of the actions and tapers, but they are less expensive and a novice angler can learn the basics with such an outfit before purchasing one of the higher-priced models.

Many bait-casting rods come in single length, which doesn't allow them to be taken apart for easier transportation. This is especially true with the shorter rods of around five feet.

Other rods, though, are equipped with ferrules, which join two parts of the rod. As I mentioned in Chapter Two, much attention should be given to the ferrules to save problems.

Because the ability of the line to smoothly pass through the line guides and tip top of your rod is so important to casting accuracy and distance, fishermen should examine these closely when purchasing a rod. While most will simply be of stainless steel, chromed brass or chromed steel, some of the more expensive rods have agate on the inside of the

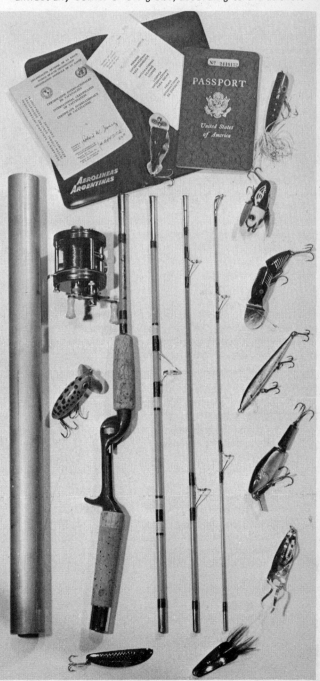

As in spinning, bait-casting can begin with a simple selection of equipment. An outfit such as the one illustrated below will take fish of many varieties in almost any corner of the globe, according to the author.

No matter whether the angler wishes to present a bait or cast with a lure, the author has found that today's bait-casting reels are almost totally free of backlash. This means one can get into action fast sans problems!

line guides. One of the hardest materials known to man, agate is a semi-precious stone, which accounts for the healthy price tag on rods using it.

Whichever type of line guides your rod is outfitted with, take the time to check them for rough spots before getting on the waters. Even the faintest abrasion will tend to weaken your line, after repeatedly scraping over it during casting and retrieve. Should you have any rough spots, sand them

down with crocus cloth or the finest grit sandpaper you can find. It may save you a lost trophy!

A close look at the windings and trim on a prospective rod may give you an idea of the craftsmanship that produced it. While the primary purpose of winding is to attach the guides and tip tops to the rod, or to blend ferrules to the rod, winding sometimes is used for decoration.

Examine it closely. Is it smooth and even, with no gaps

FISHING SITUATION/SPECIES	ROD	REEL	LINE	LURES
(1) Panfish, small bass, trout	Xtra-light 6'-6½'	Ultra light	6-8 lbs.	1/4-3/8 oz.
(2) Smallmouth & largemouth bass, pickerel, walleye	Light 5'8"-6'	Sporty	8-10-12 lbs.	3/8-1/2 oz.
(3) Big bass, Northern pike walleye, landlocked salmon, trout (general fresh water trolling, baitfishing)	Regular 5½'-5'8"	Regular	15 lbs.	1/2-5/8 oz.
(4) Northern pike, big walleyes, muskellunge, school tarpon, snook, fresh water trolling, salt and brackish water casting	Medium 5½'-5'8"	All purpose	15, 17, 20 lbs.	5/8-3/4 oz.
(5) Big, deep-water lake trout, tarpon, snook (similar species), West Coast salmon, stripers, heavy duty fresh water trolling, salt water casting	Heavy 4½'-5'2"	Heavy duty	18, 20, 25, 30 lbs.	3/4 oz. & heavier

Once fisherman learns to regulate reel properly with proper angle at time of line release (above), he will be amazed at accuracy, efficiency of this type of reel. (Below) Using Ambassadeur bait-casting reel, Bob Zwirz plays fighting tarpon along the west coast of Florida.

Fishing the Northwest Territories from Branson's Lodge, in recent years the author has caught several record lakers. Wobbling spoon resulted in victory this time.

between wraps of thread? What is its color?

While color may seem a ridiculous question, since a rod is meant to function, not beautify the landscape, it does have real meaning in the area of winding and trim. You'll find the best rods will have windings of different colors and finer thread, while less expensive models will use a coarser thread and the maker often simply paints it to achieve a two-color effect.

To some people, this is like comparing a new Rolls Royce Silver Shadow with a 1964 Buick: Both function in

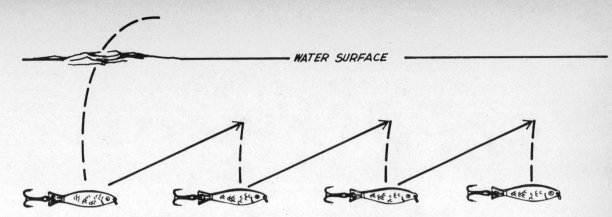

A deadly technique used when fishing a sinking plug is to reel and pause, reel and pause (above). Sinking plug raises when reeled, then sinks.

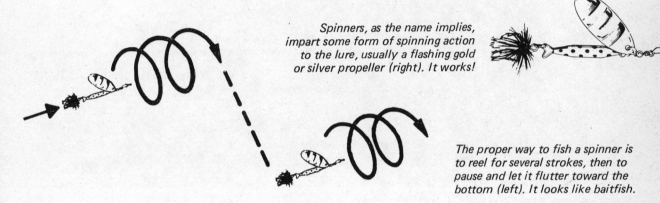

Spinners, as the name implies, impart some form of spinning action to the lure, usually a flashing gold or silver propeller (right). It works!

The proper way to fish a spinner is to reel for several strokes, then to pause and let it flutter toward the bottom (left). It looks like baitfish.

Spoons, like the one at right, take a heavy toll on all types of gamefish. It produces a wobbling action in the water, again imitating a wounded baitfish. They come in many colors or painted gold or silver, with a treble hook attached.

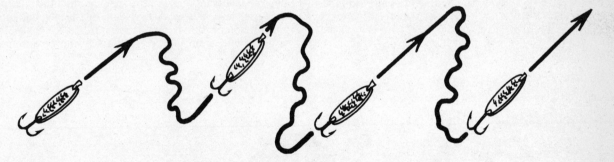

To properly fish a spoon, and to get the best results, the retrieve shouldn't be continuous. Rather, the rod tip should be given a healthy pull, then let the spoon wobble and dart back toward bottom by slack line. Erratic retrieve is best.

the appointed manner, but one has immensely more class. Or, to put it another way, personal preference is the dictating factor, as is the pocketbook.

Bait-casting rods have a novel appearance, caused by the handle chuck, that distinguishes them from any other. This handle chuck serves a vital function: The index finger of the casting hand wraps around it like a hungry largemouth does a plastic worm, thereby adding stability and aiding casting accuracy. Because the rod is whipped severely during a cast, which we'll discuss later in this chapter, the handle chuck often saves rods flying out of anglers' hands and into watery depths.

The reel seat lies opposite the handle chuck, which holds the reel solidly, usually by employing a screw-down plate

and shoe arrangement. Naturally, assure that your reel is snugged down tightly before making your first cast, or you might have to take a swim. And in late autumn, that ain't no fun!

You'll notice that the butt section of virtually all bait-casting rods is made of cork. Examine this area closely. Take it in your hand and test the feel. If it's too thick, check for a rod with a somewhat thinner butt section. When you find one that's comfortable, don't forget to check its smoothness. It must be smooth or you may be thinking about its irritation when that lunker nails your plug.

Most bait-casting rods don't come equipped with butt caps. Rather, there usually is just a metal extension of the

Wherever big fish are being sought, one will find a share of anglers using one of the modern level-wind reels.

grip. This can be quite slippery; especially if coated with fish slime. Therefore, don't overlook a rubber bulb which fits over the butt cap, providing support for the hand should your rod begin slipping away from you during a cast. If you can't find any, wrapping the butt cap with tape to build up such a bulge has proved satisfactory. If you do everything right on every cast, you won't need such an addition. But if you've got it when you need it, you'll be mighty thankful!

By its very design, the bait-casting reel demands more of an angler than any fishing method aside from fly fishing. Probably one of the oldest types of reels, its principle is extremely simple: During a cast, as the weight of the plug pulls the line from the reel, the spool holding the line turns. During retrieve, the spool turns and line is rewound on the spool. It sounds simple, but as many frustrated anglers have learned, things don't always go the way they are supposed to.

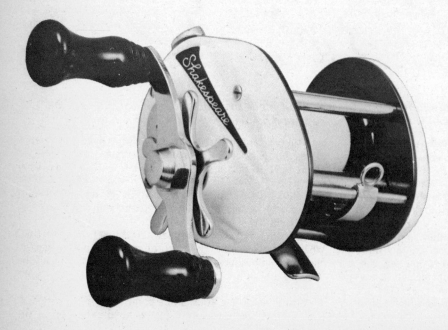

There are many top quality reels available. Among them are models such as this Shakespeare, plus those from Garcia, Daiwa, Heddon, Pflueger and a number of others.

This avid salt water fisherman knows the area in which he will be working. He has readied a Hopkins lure prior to an expected bout with sea trout.

Which brings us to the single drawback of the bait-casting reel that caused the migration by anglers to other fishing combinations: backlash. As the line is pulled from the spool, it must be controlled by the fisherman or, when the plug stops sailing and plunks down in the water, the spool will keep revolving and the excess line resembles a rat's or bird's nest in the reel. When we get to discussing casting methods, we'll cover how to control this malady — which has befallen every bait-caster at some time or another.

Some manufacturers have devised anti-backlash systems which are nearly foolproof. This "nearly" is what keeps anglers on the lookout, however, for no system is fool-proof.

The manufacturers have built into the reels incorporating the anti-backlash feature an automatic drag system on the turning spool. This puts just enough tension against the spool as it revolves, releasing line, to keep backlashes from occurring. It's similar to a governor on some trucks: Although it doesn't stop the speed of the spool, it governs the spool speed when the plug begins slowing down preparatory to reaching its destination.

Another feature you should look for when selecting a bait-casting reel is the handle. Is it balanced and is the knob comfortable in your hand? If not, look for another. That way, you can't blame your tackle if you fail to boat that wallboard specimen.

None of the bait-casting reels I buy come without a star drag, and I wouldn't have it any other way. I can't count the fish I would have lost, had I not had such a system built into my reels. Should it be exerting too much tension against your fish, so that your line is threatened with breakage, simple manipulation with a finger loosens the drag to the proper degree.

On my fresh water reels, I always go in for the level-wind design. During retrieve, this keeps the line flowing evenly and smoothly back and forth across the spool, so that it doesn't bunch up anywhere.

Another nice feature to have, which often means the difference between fish in the boat or an empty stringer, is ease of dismantling to change spools. This is accomplished by loosening take-down screws, usually found on the handle side of the reel. Naturally, if the knobs are knurled, this process is simplified immensely. And, you shouldn't need the strength of Godzilla to undo them, either.

The sideplates of the reel, while they should be strong, also should have minimum tolerance between the spool and the side to keep line from wending its way between them. Should you be fighting that dreamed-of big one and he gets to stripping line from your reel with amazing speed, guess what's going to happen when he yanks at the end of the line and it's caught between the spool and sideplate?

Speaking of line, what are the favored types used by the bait-casting fraternity? As with choice of rods, reels and lures, line is a matter that falls under the personal preference category.

This history of fishing line is interesting in itself. While prehistorians probably used some type of gut or sinew as line, much knowledge has been gathered on relatively modern specimens, horsehair, linen and silk lines, in that order of development.

Horsehair line was made from individual strands of mane and tail hairs of the horse, which then were knotted together. Twisted linen lines of early manufacture primarily were handmade, the small fibers twisted in one direction, then the twisted pieces wound around each other in the opposite direction. This line, in addition to the strength imparted through the many fibers, also tended to avoid unraveling; to twist in either direction simply tightened the strands.

The next innovation in fishing lines came with the silk worm. After this little insect finished his part of the job, manufacturing the silk, the strands were braided on a machine to form bait-casting line.

The problem with all types of fishing line constructed of organic materials was deterioration. It practically became unwritten law that linen or silk lines were good for about a half-season of normal use, at which time they should be replaced — their strength was gone.

Synthetic fishing lines showed up on the market just before the Second World War broke out, and before the conflict was over, manufacturers had perfected the techniques used today in the making of synthetic lines.

While there are many types of fishing lines available, including monofilament, braided nylon, nylon squidding, braided dacron, wire, IGFA and fly lines of many types, the ones most used by bait-casters are monofilament, braided nylon and braided monofilament.

Monofilament, in construction, much resembles one long strip of thin spaghetti. It is made of a single filament, making it nearly invisible in the water.

Braided mono, on the other hand, is a combination of from one to two hundred individual minute filaments, braided together into a single line in much the same fashion as was silk line. It tends to be used more on big fish and has the drawback of higher visibility in the water. Therefore, it usually is used in conjunction with a leader section of monofilament, to which the plug is attached.

Braided nylon line is exactly what its name implies, and comes into its own when fishing surface and just sub-surface lures. It has little weight and, when an angler wants his top-water plug to respond to each and every twitch of the rod tip, this is the line to use. Because it floats and thereby encounters little hindrance from water pressure, you can believe that every bit of action you put into the plug will be duplicated.

I firmly believe that reels should be spooled with at least fifty yards of either mono or nylon line testing from nine to eighteen pounds. Of course, this tensile strength will vary, depending upon the weight and fighting ability of the gamefish you're after.

Earlier I mentioned your bait-casting reel should feature easy disassembly. This is a must, because I feel no well equipped angler goes on the water with just one spool of line. You must adapt to changing water conditions, so having another reel spooled with a different weight and type of line could spell the difference between coming home empty-handed or with fish for the table.

Up to now we have placed emphasis primarily on fresh water bait-casting, but I can assure you that it plays a vital

BAIT-CASTING REEL

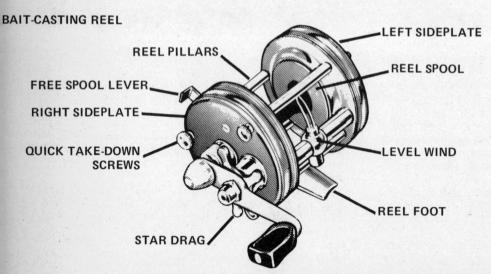

REEL PILLARS

FREE SPOOL LEVER

RIGHT SIDEPLATE

QUICK TAKE-DOWN SCREWS

STAR DRAG

LEFT SIDEPLATE

REEL SPOOL

LEVEL WIND

REEL FOOT

To properly use a bait-casting reel, an angler should know nomenclature of his reel. Drawing at left gives the run-down of each integral reel part.

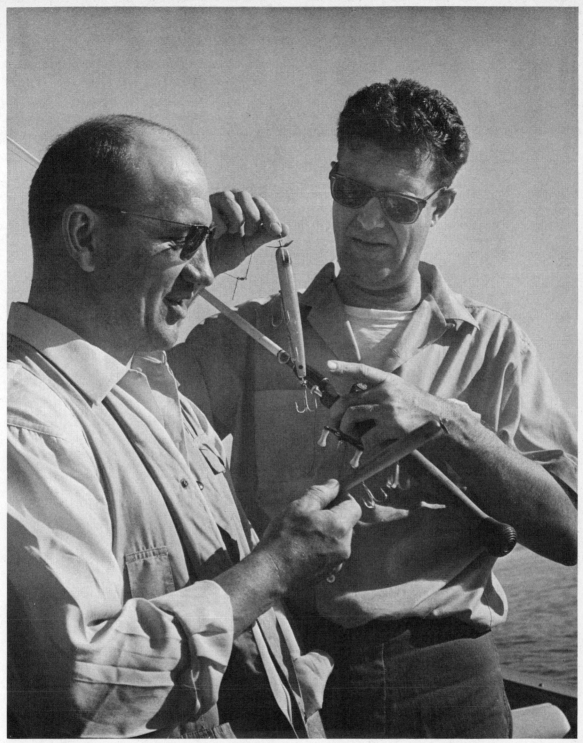

Salt water plugs are near ideal for use with bait-casting tackle. Dick Kotis of Arbogast readies a pair of this maker's Dasher plugs before looking to the heavy mangrove growth for snook and tarpon.

role in salt waters, also. Of course, because the gamefish being sought range much larger in size on the average than those sought in fresh water, beefier bait-casting tackle is needed.

Salt water reels, in design, are basically the same as their fresh water cousins, with the exception that they're larger in size, integral parts are extremely strong to withstand tremendous tensions, and the reel is resistant to corrosion.

The super-size specimens usually don't have the level-wind feature, either. And, finally, most salt water reels have brackets to anchor the reel to the rod, in addition to the regular reel foot.

While big game reels appear similar in construction, that's about where the similarity to bait-casting reels ends. These reels are built to withstand outrageous tensions from the monsters cruising deep in the oceans, and accommodate immense quantities of line. Instead of attaching to the rod with brackets or shoes, these reels are clamped around the rod. Once they're attached, they're not going anywhere!

Naturally, you won't find one of these reels mounted on just any rod. Rather, they sit atop what anglers call "big game rods," which are specifically designed to handle the punishment only the big bruisers are capable of dishing out.

A bait-casting rod that often is used for salt water gamefish, or the larger species in fresh water, is known across the land as a muskie rod. Because of the larger plugs used when after these gamefish, the rod has a foregrip, in addition to the regular butt, for two-handed casting. These rods feature the bait-casting earmark, the handle chuck, and the reel is seated opposite this protruding claw. It is capable of withstanding the torture dished out by these hard-fighting species.

Bait-casting tackle, both salt and fresh water, has to be balanced if you are to achieve any success with your casting. If your rod, reel, line and lures are not matched correctly, the result can be anything from a loss of enjoyment to downright disaster. Just as important as properly balanced tackle is consideration of the type and size of fish you're after and the conditions of the area to be fished. Such things as the presence of heavy weed beds, mangrove roots or thick concentrations of subsurface or surface deadfalls become prime factors to consider when choosing your tackle. Often these will outweigh your consideration of the size of fish you are after.

The majority of American rod manufacturers classify their rods as having extra-light, light, medium or heavy actions. First consideration in selecting one is the general weight of the lures one intends to use and the action best suited to these. Just remember that both rod action and the pound test of your line would require beefing up, if you, for example, were to specialize in taking muskellunge or large Northern pike from lily pad-choked ponds or tarpon or snook from shorelines and mangrove-lined swamps. The same holds true if one intends to specialize in fishing certain deep-water areas.

As a general rule, there is a fairly well proved formula you can use to aid yourself when becoming familiar with the various bait-casting combinations. It has been put together from the viewpoint of the type of fishing situation. As I have mentioned already, it will take some consideration on your part as to whether the basic equipment needs to be beefed up for special situations or used as indicated in a general manner.

Just about any of these outfits, light, medium or heavy, can be rigged to handle most fishing situations whether they call for casting, trolling or one of the techniques of live-bait presentation. For you, the angler, the most important thing to consider is your type of fishing. When it comes time to select a specific bait-casting combination, use common sense. For a given situation, the proper class of tackle can give you a delightful brand of light-tackle fishing.

Although I use more than one specific rod for species such as tarpon, yellowtail, stripers, croakers, mackerel, bluefish and snook, it generally falls within the following classifications: a hollow fiberglass rod 5½ feet in length with a one-piece tip. The action tends to be close to medium and the guides always are wrapped with stainless steel wire.

Depending on the area and fish involved, I'll carry extra spools with lines testing from a low of eight pounds (more usually 12-pound), up to 30-pound test for heavyweights as tarpon, whites, sailfish or large barracuda and where hang-ups might be a problem. I rarely travel without a second rod and a spare, top-quality reel.

I believe in using the lightest sensible outfit I'm capable of handling. If, for example, I think it's possible to work a white marlin on 20-pound mono rather than a higher pound test, the chances are I'll give it a good try.

For the light-tackle fisherman, such terminal setups as the Bimini twist are exceptionally useful. If you know you're going to tangle with scrappers like bluefish or barracuda, don't forget to use wire leaders. You can often use mono shock leaders (these have to be of a considerably heavier pound test than your line) when fishing for most of

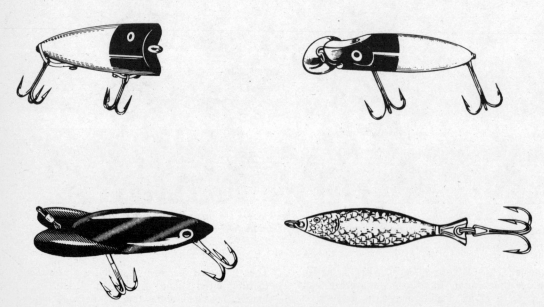

These rough divisions of plugs, surface (top left), subsurface (top right), deep-diving (bottom left) and sinking (bottom right) are used effectively both in salt and fresh water. Their performance in the water is limited only to the angler's imagination, so expand on the actions you give a plug and see what happens. Hopefully, it'll be fish on the line!

the heavier, more pugnacious fresh and salt water species. And, don't forget that such worthwhile items as nylon-covered leaders, barrel swivels and lock-snap swivels exist for special purposes.

When it comes to lures, darting, sub-surface plugs are great, as are the surface-disturbing plugs. Squids, feather jigs and wobbling spoons can be productive when a salt water angler gives an inticing action to his lure.

Such bottom feeders as corbina, pompano, kingfish, porgies, sea bass, tom-cod or halibut normally require a somewhat heavier combination, since the sinkers have to reach the best depth, then hold. These shellfish eaters rarely will react well to a cast lure, but if you're willing to fish bait, they are willing to provide sport.

If you're planning to cast or troll using bait-casting tackle in either salt or fresh water, a number of the basic lures such as spoons, spinners, jigs and plugs can be very much a part of the scene.

When deciding on the correct type of artificial lure for the fish you're after, first familiarize yourself with how the fish feeds, in what areas and depths and, most important of all, what natural foods he prefers. The salt water fisherman who learns that his quarry goes for mullet and sardines and not for bottom shellfish can be sure that certain metal squids will work, as will plugs that imitate the appearance and action of his favorite baitfish.

The selection of metal spoons, wobblers and squids having all the flash and lifelike motion of the baits they are imitating is amazing. Some, made to work like common fresh water baitfish, are of a thick, flat design. Often they have a swinging rear hook which comes undressed, wrapped in bucktail or used in conjunction with a pork rind. Squids can be controlled as to depth by the speed of your retrieve or, if they are trolled, by the speed of the boat.

The angle of your rod tip and the jiggle you give your lure will cause it to work at different depths and in a different manner. You have to experiment to learn what a lure will do under a given set of circumstances.

As already mentioned, plugs play an important part where the salt water angler is concerned. Many are just larger editions of fresh water bass models with heavier construction and better hooks. For typical inshore casting and trolling and in rivers, inland bays and backwaters, many of the successful fresh water plugs are just as effective when used for snook, tarpon, stripers and other fish that show an interest in baitfish imitations.

Tops in my book are surface and subsurface darters. The best colors seem to be white, blue, green, red and yellow or combinations of these colors. The flash of such plugs as L&S, Rebels and Mirro-Lures, to name a few, have had great success. This is due to the fact that, in action, they look like the scurrying bait in which gamefish always are interested.

The weights of metal lures, including bucktail jigs, plus the highly effective plugs, run anywhere from half an ounce up past weights you can readily handle with bait-casting tackle. Certain areas also seem to develop favorite lures which work best for local fishermen. It pays to ask questions of and listen to local experts, if you can get them to talk.

It's worthwhile at this point to say a little more on the subject of the bucktail jig and to include all types and styles of jigs dressed with bucktail, feathers or rubber skirts. I'm referring now to the Americanized version, not the Japanese, and to those weighing from between one-eighth ounce to those just under two ounces.

I don't claim I know why they are as effective in both fresh and salt water as they are, especially in the hands of a skilled fisherman. I do know that these gobs of lead are deadly when trolled or cast, particularly when they are bounced and jigged along the bottom where fish are likely to congregate.

When they are retrieved from the very bottom with regular jerks, you can have a strike at any moment. There is nearly no species of gamefish that doesn't show an interest in this lure. I've taken numerous blues out of the chumlines, as well as albacore and bonito. Cod, stripers, blacks and even school tuna are candidates for its appeal. In fresh water, the list is equally as impressive.

When you cast a surface plug, either fresh or salt water, the first thing to remember is it must resemble something that interests the gamefish you're after. The secret of success with any surface-disturber lies in creating the same performance the gamefish would expect to see from a crippled baitfish.

Surface plugs can be divided roughly into several sub-

Learning effortless casting with bait-casting equipment is not difficult and, once mastered, has few limitations.

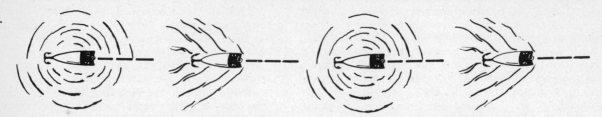

When fishing a surface or top-water plug, patience is of utmost importance. It should first be cast to a likely-looking area and left motionless on the water until all ripples caused by the cast have calmed. It then is given a healthy twitch or tug, again followed by a motionless period, after which the process is repeated. You then can expand effective methods.

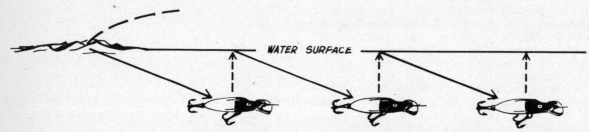

A subsurface plug is equipped with a metal lip, which makes it dive and wriggle when retrieved by the angler. It will float when not retrieved, and the combination results in many fish. After a cast, again letting the ripples die away, it then should be retrieved for a few cranks, then given slack so it will rise slightly. This process is repeated ad infinitum.

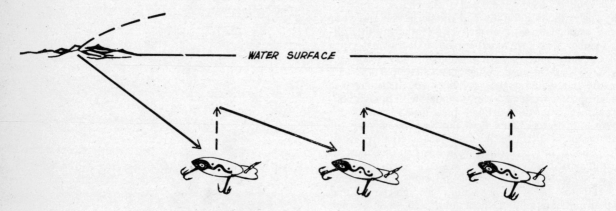

A deep-diving plug will also float to the surface when not retrieved, compliments of its wood or cork construction. The depth it attains is regulated by the speed of retrieve: the faster you crank, the deeper it gets. You should pause upon occasion to let the plug rise slightly in the water, then resume reeling. This technique is a proven big fish-getter.

divisions. There are the traditional poppers and others that work as swimmers. A third type is the cigar or torpedo shape, with either a tail propeller or a combo of both head and tail propellers. When worked by the fisherman, the plug causes a surface disturbance that attracts by motion and sound. These surface plugs imitate frogs, mice, large bugs and birds, as well as other terrestrial critters fish find edible.

Although these usually are more successful in fresh water for bass, pike and muskellunge, they have done well for salt water species when used in canals and backwaters or close along shorelines. Snook and tarpon find such lifelike commotion appealing and can be lured into a strike. In my estimation, these lures can be worked best with a bait-casting rig.

Artificials are the choice of most fishermen who favor light bait-casting in both salt and fresh water. But, there are times and fish that simply refuse to go for the hardware.

All of the so-called worms are excellent baits in both fresh and salt water. Seaworms, sandworms and bloodworms make up a great portion of the diet of many of the top salt water gamefish on both coasts. Stripers, too, are partial to the worms, especially during the early season.

Shrimp, sandbugs, clams, crabs, squid and such baitfish as kilies, mullet, menhaden and those extra-special sand eels are important as natural feed for coastal fish. The correct combination of bait-casting tackle can handle any of these assignments.

What are the best ways of fishing your presentation? It

seems that each angler has his own favorite method and, if it works, that's all that is required. However, the novice fisherman should first learn the movements that take fish for the majority of anglers.

Looking first at top-water plugs, patience is the key to successful angling. Once the lure has been cast, it should just sit on the surface, at least until all of the surface rings have calmed — and then some. When your patience is almost gone, give the plug a good twitch with your rod tip, then stop it dead in the water. Allow it to remain undisturbed until the rings have disappeared, then repeat the process. You then can expand on your techniques to include short runs, skips, twitches, experimenting on what takes fish.

Subsurface plugs are designed to float when not being retrieved, which lends to their special magic when fished correctly. After your cast, again leaving the plug motionless on the water until the ripples have vanished, reel in a few strokes on the handle and stop. The special lip on the front of the plug will cause it to vanish under the surface, wiggling and diving in a provocative manner. Stopping your reeling action lets the plug float toward the surface slightly, presenting an up-and-down picture to fish. Repeat this reel, stop, reel, stop procedure until the plug either is grabbed or ready for a new cast.

Deep-diving plugs also are designed to float when not being retrieved. But when they are pulled reelward, they get way down deep in the water, the depth regulated by the speed of the retrieve. As you reel quickly, pause on occasion and let the plug rise gently in the water, then begin reeling again. This type of lure is deadly!

A purely sinking plug will do just that, unless reeled in. It stays near the bottom and, when retrieved, rises slightly in the water. It then should be allowed to sink for several inches, whereupon the retrieve is resumed. Changing directions of the retrieve by changing the position of the rod tip, an angler can impart a darting, erratic performance on the part of the lure; one that resembles a wounded baitfish looking for a home — like inside a big bass's mouth!

Lead-head jigs take a potful of fish, both from salt and fresh water, annually. You won't find a well-equipped baitcaster without a few jigs in his tackle box.

Essentially, a lead-head jig is a moulded hunk of lead near the eye of a fish hook, with some type of dressing flowing behind to cover and hide the hook barb. This dressing can be of bucktail, feathers, nylon or even yarn, and it usually is colored in various shades. The weighted head always rides in the water with the hook barb upward, to aid in hooking fish.

A jig normally is fished in a jerking motion, followed by

Jigs, which account for untold poundage of gamefish during any particular year, are nothing but hunks of lead moulded near the eye of a hook, with some type of skirting material trailing to hide the hook barb. The hook always rides upwards.

A jig can be fished either vertically or horizontally, depending on underwater terrain and angler's preference. Either way, it should be given a healthy pull then slack, which brings it toward the rod tip then it dives back down. By varying the method of retrieval, this lure takes on a variety of actions, the more unpredictable the better. Give it a try for bass!

The bait-casting outfit is a natural wherever heavy fish tend to hide close to or in underwater foliage or hangups. In the case, a happy angler is battling a heavy Northern pike, hooked on North Caribou Lake, Ontario, Canada. It's great sport and red and white spoons, like the one this fisherman is employing, result in some spectacular jumping action.

a slight pause, whereupon the slack line generated by the jerk is rewound on the spool. During this pause, the jig heads back down toward the bottom, then shoots back surfaceward upon another jerk.

Plastic worms have accounted for untold poundage of boated fish, which just can't seem to ignore the taunting, tantalizing action. They should be fished slowly, with just a minimum amount of action — just like a real worm would act. The size of the worm, and whether you use ones filled

with scent attractors, is determined largely by personal preference and the size of the fish you're pursuing. Those big daddies in the weeds don't hesitate to try munching a twelve or thirteen-inch plastic worm.

An added attraction you might try when fish just aren't interested in your jig or lure presentation is to strip on a hunk of pork rind. The preserved skin of a pig, it comes in its natural color — white — or dyed many colors. Its waving, wiggling action just might lure a finicky fish into striking.

Now that we've covered the basics insofar as tackle and lures are concerned, it's time to concentrate on presentation of that lure in a manner acceptable to fish. Accuracy in placing the plug or bait exactly where it will produce results probably is the most important factor relative to successful fishing. Many times a big bass, pike or muskie will go for a popper landing within inches of its station, but will ignore it if the lure is a couple of feet away.

All of those stories you hear about sliding a plug right in under overhanging branches or at the very edge of tangled roots or a rotting stump are true. A larger fish actually will chase a plug at times, but why gamble on a careless presentation? With a little practice, one can become adept enough to tell those stories, rather than just listen to them.

As mentioned earlier, the bait-caster must regulate the speed of the spool during a cast, or suffer from backlash;

Author had been catching snook at edges of sunken wreck with a bait-casting outfit, which subdued this Florida shark quickly.

75

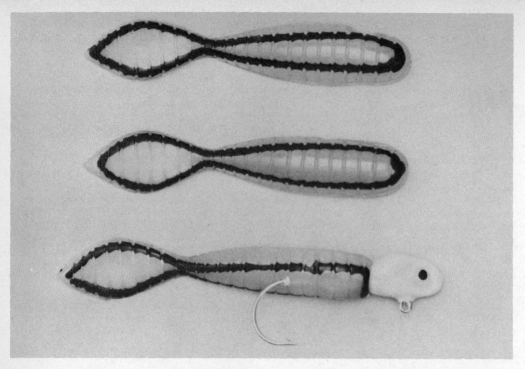

Rebel's Hot Tail grub is finding favor with many bait-casters. It has epoxy-painted head and hand-painted eyes, which resists chipping when rocks are encountered. Rig one up, fish it in the manner outlined for jigging, then wait for the results. Chances are, you'll be pleased!

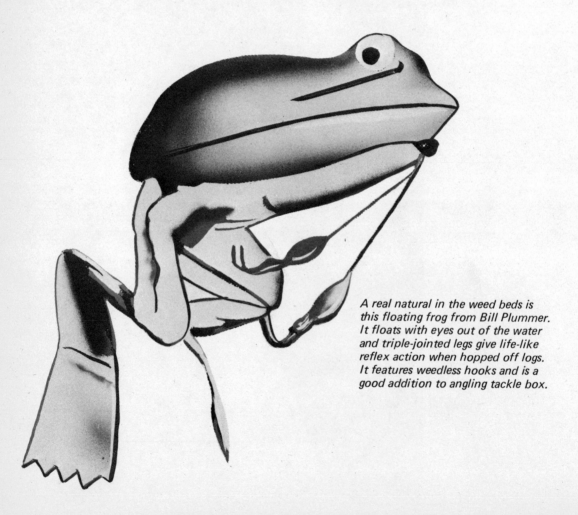

A real natural in the weed beds is this floating frog from Bill Plummer. It floats with eyes out of the water and triple-jointed legs give life-like reflex action when hopped off logs. It features weedless hooks and is a good addition to angling tackle box.

sometimes, even if his reel features an anti-backlash device. Consequently, the following describes how a cast should be made, first discussing the overhand cast, used approximately eighty percent of the time.

The rod should be held so that the reel handle is up, with the thumb on the line. If it's more comfortable, you can rest your thumb against the side of the spool during this phase, to keep the line taut and get the maximum force out of your cast.

Strip some six inches of line off the spool and let the plug hang this distance from the tip of the rod. Set the reel lever or button on free spooling and, keeping the elbow close to the body, extend the arm, hand and rod toward your intended target. When you have the bottom guide sighted on the spot where you wish the plug to land, snap the rod arm backward to about the ten o'clock position behind your shoulder. The casting arm now is cocked, then whip the rod-holding arm forward forcefully, all the while keeping a firm grip on the spool.

As the rod nears the two o'clock position on this mental timepiece, release the thumb on the spool and allow it to trail out, pulling line with it. Follow through on the cast by extending the casting arm and rod, and regulating the speed of the spool with your thumb.

Chances are, your first couple of casts will be short, because you'll jam your thumb against the spool prematurely to prevent backlash. With experience, you'll learn to guide that plug right to the intended spot.

As soon as the bait hits the water, transfer the rod to the left hand and begin reeling with the right, to take up any slack line from the cast. The left thumb and index finger should grasp the line lightly during retrieve, to clean any unwanted matter before getting to the spool. It also keeps the line winding on the reel smoothly and evenly.

While the overhand cast is most used, oftentimes environmental factors like wind or trees make this type of cast impossible. When this occurs, you can use either the sidearm or backhand cast to get your lure to where it'll do some good.

The sidearm cast is conducted in the same manner as the overhand cast, except the rod is held parallel to the water and out to the side of the angler, instead of over the head. The casting arm should nearly be fully extended, brought forward forcefully and the spool freed at the proper time. Line play can be regulated again by the thumb.

The backhand cast is somewhat more difficult, but nature sometimes dictates its use exclusively.

In this case, the rod is swung across the chest, the wrist cocked back as far as it can go toward your buttons. Then, with wrist and forearm action, the rod is thrust forward in a sweeping motion, the arm follows through by extending the rod, and the cast governed by the thumb on the spool.

The keys to all three of these casting methods are timing and release. It will take a few practice sessions in the backyard before they sufficiently are mastered, but the effort will be worth it. You'll be rewarded with the knowledge of improving your proficiency, along with more stringers of fish.

Where conditions call for accuracy in casting and power for playing your fish, nothing can beat a balanced baitcasting rig.

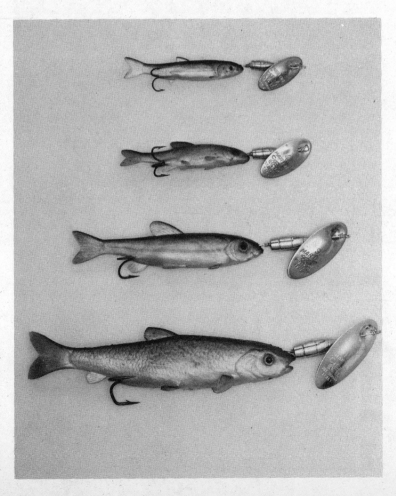

Panther Martin's Minnows come in four sizes for all sizes of fish. The bright spinner adds flash to the presentation, getting more attention.

Chapter 5

The Mysteries Of This
Means Of Taking Fish
Are Substantially Reduced
After Reading These Pages!

BASICS OF MODERN FLY FISHING

Using a balanced outfit produced by Scientific Anglers, Zwirz shows form that makes casting 100 feet possible.

IT'S PRETTY OBVIOUS that you can't fish with ease or become a proficient fly-caster, unless you've selected your equipment to work perfectly for each specific phase of fly fishing. It's possible to be a complete fly fisherman while owning just two rods, but if you want a rod especially for the smallest streams and another for the largest tarpon, you may want four rods available.

To be quite frank, I manage nicely with two, well chosen fly rods and don't feel at all handicapped unless I don't have special purpose fly lines that extend the usefulness of each one.

Almost everything you read about fly fishing tackle opens with the statement that "you must have a balanced outfit." All well and good as far as it goes, but there's a lot more to it than just that. The rod and line also must be suitable for the type of fishing you will be doing most of the time. Where a large flow calls for a heavy fly line whose drop is practically unnoticed, in ripple-free meadow waters it would be disturbing enough to put down every trout within two hundred feet.

If you are fishing small, brush-choked streams, you have become a specialist and will need a special rod and line

combination. Something like a six or 6½-foot rod along with a No. 4 or 5 fly line affords that extra finesse of presentation.

But most fishermen stick pretty closely to more conventional trout streams, rivers and lakes where conditions are average. This offers fewer casting problems and broader fishing opportunities for those who aren't quite all-around experts.

For those in this latter catagory, there is a basic rod and line combination that will prove to be quite satisfactory for everything from small stream excursions to situations where you can push your tackle to its fullest capabilities by using weight-forward lines along with the double-haul casting method.

The most effective all-purpose rod according to popularity charts, is one measuring eight feet in length and requiring either a No. 6 or No. 7 fly line. Nearly all rod manufacturers now produce progressive taper glass rods that are as comfortable casting a dry fly as they are for casting a wet one.

The modern, progressive taper is best described as one in which the tip begins to bend as force is applied, continuing to bend over its length as the force builds. At maximum, this rod is flexing and working clear into the butt section. No matter whether it's because of a hard run by a heavy fish or stress built up by the weight and forward impetus of ninety feet of fly line, the force is the same as far as the rod's action is concerned.

Before buying a rod, check it carefully by tying a short piece of line to the tip, then pulling back against the line with varying intensity. Slight tension will involve only the tip. Added force should involve more and more of the rod until, at maximum, the entire rod is in flex.

If your tackle dealer doesn't go for this test, simply settle for flexing the rod back and forth, parallel to the ground. Hold the butt against your stomach with both

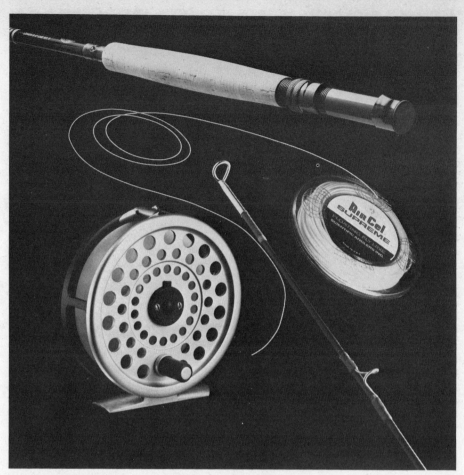

*Author contends that the complete fisherman will be
wise to purchase extra spools for his fly reel, then
learn to utilize the various types of lines such as
floating, sinking, bass bug, to match action of the rod.*

hands. As the rod receives steady increase of force, note the action point moving nearer and nearer the butt section.

Once you have your rod, the next step is to select the proper fly lines so that correct balance is achieved between rod and line. Let's discuss the types of lines for the specific methods of fly fishing.

Your most important line will be the correct AFTMA-numbered classification for the rod you've purchased. Let's say it calls for No. 7 weight. Now, no matter which type of fly line you choose, No. 7 weight will do for double taper, weight-forward and even a shooting taper.

Many fishermen who use a double taper for the dry fly and fish big waters that require an extremely long cast, will often have seventy to ninety feet of fly line sailing over their heads. Many of these anglers, with their special fishing setups, pick a line one weight lighter than the guy who sticks to more accurate casts of thirty or fifty feet.

In the case of weight-forward and shooting tapers, the reverse is true. Many casters will spool a one-weight heavier line, feeling that their rod works better for them.

But, for rule of thumb, my point is simple: No. 7 will average out just fine for most casters under average conditions.

The double taper line is the basic tool of precision fishing, especially for fishing dries, terrestrials and nymphs. And there is nothing wrong in using it for one or two wets or even for small bucktails and streamers. For dry fly

presentation, this line, in the floating type, is the best we have.

The long, progressive taper of the terminal end allows you to make feather-light presentations at all casting distances. When it becomes worn, reverse it and use the rearward section. It tapers the same in both directions from the center.

There's a choice of several special double taper lines for fishing sub-surface. On some, only the tip sinks; others sink gradually and still others sink fast and deep.

Each type of fly calls for some special treatment, while various water conditions require a specific type of line, if you are a serious fisherman and can see what each situation requires.

Weight-forward tapers are not unlike double tapers. The difference is that with a weight-forward line, one end tapers a little more abruptly to the tip, giving the ease needed when you're casting large or wind-resisting flies. It's a great line in the floater type for handling bass bugs, large salmon dries or any wind-resistant fly that calls for this more powerful, but less delicate, type of cast.

Salt water tapers and sinking weight-forward lines of varying density provide you with excellent sub-surface control of wets, deep-worked nymphs, bucktails and streamers. This type of line performs with a minimum of false casts.

Shooting taper line is a special line designed for making

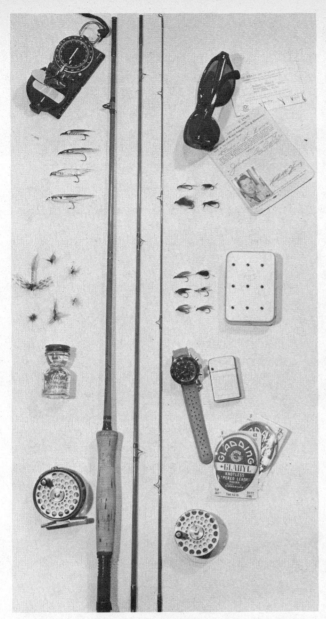

These are a few of what the author considers the basics for proper fly fishing, but in selecting equipment, he also recommends that one deal only with top pro shops.

To learn proper casting techniques, one does not need to be on water, but it does help to have a knowledgeable companion brief you, then correct mistakes in infancy.

the longest casts possible. The forward section is similar to a weight-forward line. However, in place of the normal shooting line footage, you attach lightweight mono and allow it to play out, following the fast moving head. This line is not suitable for delicate work, though.

Some of you probably will notice that I haven't mentioned level lines, but why drink vinegar when wine is on the table?

With the basic eight-foot rod, one can take advantage of most fresh water fishing opportunities that come your way. Trout, fresh water bass, panfish, landlocked salmon and a lot more are within the scope of your rig. The correct, special-purpose lines are your ticket to its full potential and your enjoyment.

But, let's say that you, like thousands of other anglers, are hankering to have a go at stripers, bluefish, pike, muskellunge, bonefish, snook, tarpon or Atlantic salmon.

That eight-foot rod and its light line leave you somewhat under-equipped. This is where a second rod will be needed.

I use rods both nine and 9½ feet in length. One of my nine-foot rods works so well with so many lines that it has become a jack-of-all-trades for me. In line weights No. 11 or No. 12, with all the special-purpose lines, large striper or tarpon flies move effortlessly up to ninety feet without overtaxing my arm.

These two balanced outfits, along with extra spools and lines, allow me to tackle almost any fishing situation within the purview of the long rod.

Up to now I've talked mostly about rods and lines, because these are the foundation blocks of your fly fishing equipment. Reels are a matter of personal preference — and

These North Carolina fly fishermen have learned about the enjoyment of tying one's own flies to match the conditions that prevail at the time.

just how much money you want to spend on one. I prefer a single-action for all fly fishing, but if an automatic is more to your liking, so be it.

But once you start fishing for large gamefish in either fresh or salt water, you'll be a prime candidate for the better quality reels that provide ample room for backing and boast trouble-free drag adjustments. When you tackle a one-hundred-pound tarpon, your reel had better be the best available. Don't forget to purchase extra spools for your

various fly lines, remembering that spool interchangeability is a must.

You also will need a selection of flies. Make sure they are of top quality, unless you like to watch your dries topple over, your wets come apart while false casting and your nymphs to look like nothing a fish has ever seen.

Pay attention to your leaders. They should be of heavy butt construction, the key to effortless casts in which fly and leader turn over without a pileup. A selection of nine

The old master, Gadabout Gaddis, takes the time to explain fly fishing tackle to a pair of Maine youngsters. Learning the basics is important.

and twelve-foot leaders should be with you at all times and in the proper range of pound test ratings to match the type of fishing you will be doing.

Make certain your leaders have a degree of stiffness, whether you buy them or make up your own. An excellent source of information is Scientific Anglers' Bulletin A1-2. They are in Midland, Michigan.

You also will need chest-high waders, a fishing vest, fly boxes, leader and streamer wallets and a landing net. For safety purposes, purchase waders with felt soles or purchase strap-on sandals or soles with steel grips. A wading staff isn't a bad idea, either. It has saved a lot of fishermen from swimming out of a tough river.

With the basic know-how and balanced equipment, there is only one place where you can learn more fully about fly fishing. The greatest classroom of all is yours on the lakes, rivers, streams and salt flats where you fish.

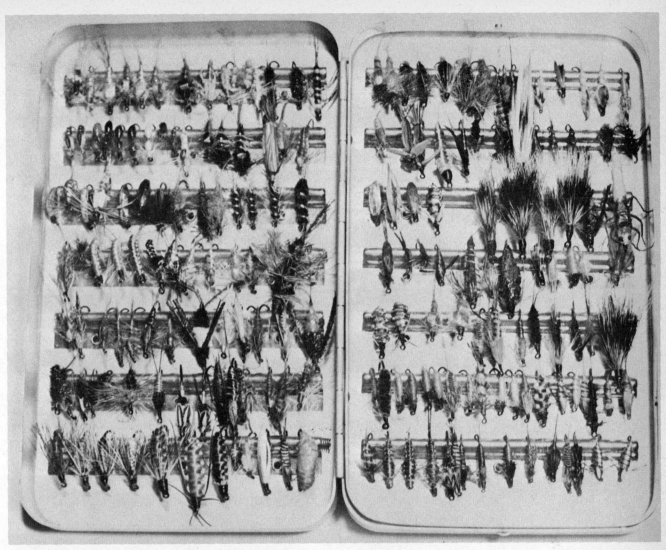

To the uninitiated, it may seem amazing that there are so many patterns of flies that qualify as nymphs, but this is only one of twelve boxes in Zwirz' collection.

Some years ago, a well known outdoor writer described myself and several others as the high priests of the fly fishing arts. While many fellow fishermen wrote me kidding letters, accusing me of everything from black magic to illegal use of the deity, in my replies I was brief and to the point; I am usually having too much fun with my fly line to have the time for sorcery, voodoo or other extracurricular activities.

Fly fishing is pure enjoyment and you don't need to know any hexes to master the art. All that is required is a properly balanced rod and a little knowledge on how to read water. I don't expect to make you an expert with this one chapter. I just hope to get you off on the right foot to build your experience on. With experience comes skill and enjoyment.

To a trout, living is serious business. In addition to such hazards as you, the angler, the trout must conduct a never-ending search for food that becomes more pronounced as he grows larger. Many times you may hear a fellow angler mutter that "they just aren't biting today." The truth is they are biting, but not in the water layer being fished and they are being so selective that, unless our angler finds the exact imitation of the natural food being favored, he's not going to score.

I once watched a sixteen-inch trout in a clear, limestone stream in Pennsylvania. It was mid-May and I stood quietly, watching as the fish carefully worked an area of riffle, looking for minute morsels, all taken from or near the stream bed. This rainbow completely ignored the occasional duns passing over his feeding station.

Now, some anglers might have tried a No. 14 dry Hendrickson to match those surface flies with total frustration as the end result. Conditions of the stream and the food choice of its trout population showed that wet or nymph imitations were on the menu. A dark ephemerella nymph, size 14, proved the trout were favoring anything that resembled the pre-emergence stage of the mayfly. During the time I fished wet, I did well, especially when I moved to a deeper stretch and fished a slightly weighted fly on a sinking line as close to the bottom as I could get it, with a slight twitching motion of my line.

Another time I was fishing a boulder-strewn run on the West branch of the Delaware River. Using a sparsely tied

By any standard, these are tremendous size trophy trout. Each succumbed to a deeply presented and imaginatively worked nymph.

light Cahill in the dry pattern, I had taken and released a good share of average-size browns, while covering every inch of productive looking surface. Foolishly, I assumed that every worthwhile trout around had been hooked and released.

Suddenly, across the river in a side eddy where I had placed a number of unproductive casts, I saw a fast swirl, a splash and a series of leaps. A large dace minnow was running for cover among the rocks of the shoreline. Under the frantic minnow lunged a dark shadow and, with a slash and half-roll, a brown of some twenty inches had one of his favorite dinners.

Now I can't say for certain that if I had fished the brown with, say a three-inch black dace bucktail, working deep and with darting motions, I would have lured it from its

station, but my chances would have been pretty good.

I'm not trying to build a case for wet flies with these two stories. I'm just illustrating the point that over a large part of any twenty-four-hour period on the rivers, lakes and streams of this country, one will be rewarded by relying on the various types of wet flies. These underwater patterns, fished skillfully, together with reading of the primary and secondary flows, will produce fish for you.

One thing to remember: When you first move into the water with your fly rod, until you know just what feeding cycle is in progress, you aren't making a mistake by probing the water from bottom to just below the surface with wet patterns applicable to the time of the month and the water temperature. The wet fly can be fished quartering upstream, giving it an occasional twitch for the appeal of motion, as it starts to swing downstream.

This fisherman uses the combination of wet fly and nymph, which is fished on a dropper.

At times, when more than one species hatches simultaneously, careful evaluation of just what is occurring and just what flyfish are actually feeding on is needed. Often a three-fly brace made up of imitations of the prevalent hatches may show you which fly the fish are taking.

It would be nearly impossible for me to list here all the wet fly techniques, as well as the more sophisticated methods used for proper nymph presentation. Instead, I will concentrate on making fishing with the nymph a little less mysterious. By understanding the nymph and its usage, the fishing of wet flies will be a valuable extension of your fishing tactics.

Nymphs are the immature forms of certain aquatic flies. As the caterpillar turns into a butterfly, so a nymph turns into the adult mayfly. The nymph lives underwater among the rocks and stones of stream beds. They may be enclosed

*Once you are on the water, it is important to take the
time to determine what species are hatching in the
local area, then properly matching your fly to hatch.*

in tough shells or cases, while others protect themselves by
forming little houses of sand grains and tiny sticks around
themselves.

When they complete their underwater stage, they surface
to emerge as flies and reproduce. There are nearly ninety
forms of mayflies, caddises and stoneflies that are
important to anglers. Many can be fished with identical

patterns, since they vary only slightly in color, size and
emergence habits.

Your choice of pattern and its proper presentation lies in
your knowing what is happening when you stand there,
ready to fish. It's frustrating to see fish all around you and
not have any idea how to handle the problem. It's bad
enough when you can't see them nymphing in deep water,

There probably is no more exacting sport than that of zeroing in on a wily bonefish cruising flats. The one taken here by the author was lured on by a wet imitation of shrimp.

but it's cruel and unusual punishment for an angler to see the feeding in progress and not be able to score.

I've seen inexperienced anglers stand in a stream and continue to cast dry flies at tail swirls, positive that they were seeing true rises to the flies they were watching float downstream, never realizing that the trout weren't touching the floating flies, but feeding just below the surface in what the late Jim Quick liked to call "slurping."

To do this, a trout will position itself in a feeding channel, then will refuse to move more than an inch or so in any direction. It raises and lowers its head as need be, sucking in the helpless nymphs approaching in the surface slick or just below. It takes a careful cast on a fine leader to fool him with an artificial. You have to offer an exact imitation of the prevailing nymph.

This is a prime example of the need for streamside investigation on your part. A few minutes spent on checking, before casting a bad fly choice and putting the fish

Unless an angler reads water intelligently, all the fly patterns in the world will not help him take a fish. This fly fisherman is concentrating on pocket water.

down with foolish casts that won't produce results, will add to your enjoyment. Without keen observation you'll be out of luck ninety percent of the time in the exacting world of troutdom.

A second form of slightly sub-surface trout activity often is referred to as bulging. The fish are moving about freely, throwing caution to the winds. A huge brown trout will move up and forward, giving you a flash of fin and its broad back for a split second. Tails slap the surface and heads smash through in last minute snatches at fleeing naturals.

In a river with good size trout, bulging can result in just two things — either you figure out the right fly and

As all fish feed on some form of natural food, it is not difficult to understand why they will accept a believable imitation of a wet fly or a nymph. This trophy fell for the subtle charm of a wet fly.

presentation and take fish or you end up talking to yourself.

There is another instance of peculiar conduct among trout. It's called tailing. The trout are grubbing the bottom for tasty stenonema nymphs and their tails protrude above the surface at intervals. They push and poke the nymphs from under the gravel and stones, dislodging them with their snouts.

Tailing goes on day and night in all depths of water where there are trout. I've watched for hours with varying intensities of polarizing glasses in shallow streams and have gone underwater to observe within a few feet of working trout. No matter what the depth, they look the same — tail up as they push and burrow, then down with the tail and a step backwards to suck up the dislodged nymphs.

When I want big trout, I go deep. I have learned how

*In any type of fly fishing, the tackle — meaning the rod, line and
reel — must be balanced to make a presentation that seems effortless.*

hatches occur and the approximate dates and times of day, so this is particularly effective for me. Year in and year out, emergence dates for any species of nymph stay fairly close to schedule.

Anticipating the great action resulting from emergence of the big stonefly nymph, I'll fish the deep runs and pools with a slowly worked stonefly artificial. The same holds true for the caddis nymph. When you learn a stream, you can pre-guess the emergence of a particular nymph. Examining stream-side foliage can bring you up to date on nymph activity. It's just like looking at the calendar when

you find a specimen adhering to the bottom of a leaf or branch.

Knowing the species will give you a good, educated guess as to which forms will be emerging over the next week. The thinking, planning and analyzing are all part of the fun of fly fishing.

The smaller the stream and flow, the more correct the pattern and casting have to be. On larger streams and rivers, one can get away with a careless cast or two and the use of more interpretive patterns that sometimes mask personal indecision. Such large buggy patterns like the gray muskrat

Even the fighting Atlantic salmon, fresh from the sea, can be taken on a deftly presented wet fly pattern.

nymph and the fledermouse often will produce fine trout that just can't resist a meaty, buggy appearance.

Some experimentation on your part is called for so that you may learn where and when to use offbeat patterns which have proved successful for others. This also holds true of unconventional nymph manipulation as against matching the actions of particular nymphs, as they emerge.

Needless to say, one should start learning about the various naturals and their artificial copies. Know emergence schedules and the aquatic behavior of the more important nymphs. It will take some research, but this should pay off with results the first time you work a nymph through a feeding channel.

There are several good books that you can read, among them: "Fishing the Nymph" by Jim Quick; "The Practical Fly Fisherman" by Al McLane; "Streamside Guide" by Art Flick; "Matching the Hatch" by Ernie Schwiebert; "Complete Book of Fly Fishing" by Joe Brooks; and my own book, "The Young Sportsman's Guide to Fly Fishing."

As for nymph patterns, I recommend hook sizes 10, 12 and 14 for American March brown, quill Gordon, Hendrickson, Ginger quill, black stonefly, yellow may and green caddis.

In wet fly patterns, the same hook sizes are suggested for quill Gordon, blue dun, March brown, leadwing coachman, light Cahill, coachman and gold-ribbed hare's ear.

Regarding tackle for wet flies, nymphs and streamers, I suggest you choose a semi-parabolic action rod, seven to 8½ feet for average waters and up to nine feet for the big Western waters.

As for leaders, try 7½ to twelve feet in 3X, 4X and 5X (heavy butt construction). Use 2X for large wet flies at night in a big water or big trout situation.

The fly line you use depends on the depth of water, rate of flow and specific conditions. A well outfitted fly fisherman should have a sinking line, deep sinker and an intermediate sinker available. A floater also is a good bet for those times when wets are taken just sub-surface.

This terrestrial is a tie of the red ant. While the list of effective terrestrials is long, this one, when well tied has proved to be especially deadly.

What happens during those relatively short periods when fish reverse their preference of feeding beneath the surface and a stream becomes alive with the rise of actively feeding fish breaking the surface?

This is a time of great excitement for most anglers, with no worries about whether the fly is deep enough for sub-surface fish, just concentration on careful, pinpoint casting while enjoying a stream bursting with visual activity.

There's no reason why you can't use the same rod for fishing dry flies that you use for wets, nymphs, streamers and bucktails. Modern taper rods have just enough semi-parabolic action to overcome the difficulty of switching from a delicate dry fly to a brace of wet flies.

I'm not saying that if you can afford two types of rods you shouldn't own them. But should you only have one, you have little to fear if it is one termed all-purpose by the manufacturer. If designed by one of the well-known manu-facturers, these are quite adequate for the various methods of fly fishing.

One thing is necessary: You have to have a floating fly line if you want to enjoy those special magic moments with floating artificials. Modern floating fly lines offer unsur-passed performance with a minimum of line preparation. Cleaning your line after each day's use is not necessary and, with the special preparations available, cleaning your line,

Fishing a fast run in New York's Neversink River, this angler has matched his dry fly to prevalent hatch. Success is obvious result.

This is the author's selection of flies that will work anywhere and are excellent for trout. At top are black gnat, Adams spentwing. In the center: brown bivisible, female Beaverkill with egg sack, Henderson; bottom: quill Gordon, light Cahill.

*While Western waters tend to call for a more heavily
dressed pattern, in big water fishing such sparsely
dressed patterns as this quill Gordon are most effective.*

when you do, takes only a few minutes.

Leaders for dry fly presentation run lighter than those used for wet types. Leaders with heavy butt construction are best and a selection in 3X, 4X and 5X calibrations will do for most occasions. Since your leader often gets shorter as you change flies, it pays to carry several spools of material corresponding to that from which your basic leader is made. It's easy to extend your leader by tying on an extra bit with a blood knot.

If you fish the big, heavy flows that often hold trophy fish or prefer to cast at dusk for the larger browns, then take along a couple of leaders testing 2X. The rule is simple: For big fish at twilight, use bigger flies.

For most wet and dry situations, leaders measuring nine feet long are fine, an exception being when you are fishing the dry fly in low, clear water. This situation calls for twelve-foot leaders.

A dry fly flotant, such as Silicote, has to be applied to the fly if you want to ride high and dry on the surface for any length of time. Just make one dip into the dope, then a few false casts to dry the flotant and your fly is ready to tempt the fish.

Dry flies are intended to be reasonable imitations of various aquatic or terrestrial insects floating on the water's surface. Mayflies, of prime importance to an angler, rest on the surface with a natural posture that borders on perfec-

One always must remember the various species of flies that hatch in specific types of water flow. If one can choose water for a specific hatch, fish will be there.

tion. The live ones don't tip over on their noses, their tails don't sink nor do they capsize like an unbalanced canoe.

A trout worthy of the name quickly learns just how each species should look as it floats by. Poorly conceived and tied flies rarely get a fish in slow or medium water. The trout has enough time to give the artificial the once-over and reject it. Only in fast, broken water will his caution be lacking, because of his almost spontaneous need to accept what appears to be natural food. Streams that are shallow and small will offer you the greatest opportunities for luring fish to the dry fly. This is true when fish are not actively feeding and applies to trout, bass and sunfish. In shallow water, visual contact with the fly is easier for the fish and he seems reluctant to let any easy meal drift by just a few inches overhead. In slightly deeper water, an adept angler actually can create a hatch in a trout's mind by repeatedly and carefully placing his fly over the fish.

On occasion, I've located a good fish with the help of my Polaroid glasses, then lured it to the surface with careful, accurate casts of a dry fly. In each instance, the fish has been scrounging along the bottom for food and it only took a cast or two to bring him rocketing up for a seemingly easy meal.

Things are different when fishing large rivers like the Snake, the Madison or the main stream of the Delaware. In challenging waters such as these, there is no substitute for knowing how to read the water and knowing the approximate dates and times for the hatches of fly species that spell surface activity.

Keen, clinical observation is the greatest aid to building personal experience. If you can lay a cast about twenty feet and drop your fly lightly on the water's surface, you'll find yourself eventually playing a fish. If you learn to drop that fly delicately and let it drift to a likely feeding station, you

*Although not thought of as dry flies, few creations are more effective
than patterns such as these using deer or caribou hair. Big trout
will suck them in, as will bass and many other types of game fish.*

certainly will take your share of fish.

Earlier, I talked about false rises that trout make when
flies are emerging in numbers. A novice thinks all those
splashes and rolls are signs of dry fly or surface takes by the
fish. Actually, the trout are chasing the fast rising nymphs.
They come to the surface so quickly that they break
through in their nymph-feeding frenzy. A sudden swirl, a
dimple in the water and a floating fly is gone.

The trout are rising to the surface to continue the feeding they started originally on nymphs, while the hatch was
progressing sub-surface.

Once you see this definite surface take, it doesn't matter
whether the flies involved are newly emerged, returning to
lay eggs or just spent flies dropping onto the surface. To
take a surface feeding fish you must use an artificial similar
in form, color and size to the natural ones present and you
must present the fly delicately.

There are times when more than one type of fly will be
present on the surface at the same time and the trout will
select one particular species on which to feed. They will,
for no apparent reason, completely refuse all the others, no
matter how many they may have had the day before.

Fishing Colorado's Frying Pan River, these two anglers are casting drys, using upstream quartering technique with floating fly lines.

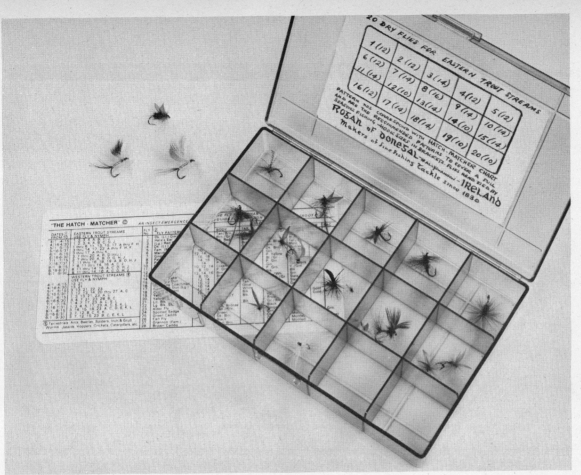

New anglers should utilize a system for choosing and identifying their flies. This outfit and chart was devised by Hatch Matcher.

This means you have to be especially watchful to determine just what the fish are taking. If mayflies and caddis are present, you won't catch trout with caddis if they are interested only in mayflies. You could, if you've done your homework, try a No. 14 dark quill Gordon that matches the mayfly hatch on which the trout are feeding.

It's important that you be able to visually follow the pattern you choose when casting. Most fish are lost because the caster doesn't know exactly where his fly is drifting. Fish don't hook themselves. You can't strike and hook them if you can't see your fly and leader.

If you have poor vision you are better off choosing patterns from the bivisible types. The contrasting color is a great help. Also a great help are hairwing flies and the lesser-known Trude patterns.

A thing that astonishes me continually is how many fishermen just shrug off the fact that line drag ruins almost every cast. If your fly is drifting slower than the naturals around it, you're not going to fool the fish. They learn quickly. A floating belly in your line will almost always cause line drag on the fly, if you don't mend the line during the downstream drift.

In addition to mending your line, it is important that your rod be held high so your fly line doesn't touch the water along the entire length you have cast. There are a lot of techniques for controlling a fly line in various flows of water. Some you will learn naturally; others you can pick up from any of the good books on fly fishing that are available.

Personally, I use several types of flies, each designed with a special purpose and specific water in mind. I prefer sparsely tied patterns for quieter, less turbulent flows. For probing rapids and the fast flows found at the head of large pools on big rivers, I keep heavier-hackled flies, bivisibles and hair-body flies ready.

I also carry a special box with appropriately tied copies of ants, flying ants and various beetles, because I know that there are times when such terrestrials will find their way onto the water surface. When the wind blows land insects onto the water, these terrestrials work like magic.

Another important consideration is your casting position in a river. You should be downstream of the area you intend to work. Casts made quartering upstream are easier to control and you are in a better position to hook your fish by instantly tightening your line once you notice the strike. Being downstream also allows your fly to float farther before becoming subject to leader or line drag.

A good basic selection of dry flies that will work effectively under almost any appropriate situation includes the light Cahill, quill Gordon, black gnat, spent wing Adams, brown bivisible, female Beaverkill with egg sac and the justly famous Hendrickson. I recommend sizes No. 10, 14 and 16. To imitate the most common terrestrials I go for black ant and the various beetles.

Now, each phase of fly fishing has more tricks and variations to it than can be covered in a single writing. By concentrating on basic problems first, you can learn how to catch enough fish to satisfy yourself that you are making progress at it.

The extras and fine points will reveal themselves to you as time and practice improve your skill, understanding and patience.

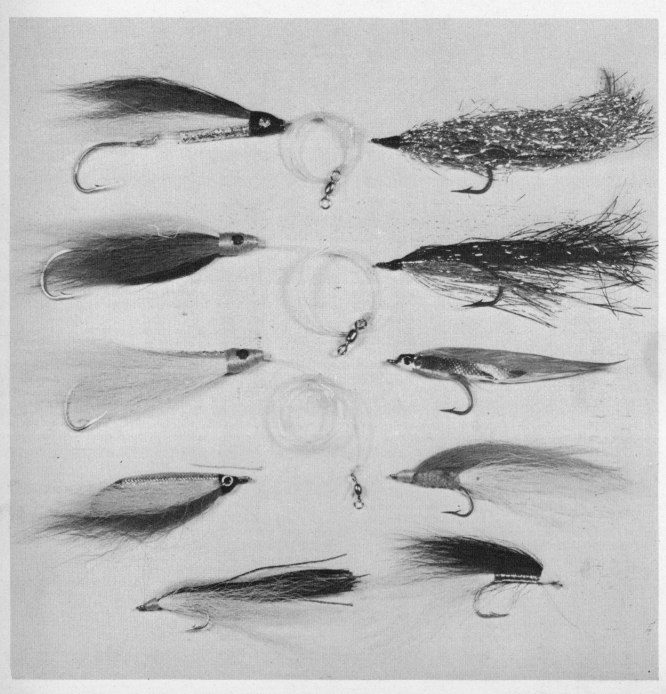

This is an array of salt water flies used by Zwirz for such species as white marlin, dolphin, lake trout, dorado, stripers, snook and tarpon. Northern pike, muskies and dozens of other varieties also delight in striking them.

One of the top flies is the streamer-bucktail. You cast it or troll it and, if you use it properly, it will catch larger fish than you might goad into striking with smaller, more delicate flies.

There's a great deal of misinformation about streamer flies. Some fishermen insist they are strictly an early season offering or just something to fall back on when streams are badly roiled and high. The fact is that streamers or bucktails will work on just about every fish that feeds on minnows and baitfish that these flies are tied to imitate. Not only are they productive on fresh water, but if you're a salt water angler, they are your best all-around choice.

Many anglers have another opinion that, because of the basically negative approach, use of streamers almost guarantees them unrewarding fishing. They look at streamers as a lesser art than dry fly fishing or fishing the nymph. You can always tell these types at a glance. They cast and work their streamers as if they were beating dust out of a rug. A streamer has to be fished with the same thought, skill and patience that you use with dry flies and nymphs, otherwise you'll be getting nothing but exercise for your efforts.

From this point on, the word streamer will refer to all streamer-tied patterns, as well as those using bucktail,

In this greatly enlarged photo, the delicate details of the grizzly optic are clearly visible. Described as the Homer Rhode type fly, the author calls it a favorite.

marabou and similar material.

Some streamers are carefully formulated and tied to imitate actual baitfish species. Among these are smelt, long-nose dace, golden shiners and spearing, naming a few.

Then we have the attractor patterns — highly visible flies that work under an amazing number of circumstances. These are probably best in off-color water and with fish that react more to instant stimuli rather than to the exacting requirements of imitation. Rainbow trout, brookies, tarpon, snook and even large and smallmouth bass often react this way.

Brown trout, on the other hand, often are selective about what they will or will not accept. Because of this, it's a good idea to use reasonable imitations of baitfish actually present when specifically fishing for larger browns.

Throughout this chapter, I've tried to emphasize that

any form of purism will tend to reduce your chances of success. Choosing the correct tools and using them at the right time to your best advantage is the secret of increasing your seasonal score of fish caught.

There are many different conditions in which you may find yourself fishing. Fast to medium flows will require different methods than you will use on lakes and ponds. Brackish and salt water are special fields that require knowledge of the species involved, as well as the requirements of the artificials used to entice them.

Wet fishing specialists have proved that, over a long period of time, sub-surface patterns take more and larger fish, if you concentrate on using baitfish imitations. This holds true for the early season as well as when the water becomes low and clear. Once waters reach their points of normal flow, it is important that your leaders, wading

Northern pike are especially avaricious when it comes to seizing on anything that looks like a baitfish. This one, just netted by the guide, is no exception in Ontario.

tactics and casts be as refined as your patterns and presentation.

It's not at all unusual for large trout to refrain from feeding during less important fly hatches. It's quite common among wise, old browns which have become, for the most part, cannibalistic in their feeding habits.

Once on the East Branch of the Delaware River, my intuition paid off with a twenty-three-inch brown. I had fished a medium-fast flow that ran for about a quarter of a mile over large boulders, some submerged and some protruding. Since a hatch was actively taking place and fish were feeding on the surface, I fished the dry pattern.

In less than an hour, I had released eleven trout. Just for the heck of it I pulled the 5X leader I had been using, substituted a 2X, nine-foot tapered Platyl, tied on a black-nose dace (bucktail) in size 6 and cast to the same water I had already fished.

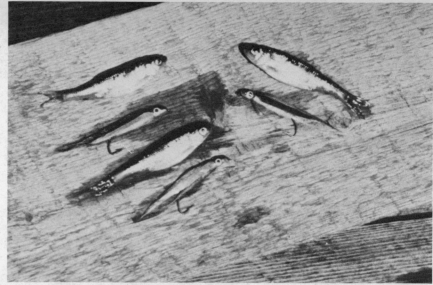

Note how the artificial streamers closely resemble small baitfish. Streamer pattern flares slightly in water for closer resemblance to the fish, its shape, movement.

Some of the largest trout fall to well handled streamers. This one is miracle marabou, which was created by the author and his wife, Glad.

I drew a complete blank.

Then I decided to practice what I so often preach. Off went the floating fly line. In its place I seated a spool containing a WetCel II line. Halfway down this deep run, just as I was mending line from the quartering upstream cast, I caught a glimpse of a dark form as it moved out from the shadows of a large, flat, underwater rock formation.

Through my Polaroids, I watched it follow that big

bucktail almost to my side of the flow. At this point, I delivered two twitches to the rod tip, which translated into two measured, darting moves on the part of the streamer.

The rest of the episode was made up of those things that keep fishermen smiling from one season to the next. While all this was taking place, smaller fish continued to surface feed in the areas not spooked by my casting and the eventual landing of that beautiful brown.

Attesting to the deadliness of streamers/bucktails is
this Field & Stream first-place record trout taken
from Snowbird Lake, Northwest Territories by the author.

Assuming you have read the section on using wet flies and nymphs, you know that I strongly believe in fishing the wet patterns when there is no visible reason for fishing the dry. That big brown probably had seen the dace pattern moving over its position when I fished it with the floating line. Even with the leader sunk, it still wasn't close enough to his station to entice him.

But, when it came into view right along the bottom stratum where he was hiding, the temptation was too much. For reasons of its own, the brown wasn't interested in surface fishing that day, preferring to keep to its cover. The large, minnow-like fly, sighted at his level, proved more than he could resist.

The greatest single item that leads to the better scores chalked up by modern streamer fishermen is the fly line.

Until recently, fly fishermen weren't getting their offerings down as deep as they thought. In the fast, deep channel areas of the big trout rivers, flies rarely were moving down along the bottom where the larger fish station themselves.

It's true that these large fish can be found at times at other depths and they do cruise during feeding sessions. But the majority of their time is spent taking cover from the current's force and from their natural enemies.

The fly that seeks them out down where they live will mean strikes for the angler.

You'll discover that high-density fly lines that sink fast are just the thing for larger waters and for those deep, swift runs that hold excellent pocket water.

On the other hand, you can pick one of the new floating-sinking lines where just ten feet of tip section sinks

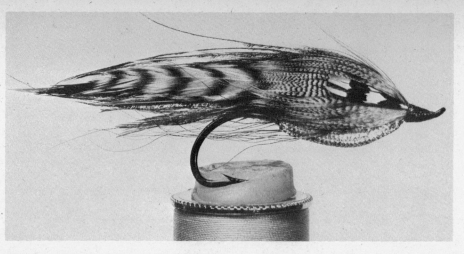

A favorite for big waters, this was patterned by Carrie Stevens, but it now uses mylar tubing for the body.

Below: Fine Alaskan catch was taken on bucktail. Rod is Wright McGill, reel is Pflueger Medalist, line is Scientific Anglers. (Bottom) Glad Zwirz presents streamer fly to this smallmouth bass for instant action.

Fishing out of Branson's Lodge in the Northwest Territories, Zwirz used spinning, bait-casting and fly fishing gear to collect these trophy lake trout. While he was fly fishing, all of his fish were taken on large streamers or bucktails.

for shallower streams. With the rest of the line floating, it's easy to pick up the fly for another cast. Because of the water moving against the tip and leader, you'll be fishing only slightly sub-surface and rarely as deep as you may have thought. Because of this, I always carry a fast sinking, a floating-sinking and a true floating line with me.

There are plenty of ways to work a river with a streamer or bucktail. If the problem is one of presenting the fly deep, an upstream cast may be the answer. Where foliage or rock formations hem you in, an upstream cast can be a must at times. The problem with an upstream cast is to mend your line fast enough to retain control of the fly. Added to that is the additional problem of possibly spooking the fish with the leader or fly line.

But, all casts present some problems. The most serious of all is an improperly mended line. Nothing is a bigger giveaway than to have your streamer drifting by a wise, old fish faster than the current itself. Little short bursts of speed — yes! Moving downstream hell-bent — no! Each and every darting motion, each pause and head-dive, must simulate the lifelike actions of baitfish present and recognizable to the gamefish you're after.

When it comes to big trout, it is the impatient angler who cuts off his own action. I was fishing the upper Connecticut River when I noticed a large fish stationed in front of a boulder. He rose to a grasshopper not sixty feet from me. I immediately fished him dry, using hoppers, muddlers and finally a rat-faced McDougal. Not a touch.

I then moved upstream from him and, with a sinking line, drifted a miracle marabou right in front of his nose.

For nearly six minutes I let that pulsating marabou dance and dart about. Then I gave the fly two or three long forward sweeps with my rod tip.

He nearly took the rod out of my hand with his surging, lightning fast strike. He may not have been hungry, but at that precise second he had come to hate that intruder. Patience and persistence paid off with a nice trout.

Using this downstream presentation to a known fish or a likely station, you don't have to worry too much about the fish noticing your leader or line. It rarely is a problem. Neither is the business of controlled speed or mending the line.

I get real enjoyment from locating such wise, old fellows, for they have eluded all of us fishermen for the time it takes them to grow into real heavyweights. I find it a greater challenge to find their weakness.

With fly fishing, such a veteran could take wet flies at dawn or at dusk or maybe a deeply drifted nymph or the natural presentation of a streamer that is a believable resemblance of a big trout's favorite baitfish. My experience is that, day or night, throughout the season, imaginatively handled streamers are hard to beat where trophy trout are involved.

When it comes to streamers, here are a few of my favorites that I am never without. The miracle marabous (the five major baitfish patterns), silver darter, gray smelt, male dace, Doctor Oatman, blacknose dace and muddler minnow for the close imitations. For attractor patterns I carry the Mickey Finn, white marabou, atom bomb, Sanborn and parmachene bell.

Chapter 6

FLY ROD ON SALT WATER BIG GAME FISH

This party, fishing with Zwirz in Nicaragua, play big tarpon fresh from their ocean grounds. The tarpon rates as the greatest acrobat in either fresh or salt water and usually accepts a wide variety of lures and baits.

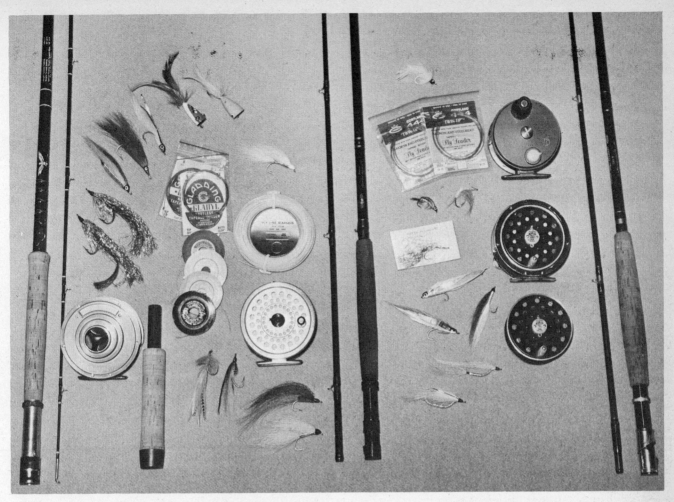

This is a typical selection of big game fly rods, reels, fly lines, leaders and salt water flies carried by author.

SINCE I FISH with a fly rod on both fresh and salt water, I can tell you there are a lot more tricks to the trade than many anglers realize.

Many say that being on the water is the essence of fishing enjoyment and that you don't necessarily have to hook and land fish to enjoy the sport. I believe it holds true for the majority of us, when I say that true fishing enjoyment stems from hooking, playing and landing many trophy fish. So let's take a look at what's going to help us land those large fresh and salt water gamefish.

Starting with the fresh water scene, there are few of the larger gamefish one can't entice to the fly. The major problem for the fly fisherman is one of specifics in relation to the accessibility of the fish you want to catch. For example, if a lake trout is forced to seek a depth of beyond thirty feet, because of water conditions, for all practical purposes he's beyond the reach and handling capabilities of conventional fly fishing tackle.

Some fish may go for a cast fly at depths as deep as fifteen feet, if you use the proper fly line — say, an intermediate or fast sinker. With a little bit of luck, it's not at all unreasonable for you to be able to beat a fifty or sixty-pound monster laker using the long rod.

This holds true for Northern pike and muskellunge, also. With the introduction of the Keely fly in recent times, it's a relatively simple matter to snake a bucktail or streamer

through the outer edges of weed beds and deadfalls and, in all instances, the basic step is your presentation.

If your cast is imaginative and accurate — the more imaginative and accurate the better — the greater your chances are of a trophy fish striking. But this, in itself, isn't enough if you want the odds in your favor with any degree of consistency.

There is a need for research on your part. A problem of many fly fishermen is that they have cut their teeth, so to speak, flyfishing for such fish as bass, trout and panfish. Few of them can visualize the smashing strikes, wild leaps and powerful runs of large tarpon or sailfish. Nor can they realize the beating that terminal tackle takes from an irate muskellunge, snook, albacore or even a heavyweight bluefish.

The highest degree of casting skill, the finest selection of tackle and flies are wasted if the fly fisherman does not make use of terminal rigs. These are used by experienced fly-casters when fishing for trophies, especially when they're after the greatest aerial performer of all, the tarpon.

When I want to test new, heavy-duty fly rods, reels or other equipment, I go for the toughest of fish, the tarpon. Any gear that can weather the storm created by these fish will fare well on other large species that can be taken on flies, including white marlin or sails.

In one instance, my wife and I were fishing out of our

favorite haunts on Florida's West Coast for tarpon and snook. Most of my fishing was done with the fly rod, especially during the week we fished exclusively out of Remuda Ranch in the Ten Thousand Islands area in the company of our long-time friend, the crackerjack light-tackle guide, Ray Bradley.

The tests we conducted during this session had to do with various salt water rod tapers, heavy-duty reels and terminal tackle for heavy, hard-fighting gamefish.

The reason for this all-out, conscientious checkout of fly-fishing tackle centers around our mutual need for definite data on hooking, playing and lasting qualities of certain items of equipment when they are abused by big fish. Leaders were particularly subjected to more than the usual scrutiny during these sessions.

Along with our findings relating to leader construction came the somewhat startling revelation that few rod manufacturers have the faintest idea of what must go into a true, big-fish salt water fly rod. Several highly touted fly rods actually snapped in two at the butt when subjected to power-casting techniques that a number of our older, time-tested rods have been taking for as long as ten years.

We also found that leaders and leader material offered by one well known mail order house didn't test anywhere near the claim stated on the label. Here are a few of the opinions formed by Ray Bradley and myself, along with

Ray Stephens of Remuda, who formerly was with the Florida Fish and Game Department.

Lot's of people will tell you that you can't hook a tarpon using a fly rod. That's rubbish. Using a combination of a razor-sharp hook, some special leaders we'll talk about later, and a rod with the backbone and power in its tip section, it is possible to sink the hook more often than many anglers would be apt to believe. And, the fly is less likely to be shaken loose than would be large spoons or plugs.

Experienced anglers agree that almost any heavy-duty fly rod that can handle Nos. 9, 10 or 11 fly line is suitable when after large gamefish. This might be true when fishing for fresh water gamefish. Lake trout, muskellunge and Northern pike will hold onto bait and lures too long for

Although considered to be in the realm of fresh water angling, this Atlantic salmon was taken by Bob Zwirz, as it started up a Canadian river, fresh from sea.

their own good, so far less rod power is needed to sink a hook.

On the other hand, many large salt water gamefish are quick to toss artificial baits, lures or flies, so it is necessary to strike them instantly with all the power your rod and terminal tackle will stand. A fly rod on which the tip section is too soft will be of little help, because it will collapse at the instant of strike.

During the tests, we also discovered that our rate of success in hooking snook and tarpon increased greatly in reverse ratio to the amount of line between us and the fish. Nearly forty percent more fish were hooked solidly when only forty or fifty feet of fly line and leader were off the rod tip. Thirty to forty feet increased our success rate.

To find out why, try this little test. Let out fifty feet of fly line and leader, then tie the tippet securely to an immovable object. Now, grab the fly line where it leaves the tip top and give it a pull. You'll notice quite an amount of stretch. Combine this with a rod that doesn't have any backbone and tip power and you have a rig that's pretty poor when trying to hook a hard-mouthed fish.

When a fish takes your fly or streamer, you have to strike immediately with all the sweep and power possible. Also quite important is your retrieve. The index finger of the hand you have on the forward section of the grip is used as a line control stop. At the end of each action-inducing retrieve of a foot or more of line, the index finger has to snug the fly line firmly. Then, as you bring the next

113

foot or so of line in, release the pressure while using your finger as a line guide.

Longer casts should be made if fish are seen, or thought to be moving at greater ranges. But, as I said before, your chances of hooking are greatly reduced with each foot of line over forty or fifty feet. When you have eighty or ninety feet of line between you and your fish, your greatest assist will come from the resistance of your line against the water. The fish must hook itself to a degree.

Rods ideal for most medium to large fresh water species can often be used for such salt water fish as bonefish, ladyfish, small tarpon and similar small fish. Usually these rods won't perform too well if you use them on the more difficult, larger species, nor will they use the lines required on a windy flat or pass. This calls for a rod of nine to 9½ feet, capable of throwing No. 10 or 11 special purpose fly line.

As I've attempted to show, any combination of tackle that can handle fifty to seventy-five-pound tarpon can handle any big, fresh water gamefish, along with sailfish or white marlin, that you can break before it decides to sound. You'll have far more control if you hook these large fish in

Above: Author prepares to release tarpon taken off a fly rod and a popping bug in waters of Florida. (Left) This amberjack was hooked by Carl Osborne off Hatteras, N.C.

4

Bonefish is but one of the popular species that fly rodders have learned to take with specialized gear.

relatively shallow water. They wear themselves out when the fight is punctuated with leaps and surface greyhounding.

Fresh water leaders of heavy butt construction can be used on all fresh water species no matter what the size. It's an advantage to use a twelve-inch shock tippet at the outer end of your leader in the case of Northern pike or muskellunge. A twenty-pound-test shock section is also reasonable. If you want some insurance in case you tangle with a record fish, the leader section to the rear of the shock tippet shouldn't test over twelve pounds breaking strain or you can kiss your chance at an IGFA record good-bye.

Shock sections aren't even necessary if you're casting for bones, small snook or tarpon, Arctic char and other fish of this weight class. Leader test strength can be pulled down, often substantially, by knots, wear and abrasion.

Check your leader. Bradley, Stephens and I have machine-tested twelve-pound mono that didn't break until it registered well over thirteen pounds, while another bit the dust at ten pounds. Remember, too, that a number of manufacturers offer well-tied, ready-to-use leaders in addition to coils of leader material.

Going on the proven theory that the butt section of your leader should measure at least two-thirds the diameter of the end of your fly line, you might find it to your advantage to tie a permanent leader butt to your line using a nail knot. This can be of thirty-pound test (.021-inch), and measure a good thirty-six to forty inches long.

Here your leader should have a butt section of twenty-five-pound test (.018). If you don't want to use a permanent leader butt I recommend a removable one, using the thirty-pound section, followed by normal sections of smaller diameter to form a leader that can handle the big game fly.

Here are some of the favorite leader combinations used by experienced guides who use the fly rod for big game-fish. For giant tarpon, sailfish, white marlin and big snook, especially if the latter are lying in mangroves: A nine-foot leader if you're using a permanent butt section, twelve feet if you're not. With the nine-foot butt, thirty inches of twenty-five-pound test (.018"); thirty inches of twenty-pound test (.016"); twenty-four inches of fourteen-pound test (.014"); twelve inches of ten-pound test (.011"); twelve inches of thirty-pound test (.021"). With a twelve-foot butt try thirty-six inches of thirty-pound test (.021"), followed by the same combination as listed above.

The shock section has two roles. It offers some protection against the fish itself, while also helping the terminal section resist breaking because of abrasion caused by sand and other natural obstacles. If a big fish, especially a tarpon, manages to put a leader across its gill covers or over its scaly back, the odds are that you've lost the old ball game.

When a fish takes your fly from the side, then you stand your best chance of hooking the heavyweights. A fish charging toward your fly during the retrieve has the best chance of creating slack because of its forward momentum.

Smaller, less savage salt water fish along with trout, heavy bass, lakers and so on, can be handled easily on the leaders described. Instead of using the shock section, use a twenty-four-inch tippet, ten-pound test. For big Northerns or muskellunge, a twenty-pound shock section will do instead of the thirty-pound test you use for heavy salt water species.

These highly satisfactory, special purpose fly lines and heavy-duty reels along with a lesser number of rods, now fill the needs of fly fishermen after big game. They will assist you, too, if you are looking for a new challenge in sport fishing.

Lying close in to the mangroves of Florida's Shark River, in the Everglades, Zwirz hooks snook with precise cast.

HOOKING AND LANDING a fish often depends on what you know about leaders, knots, swivels, sinkers, hooks, bait attachments, lures and special rigs. The finest rods, reels and other special gear are no good if you don't know how or can't use your terminal tackle in an effective way.

You must know what lures, plugs, baits and riggings are available and how to use them. So, let's take a look at terminal tackle one aspect at a time. First we'll cover knots, most of which are applicable to fresh and salt water rigs. Then we'll cover the others within the basic framework of each fishing category — fresh or salt water.

Every Boy Scout has to prove he knows how to tie certain knots in order to advance in rank. That wouldn't be a bad requisite for a lot of fishermen, either. More fish have been lost due to faulty attachments between line and lure than for any other reason. Sometimes a line cuts into itself, but more often than not a tie comes apart at a crucial moment. We all have seen novice fishermen casting lures and plugs only to lose at least half either during the cast or at the moment they are subjected to a strike. Indeed, we all probably have been guilty of losing a few plugs this way.

Since everything depends on the knots we tie, joinings and special methods of making terminal attachments, let's first look at some knots that have proven themselves reliable, along with several other important items pertinent to this part of your fishing preparations.

The first knot we'll look at is the improved clinch knot, probably the best knot available for tying a lure, plug, swivel or bait hook to your line or leader. You have to pass the end of your line through the eye of the lure or whatever you're using, then double it back over itself, making three or more twists. Next, pass the free end between the eye and coils, slip it through the main loop and pull it up tight.

One of my favorites for an exceptionally strong connection between the line and the eye of a lure, swivel or bait hook is the end loop knot. Simply bend your line over four or five inches from the end to form a U. Bend the U back and around itself in a figure eight, then slip it through the opening created by the backward turn. Pull it tight and that's it.

Great for joining two strands of leader or line, the blood knot also can be used by leaving one end about four or five inches long to act as a single dropped strand for fishing two or three wet flies. To make the blood knot, you loop the two ends of the line to be joined, then twist each end around the other line back toward the loop making at least four turns. Then, pull up on both ends of the leader. As

A close look reveals the intricacies of this veteran angler's terminal rig. It holds many of the items to be discussed. Catch was made in North Carolina surf.

Chapter 7

Capturing A Creelful Depends On More Than Knowledge Of Fish Proper — Like Your Tackle!

Understanding TERMINAL TACKLE

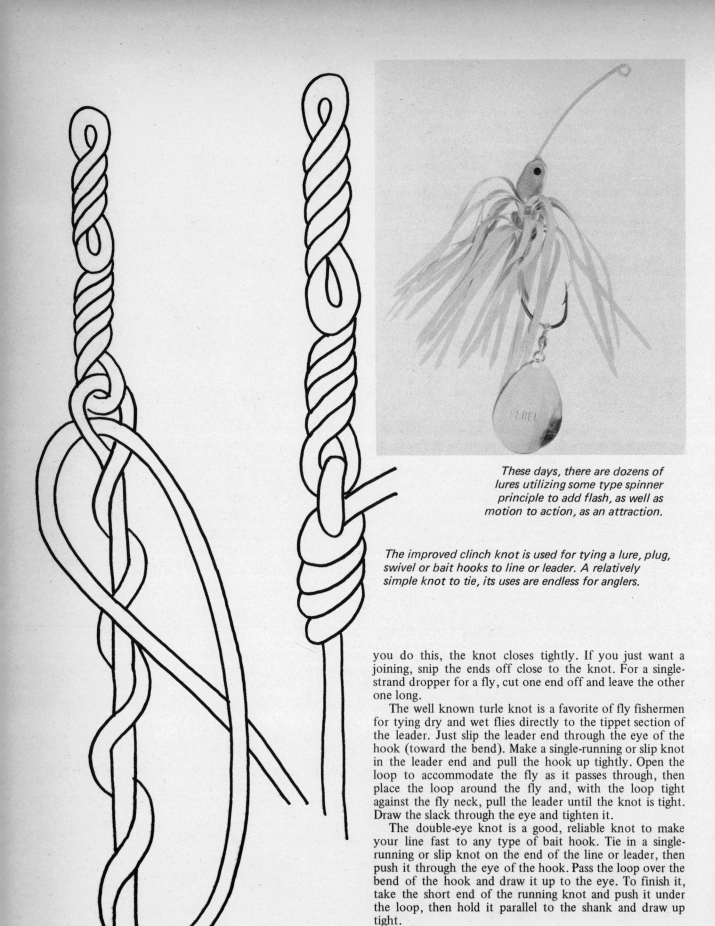

These days, there are dozens of lures utilizing some type spinner principle to add flash, as well as motion to action, as an attraction.

The improved clinch knot is used for tying a lure, plug, swivel or bait hooks to line or leader. A relatively simple knot to tie, its uses are endless for anglers.

you do this, the knot closes tightly. If you just want a joining, snip the ends off close to the knot. For a single-strand dropper for a fly, cut one end off and leave the other one long.

The well known turle knot is a favorite of fly fishermen for tying dry and wet flies directly to the tippet section of the leader. Just slip the leader end through the eye of the hook (toward the bend). Make a single-running or slip knot in the leader end and pull the hook up tightly. Open the loop to accommodate the fly as it passes through, then place the loop around the fly and, with the loop tight against the fly neck, pull the leader until the knot is tight. Draw the slack through the eye and tighten it.

The double-eye knot is a good, reliable knot to make your line fast to any type of bait hook. Tie in a single-running or slip knot on the end of the line or leader, then push it through the eye of the hook. Pass the loop over the bend of the hook and draw it up to the eye. To finish it, take the short end of the running knot and push it under the loop, then hold it parallel to the shank and draw up tight.

The perfection knot is for placing a loop on the butt end of your leader or when you want to use a loop to connect line or leader to a swivel or a lure or plug with a built-in swivel, so the lure can be changed without going through the trouble of re-tying a clinch. Take a turn around the leader or line, hold the crossing between your thumb and forefinger; take a second turn around the crossing and bring the end between the turns again and tighten it.

The dropper loop knot is basically for salt water use, but is great for looping a snelled bait hook to your line or leader when making up a fresh water bottom rig as well. Make an overhand multiple fold in your line in the desired

End loop knot is one of author's favorites and begins with nothing more than a double loop of whatever type of material one is using. Pulled tight, it is firm.

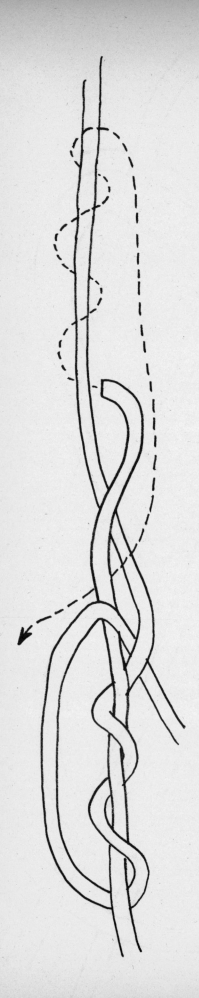

Illustration at left shows the requirement for tying the blood knot. It can be tied so that one strand is longer, allowing a single dropper strand for fishing two or three wet flies. (Above) Same knot, when tight.

spot. Squeeze a small, tight loop in through the middle, pushing it between the turns. Put your finger in the loop so you can't pull it out; pull sharply on both ends of the line and finish by pulling up tight on it.

As for fresh water gear, if you didn't have a suitable leader, the presentation of a fly would be difficult, to say the least.

Normally this important section between your line and fly is a delicate, almost transparent joining, except when you are using bait-casting or spinning tackle for large or particularly destructive fish. In these latter instances, your leader should be made of material that resists separation or cutting.

Special-purpose leaders are made from braided bronze, piano wire or heavy-duty nylon. The first two also come with nylon plastic coverings for added pliability and protection. If you intend to fish for Northerns, muskellunge, togue — or any fish with a good set of teeth — I recommend you begin by using the right type and test of leader. Check with your tackle dealer and look at the manufacturer's liter-

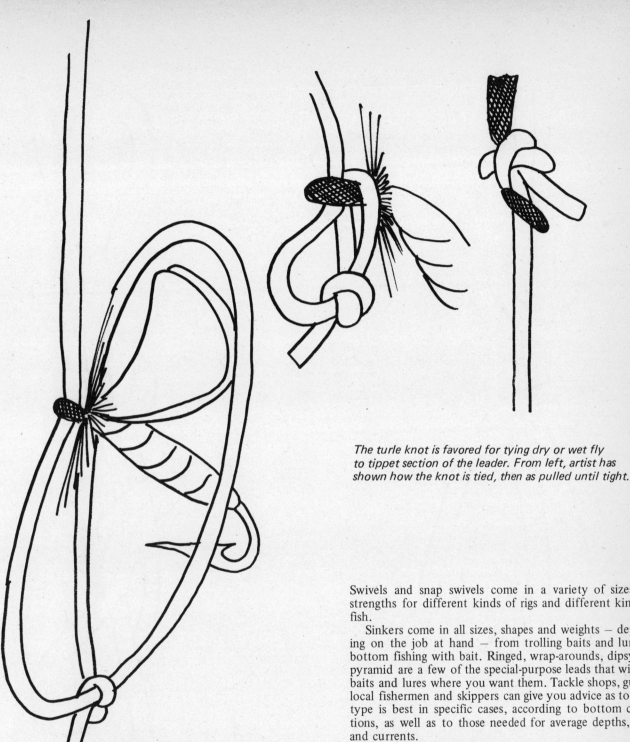

The turle knot is favored for tying dry or wet fly to tippet section of the leader. From left, artist has shown how the knot is tied, then as pulled until tight.

Swivels and snap swivels come in a variety of sizes and strengths for different kinds of rigs and different kinds of fish.

Sinkers come in all sizes, shapes and weights — depending on the job at hand — from trolling baits and lures to bottom fishing with bait. Ringed, wrap-arounds, dipsy and pyramid are a few of the special-purpose leads that will put baits and lures where you want them. Tackle shops, guides, local fishermen and skippers can give you advice as to what type is best in specific cases, according to bottom conditions, as well as to those needed for average depths, tides and currents.

Remember, though, that heavy tackle usually will require heavy sinkers, but special equipment such as lead-core or wire lines can help keep a lure down with a minimum of extra weight.

There are several types of artificial baits, each designed to be used when fishing a certain depth and to imitate specific kinds of natural bait. Successful lures have built their own names by proving themselves in certain areas or on different gamefish. Any tackle shop should have an ample selection, especially of those types that are popular locally.

Spoons are made to dart and dive and use several design concepts as to what best imitates the action of living bait. These range from such fixed-hook types as the Johnson

ature before you select a leader for use on a fish you don't know. If you are a bait-caster who uses anything but mono, you'll need at least the nylon type. All three are available in different lengths and pound tests.

If you tie an average spinning lure directly to your line, expect a badly twisted line in no time at all. Depending on the in-water action of a lure, this could be your fate after just a couple of casts or in less than an hour of trolling.

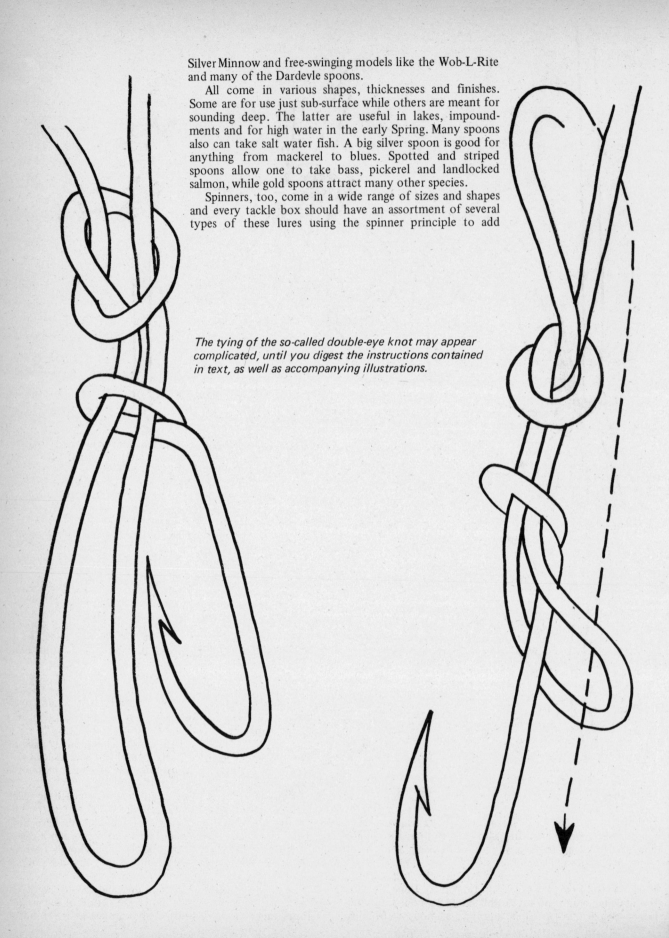

Silver Minnow and free-swinging models like the Wob-L-Rite and many of the Dardevle spoons.

All come in various shapes, thicknesses and finishes. Some are for use just sub-surface while others are meant for sounding deep. The latter are useful in lakes, impoundments and for high water in the early Spring. Many spoons also can take salt water fish. A big silver spoon is good for anything from mackerel to blues. Spotted and striped spoons allow one to take bass, pickerel and landlocked salmon, while gold spoons attract many other species.

Spinners, too, come in a wide range of sizes and shapes and every tackle box should have an assortment of several types of these lures using the spinner principle to add

The tying of the so-called double-eye knot may appear complicated, until you digest the instructions contained in text, as well as accompanying illustrations.

124

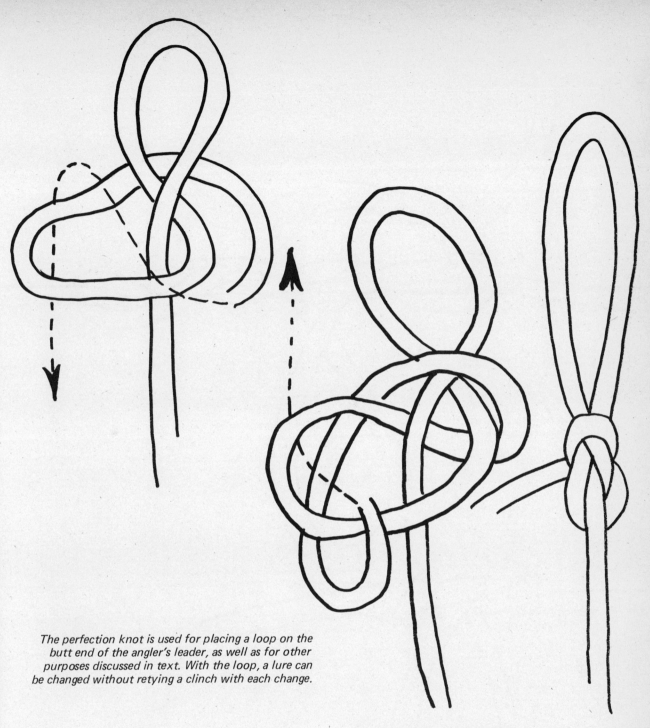

The perfection knot is used for placing a loop on the butt end of the angler's leader, as well as for other purposes discussed in text. With the loop, a lure can be changed without retying a clinch with each change.

motion and flash to their basic action. Some are designed for fishing in combinations with bait while others are used solo, having all their appeal built into their overall look and action.

Plugs — actual body design artificials — are shaped and painted to imitate baitfish and other natural baits of interest to gamefish. You can get them for surface, sub-surface and for bottom stratum use, the latter being where the action often is for big fish. Your tackle box is incom-

plete without a selection from each category, thus being prepared for the conditions you meet, ranging from the type of water to the whims of the fish.

Many plugs have been designed with the largemouth bass in mind, but have proved excellent for a wide range of fish. There are so many successful plug designs that I could not begin to list them all. A leisurely visit to your tackle shop and a careful examination of each type of plug will put a few goodies into your tackle box. Like spoons, many plugs work well for salt water fish such as tarpon and snook.

The risk run by fresh water fishermen through the use of faulty gear can be multiplied ten times for the sportsman who fishes heavier salt water species. Fresh water trout, a trophy muskellunge or a large Florida black bass are one thing on light tackle. Giant tarpon, snook, sails, kings and

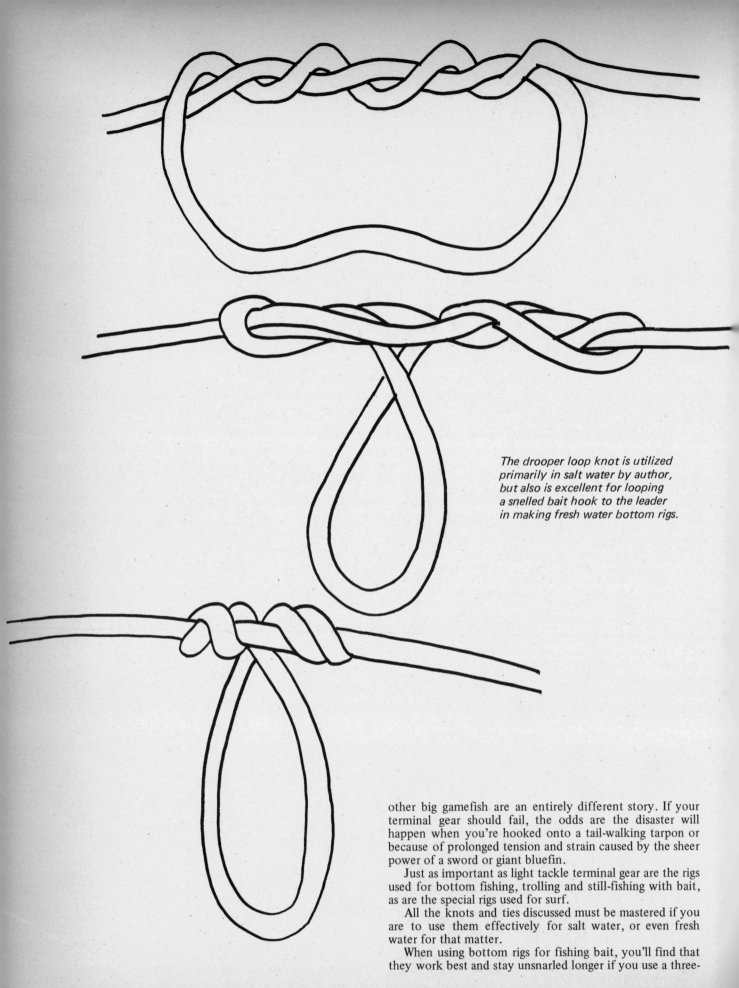

*The drooper loop knot is utilized
primarily in salt water by author,
but also is excellent for looping
a snelled bait hook to the leader
in making fresh water bottom rigs.*

other big gamefish are an entirely different story. If your terminal gear should fail, the odds are the disaster will happen when you're hooked onto a tail-walking tarpon or because of prolonged tension and strain caused by the sheer power of a sword or giant bluefin.

Just as important as light tackle terminal gear are the rigs used for bottom fishing, trolling and still-fishing with bait, as are the special rigs used for surf.

All the knots and ties discussed must be mastered if you are to use them effectively for salt water, or even fresh water for that matter.

When using bottom rigs for fishing bait, you'll find that they work best and stay unsnarled longer if you use a three-

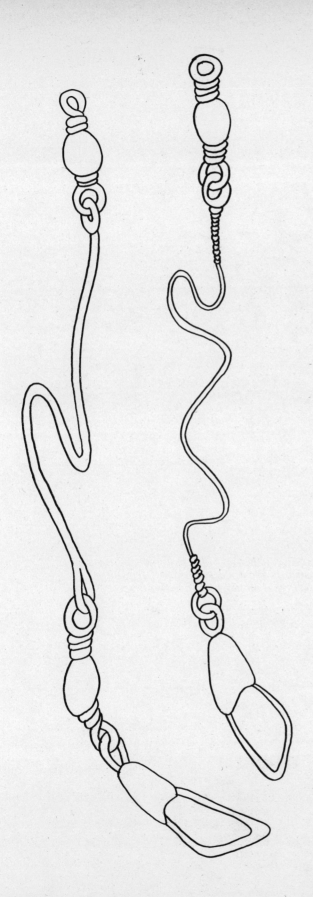

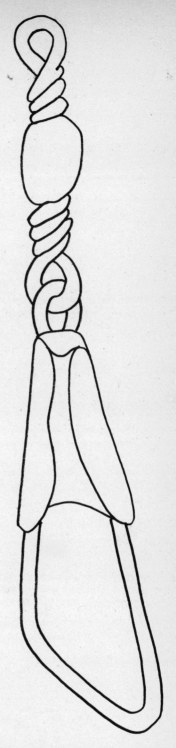

Left: There are various types of leaders available, but their lack can complicate proper presentation.
This subject is dealt with more extensively in the text. (Above) Swivels are a near must for any type of serious fishing and are designed for specific fishing.

way swivel in tying your rig. These never present a problem when one is after the majority of the bottom feeders, but blackfish may cause them some trouble.

Because the blackfish likes to hang out in obstruction-littered places, I recommend this blackfish rig: Take a sixteen-inch nylon leader and tie it in about four inches above your bottom sinker. I only use one hook, but you can tie another ten-inch snell, with hook, about halfway up the long leader. A bank sinker will tend to hang up less than

Fishing in the rugged surf, Zwirz wouldn't have this heavy stringer of fish, unless all of his terminal tackle and accessories were reliable and well planned. Fish in this instance are stripers and pollack. (Below) Deep-working plugs such as this model from Rebel that imitate the common baitfish types are the most deadly attractors.

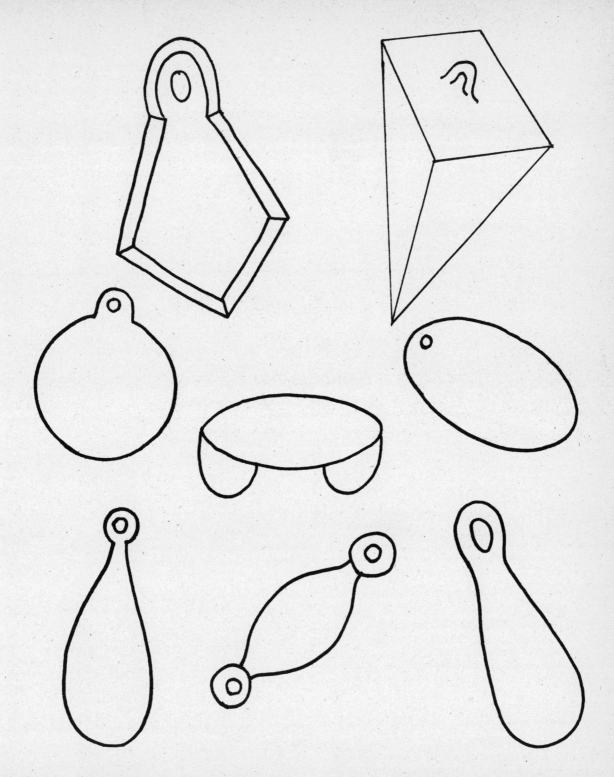

the pyramid type. This rig also is good for Winter flounder, whiting and other bottom feeders.

For the standard bottom rig, you'll use the three-way swivel as I mentioned above. A basic rig, it can be used almost anywhere — in bays, from bridges — when bottom feeders are your target. It can be a double-barreled threat, if you add another snelled hook just far enough above to clear the one at the bottom. On occasion, if after hake, whiting or smelt one can add a third hook, although I advise against it. A third hook simply adds to the chances of the line

There is no end to the shape, size, design and even the purpose of the sinkers available to today's crop of serious fishermen. Tackle shops and professional guides can best suggest the needs for local waters.

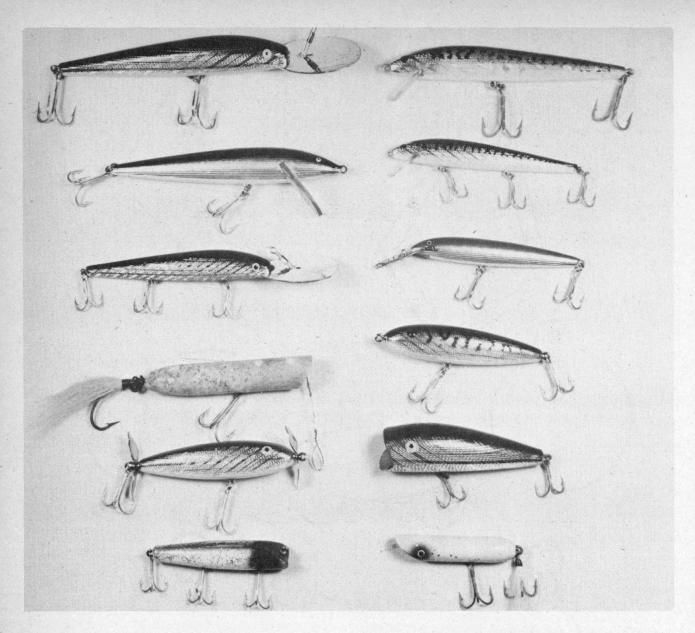

Most plugs attempt to imitate the body design and the swimming action of the common baitfish. Of this array, some are used primarily for surface use, others work best for sub-surface fishing, still others, down deep.

wrapping or tangling. All these bottom rigs can be used with three to twelve-ounce bank sinkers, depending on whether you are in sheltered waters or on a combination of water depth and rate of tide or currents.

A fluke or Summer flounder rig requires a leader of twenty-four to twenty-six inches in length attached three or four inches up from your sinker. You can use the three-way swivel. Often I'll splice in a pair of fluke spinners just ahead of the hook to attract any fish that may miss seeing the bait at a distance. These rigs are produced commercially as are most of the other popular bottom setups.

The spreader type rig has been a favorite of flounder fishermen. It is easy to use, but is beginning to lose its popularity among newer salt water anglers; while it is trouble-free, the rig makes it hard to feel a light nibble, so many fishermen use the basic blackfish rig instead.

The high-leader rig was tied originally for sea trout (weakfish). The basic rig will work well on other fish that are likely to frequent the bottom. Blues, pollack, stripers (rockfish) and other active feeders will never realize it is primarily for weaks. Often tied as a two-hook outfit, the extra bottom hook takes the bottom-grubbing fish, while the upper primary rig satisfies the others. To make a high-

leader rig, tie in a three-foot leader three to four inches above your sinker. A shorter bottom snell can be tied in four inches above the sinker.

The egg-sinker rig is an inshore, calm water outfit that works on the same principle as the fish-finder rig. The line feeds out of the sinker without any feeling of weight or tension. This makes it good for skittish fish that might drop the bait if they felt any weight.

Swivels are available in varying sizes and strengths ranging from small ones used for light, inshore fishing to heavy-duty types for use when after big gamefish. For more cast-

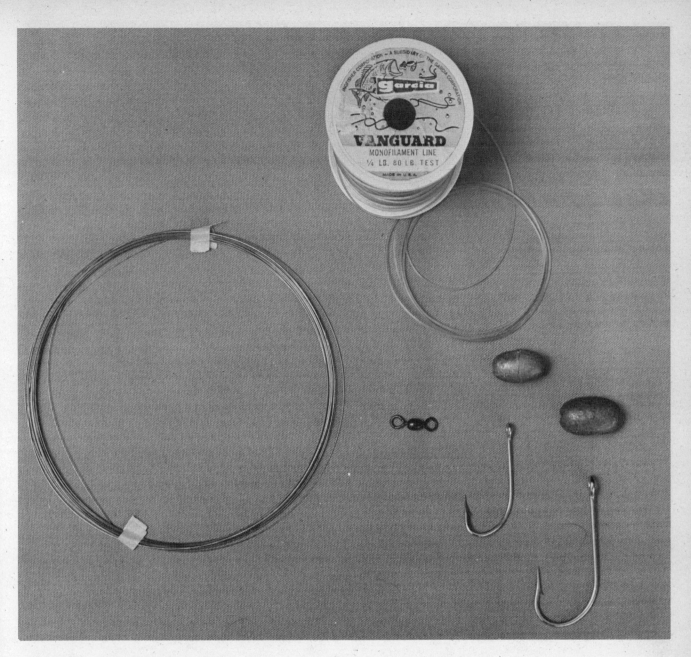

In choosing wire leaders, hooks and other accessories, make certain that you use top quality products, then rig them correctly. (Right) Blackfish rig uses a nylon leader tied above a bottom sinker. It works well with types of fish that feed on the bottom.

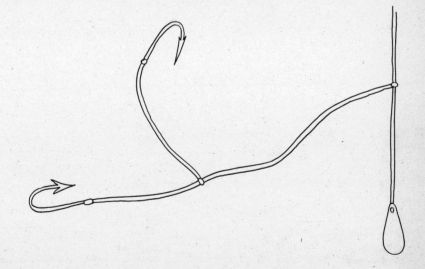

ing and trolling situations, the combination snap and barrel is used. Don't forget the three-way model for bottom rigs or special weighted trolling setups. Stay clear of poor quality swivels. A lot of fish have been lost because of junk terminal tackle imports now on the market.

Salt water sinkers are a lot more than just globs of lead weight. They come in many weights and are designed for several functions.

Bank sinkers are probably used most often by fishermen. Adequate in all but exceptionally deep water, bank sinkers are good for sandy or rocky bottoms.

Egg sinkers, as stated earlier, are great for inshore fishing for nervous or shy fish. They not only fool the feeding fish, but allow one to feel the faintest nibble.

Pyramid sinkers are at their best for fishing baits in the surf. They also can be used for general fishing and on sandy

Some time spent with a knowledgeable tackle dealer or even a guide will do much to help one understand what hooks and accessories should be purchased, if one is to be properly equipped for the specific types of fish.

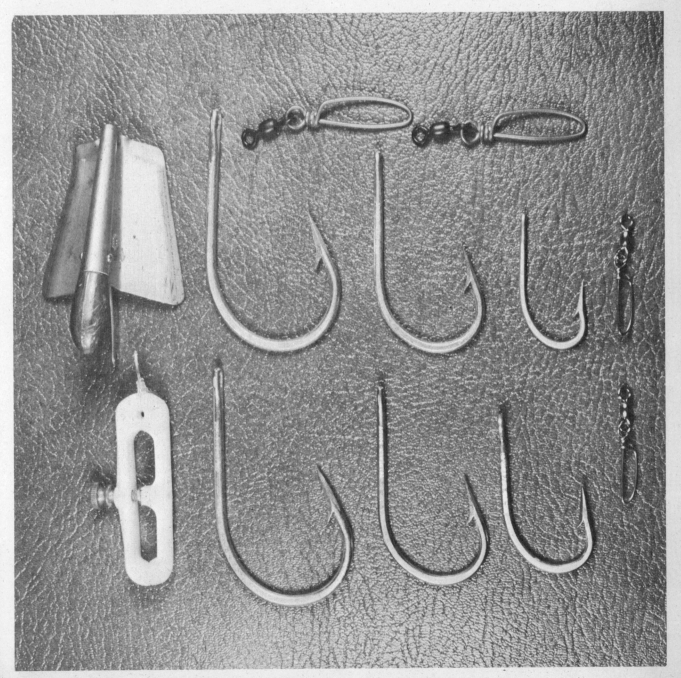

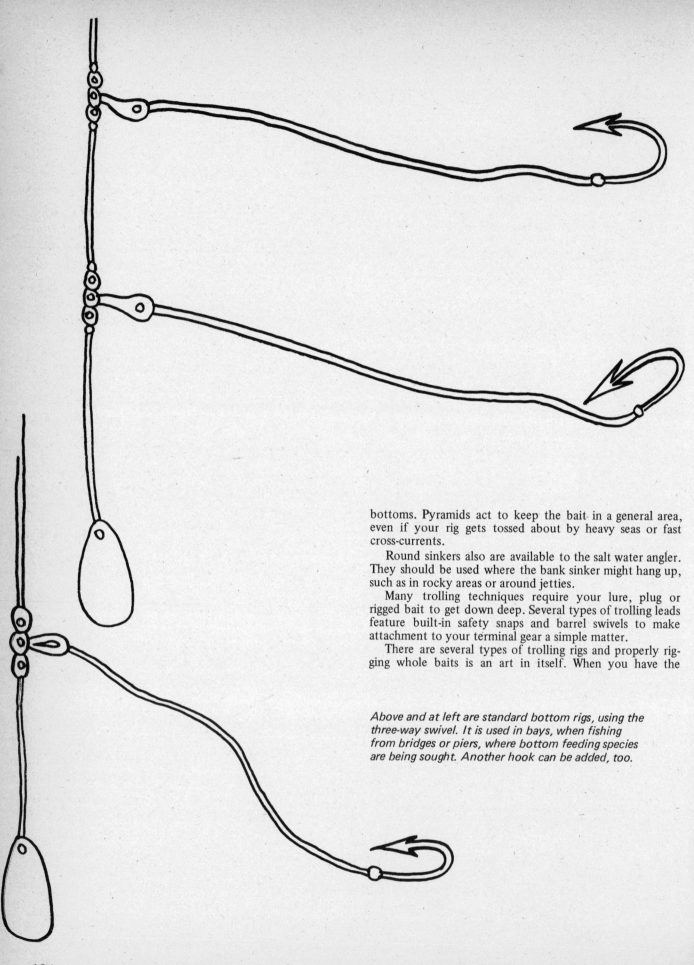

bottoms. Pyramids act to keep the bait in a general area, even if your rig gets tossed about by heavy seas or fast cross-currents.

Round sinkers also are available to the salt water angler. They should be used where the bank sinker might hang up, such as in rocky areas or around jetties.

Many trolling techniques require your lure, plug or rigged bait to get down deep. Several types of trolling leads feature built-in safety snaps and barrel swivels to make attachment to your terminal gear a simple matter.

There are several types of trolling rigs and properly rigging whole baits is an art in itself. When you have the

Above and at left are standard bottom rigs, using the three-way swivel. It is used in bays, when fishing from bridges or piers, where bottom feeding species are being sought. Another hook can be added, too.

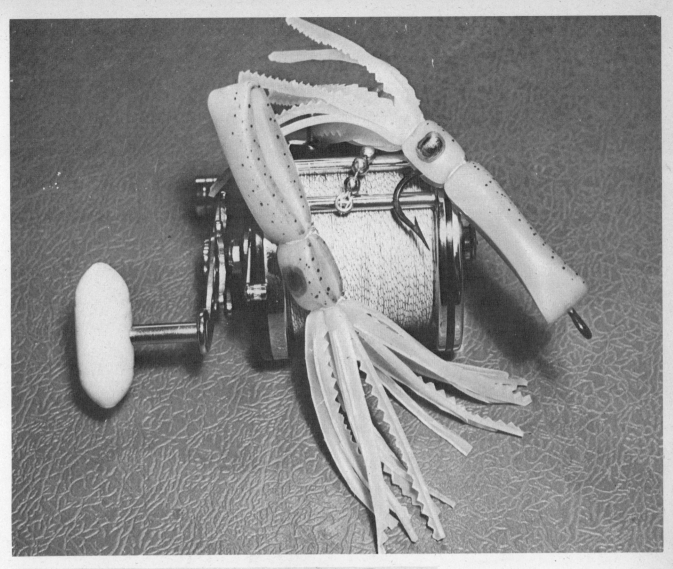

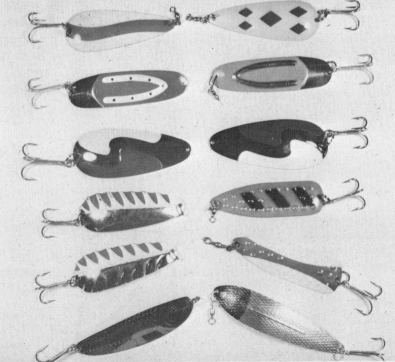

Left: Spoons are made to dart, dive and, in general, imitate the action of live baitfish; types and designs are numerous. (Above) Man's ingenuity makes it possible to imitate nearly anything in the bait line, including those such as the Bingler Squid.

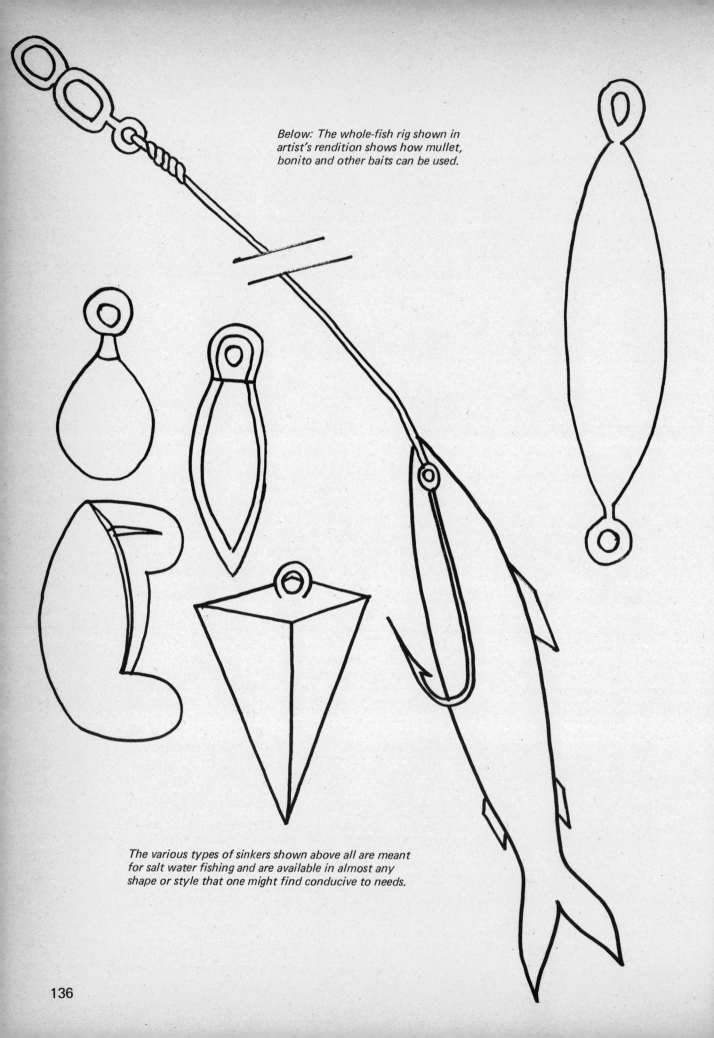

Below: The whole-fish rig shown in artist's rendition shows how mullet, bonito and other baits can be used.

The various types of sinkers shown above all are meant for salt water fishing and are available in almost any shape or style that one might find conducive to needs.

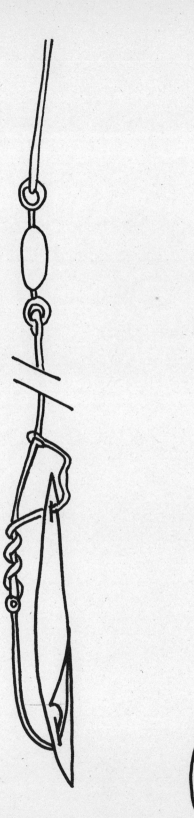

At far right is a strip-bait rig, which finds favor for medium or large salt water species. The text explains fully how to cut the bait for best results. The other rig is a spinner setup known as the Cape Cod, which is designed for catching big stripers.

services of a skilled mate or charter boat captain, it would pay to observe carefully and remember well.

Many of the most sought-after gamefish have strong perferences for rigged bait or artificials, so one should have an idea of how to approach trolling. Stripers, blues, bonito, albacore, wahoo, school tuna, swords, marlin, sails, kings and even bluefin tuna are among the possibilities.

Depending on the type and size for which you're trolling, you can use mullet, bonito or other favorite baits with a whole-fish rig. With the backbone removed (using a special tool), so the fish swims more realistically, work a wire leader into the mouth of the bait and attach to a one, two or three-hook lashup.

Simpler to rig, strip-bait often is all you need to get a strike from medium to large salt water species. The bait is a formed strip of squid or a cut from the favored baitfish available. It is tapered, widest in the middle and sharpest at the tail end.

Punch two holes, one in the head and the other where the hook is to be passed through. Pass the hook point into the strip; with a section of leader that stays after you bend your leader through the bend of the hook, pass it through the strip and take a full turn around your leader just ahead of the bait. This will secure the hook to the bait and help keep it laid out straight, even if dragged in the boat's wake.

The spinner rig for stripers is known as the Cape Cod and is used with sea worms or striper-length pork rind. It's not too different from the Montauk or the June bug familiar to fresh water anglers. It's a great early-season teaser of stripers and works miracles in all inshore trolling.

Chapter 8

PROFESSIONAL TRICKS WITH SPINNING TACKLE

EVER HEAR OF the bubble?

It's one of the simplest and most practical, though often overlooked, accessories available to the fly fisherman. A bubble can turn you from a mere hardware slinger into a crackerjack fly-caster. Used correctly, this little magic ball comes with a hatful of tricks that will help you land more, and oftentimes larger, fish.

The technique for using the bubble has been common knowledge in Europe for many years, but was ignored in this country until the late 1940s. Even then, its use was limited primarily to steelhead fishermen on the West Coast and a few others who used it with regular spinning tackle after realizing it offered a way of reaching surface feeding trout in rivers such as the Madison and the Snake.

When should you use a bubble?

Well, how often have you spent a day casting spinning lures to active trout that you could see, then come up empty-handed? Then along comes a guy with a fly rod, a reasonable imitation of the prevailing hatch of flies and begins reeling them in from the runs you found fruitless. It's a simple matter of supply and demand. The trout are looking for a specific imitation that the fly fisherman provides, but you don't.

When consistent fly hatches begin on typical trout waters, much of the effectiveness of spinning techniques is lost. Spinning hardware works during the early season and after hatches have fallen off, but is a waste of time when the fish become highly selective in their diets. In a heavily fished stream, most trout will become lure-wise rapidly or they will be caught on a treble hook early.

Spinning with a bubble can offer you advantages no matter what part of the country you fish and can be used with bass bugs and live-baits in addition to wets, dries, nymphs or streamer bucktails.

139

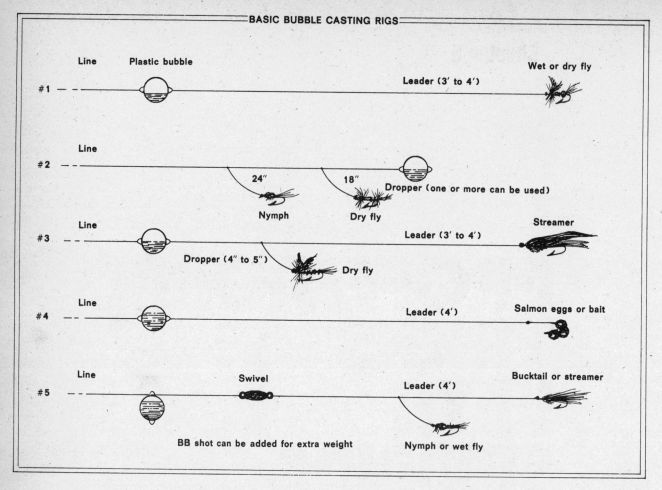

BASIC BUBBLE CASTING RIGS

#1 Line — Plastic bubble — Leader (3' to 4') — Wet or dry fly

#2 Line — 24" Nymph — 18" Dry fly — Dropper (one or more can be used)

#3 Line — Dropper (4" to 5") Dry fly — Leader (3' to 4') — Streamer

#4 Line — Leader (4') — Salmon eggs or bait

#5 Line — Swivel — Leader (4') — Bucktail or streamer — BB shot can be added for extra weight — Nymph or wet fly

The bubble technique is equally effective whether the angler chooses ultralight, medium or heavier action spinning tackle.

The bubble technique is effective on large or smallmouth bass, all the trout including steelheads and on such fish as bonefish and brackish water stripers. It can even be of help, if one knows how to use conventional fly-casting equipment and has it in hand.

Designed and made in several different forms, the bubble is basically a clear, hollow float. It may have a simple stopper that will allow you to fill it with water or mineral oil or it may have a spring-actuated part that you depress to let liquid enter. Outside the bubble has provisions for fastening your line and the special leader arrangements we'll be talking about.

There are various ways to use a bubble when fishing with flies and the drawing shows the basic bubble spinning rigs. Depending on the need, the technique for using each rig is varied by adding or removing liquid and, in certain cases, split-shot and by the type of fly being used.

With a bubble, it's possible to fish the lightest salmon eggs, grasshoppers, grubs or other bait, as well as present flies and other generally weightless lures down in the bottom stratum of heavy, deep running rivers.

In my opinion, though, the bubble — as produced today — could be improved. It should be clearer, easier to fill and have easier tie-on abilities. The smart fisherman will prepare several rigs before setting out. Don't wait until the right situation presents itself, then try to prepare the bubble while fish are jumping all over the place. I use mineral oil instead of water and use an eye-dropper to pre-fill. Mineral oil won't evaporate as quickly as water during warm weather.

What rig to use? A little common sense coupled with a

Dry fly/nymph combination shown on left is illustrated in greater detail in the line drawing on opposite page. Demonstrated at the right is a more typical setup for dry fly fishing.

little knowledge of the type of fishing one is likely to be encountering will dictate just what rig to use. If I'm using nothing more wind-resistant than a single dry fly or a dry and a nymph, I'll weight my bubble only to the point needed for satisfactory casts. Wind and the width of unwadeable water are the two factors I consider as to which rig and set-up will work best.

If the waters I'm fishing are big, I'll usually use a No. 2 or No. 3 rig. I also may substitute a nymph for a dry or a large wet fly for a streamer depending on the season and other conditions. As you can see, knowledge of hatches and prevalent baitfish is needed and this is where schooling is to

your advantage. Knowing one hatch from another and having an idea of the various hatch timetables, especially the mayfly species, can pay off.

In my own preference, with the No. 5 rig, the bubble is attached to the line in such a way that it rides free. This way, it drops no farther than the barrel swivel tied about four feet from the tippet of the terminal end of your mono.

On big rivers, where you find trophy-size trout usually lying deep along the bed and behind or close in front of

Use of partly filled bubble enables spin fisherman to reach pockets and control presentation depth of fly or natural bait.

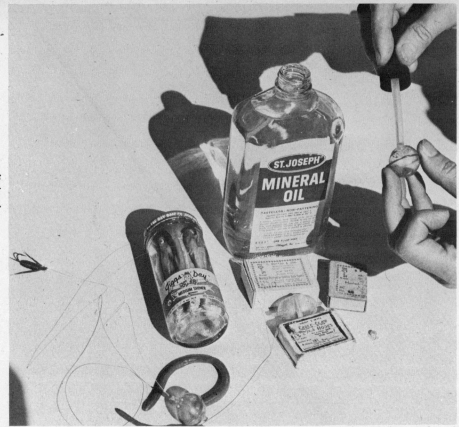

Use of an eyedropper facilitates filling of plastic bubbles to right weight for satisfactory casting.

Many of the fly patterns used for conventional fly fishing, some of which are shown below, can be used while fishing the bubble system.

142

Weighted bubble and streamer are right combination for use in deep runs and pockets of deep, flowing water.

obstructions that break the flow, it is important to put your fly, bait or lure right down where the fish are stationed and not where you wish they were. This holds true for secondary flows bordering the primary feed lines, also.

In really fast, deep runs, add a couple of BB shot to make sure the bubble rig sinks deep enough and quickly. Remember to leave an air pocket in it even when going deep. The air pocket will keep your rig just off the bottom as it moves downstream. Again, experience will teach the right combinations of liquid and weights for specific stream and river conditions and the most effective ways to present the lures or bait you've chosen to use.

Sometimes largemouth bass will seem to be turned off by the usual offerings of wood or plastic and go only for a bass bug of one type or another. While this is great for an angler with a weight-forward fly line, it doesn't do too

much for you, if you can't cast with a fly rod or only own a spinning or spin-cast rig.

The solution to this is easy. Give him what he craves by using any of the first three rigs with the rod and reel at hand. Don't overlook the attractiveness of a dropper tied in ahead of your bass bug. A wet fly, twitching just below the surface, usually works on the most stubborn bass. It also works in shallow areas on smallmouth bass.

Bass are nosey. They'll investigate anything that moves, slurps or gurgles and they have been known to pounce on the bubble, itself, completely ignoring the bug. Therefore it makes good sense to slip a small split ring into one eye of the bubble. It only takes a second to attach a treble hook and, believe me, it's worth the trouble. Last year I got a twenty-six-pound Northern pike from the edge of a weed bed this way. I had figured the bed for a bass or two.

143

Amount and weight of liquid used governs depth at which bubble will work. Sometimes split-shot is used in deep-water situations.

Trout are not only species readily taken on bubble technique. Smallmouth bass (below) and steelhead are perfect targets.

Lake or pond fishing requires fine tapered leader between bubble and fly as fish see heavy monofilament too easily.

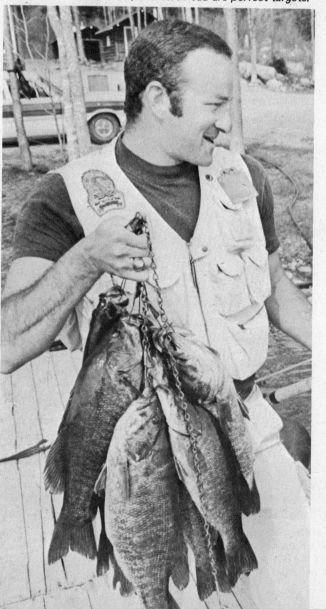

In the years since I learned about spinning with flies, I've tried the technique on stripers in shallow bays and brackish tributaries. It's a simple thing to cast small surface disturbers, drift natural baits like shrimp or to work a couple of fair size bucktails with an erratic retrieve through likely looking feeding areas.

I've used the same approach on bonefish down in Florida. You can cast even the lightest bonefish flies. The bubble will cause no more spooking than a bucktail jig or when casting a heavy, weight-forward fly line in a good, stiff breeze.

Many of my expert fly-caster friends have found, much to their distaste, that there are waters that are impossible to reach using a fly line, leader and fly. If you know that an exceptionally good fish is present, you can rig a spinning rod, a bubble three-quarters full with a BB or two if needed, and maneuver your nymph, streamer or hairwing dry fly right into position above the fish.

With such hard-to-reach fish, it will be a case of strike at first sight, because these fish rarely see a fly, especially a fly that can be controlled for a long enough, drag-free drift. This is the reason the fish aren't too suspicious of a delicate-looking fly, but will suspect typical spinning lures.

Your success with spinning flies rests squarely on your shoulders. A little money spent on terminal gear, some imagination and you'll probably find you're taking fish under conditions that used to be beyond your scope.

If you don't know how to handle conventional fly-casting equipment yet, what you'll learn by using flies with a bubble certainly will give you the push needed to add real fly rod handling to your fishing repertoire.

But, before you run off to try it out, here are a few suggestions: When using dry flies, dress them first with a silicote solution. Attaching the bubble to the terminal end of your line will give you an excellent rig for skittering a dry fly across the surface. This is a deadly technique to use on trout, especially during the hatching periods of the so-called salmon fly.

If you are tall or are standing on dry ground, use the longest leader you can and still be able to cast. With a wise fish, use a long leader.

When you're ready to cast, you'll find the side-arm cast more convenient than the overhead or snap cast. You'll need a pendulum motion to handle that four or more feet of bubble, lures and mono.

These Constitute The Fisherman's Ideal, But Ideals Can Be Adapted At Less Than Monumental Cost!

equipping today's SUPER BOATS

Ouachita's "U" Model Convincer is a family-sized sixteen-footer, with running and interior lights, deck cleats, rod holders, bow and stern anchor pads, motor well, interior paneling and carpeting among its standard features. Options are varied and the 801-pound fiberglass Convincer — with upright flotation — comes in a variety of colors. It will hold 95 hp engine.

Chapter 9

ART OF THE secret behind today's top pro fishermen and their success involves their highly sophisticated fishing boats. The trend continues toward well equipped, fast-moving craft that, in most cases, can be trailered easily and launched and handled by even the lone angler.

During any year of fishing, I have found that I must have distinctly different boats at my disposal if I am to roam the wide areas that I cover on both the fresh and salt water scene. But only when fishing the largest of big game species do I or my associates find need for a larger sportfisherman. The only other exception is when I find myself a guest on someone else's cabin cruiser. That I can afford!

Of the two boats that serve as our workhorses, one is from Ouachita Marine and Industrial Corporation, the other the product of Molded Fiber Glass Boat Company. The Ouachita is a Model UT, a boat the industry refers to as a super-bass boat. I refer to it as a super fishing boat, since I use mine not only for bass, but for most all fresh water species that require a boat and while night fishing for stripers, weakfish and other in-shore salt water species. It serves remarkably well under numerous conditions.

The same is true of my MFG Fishin' Caprice, though somewhat in reverse. This roaring monster not only provides me with a safe, stable platform on salt water, but has proved a fantastic asset when fishing such rough areas as the Great Lakes, the St. Lawrence River and other of the larger waters around the country. Like the lighter Ouachita, it

Among Johnson Outboard's line are three V-4 models — the 135, 115 (shown) and 85. All have MagFlash CD ignition, thermo-electric choke, built-in shock absorbers and more.

Glad Zwirz operates one of boats author has used with success, a Ouachita "UT" Model Convincer, fitted with Evinrude 60 hp Triumph. Boat has Zwirz-added comforts.

Author's other mainstay is MFG's Fishin' Caprice, used in salt water (above).

Ouachita UT features bow and stern Worth Remote anchors, spotlight, a Vexilar Sona-Graf, good trolling motor and padded seats for fishing in style.

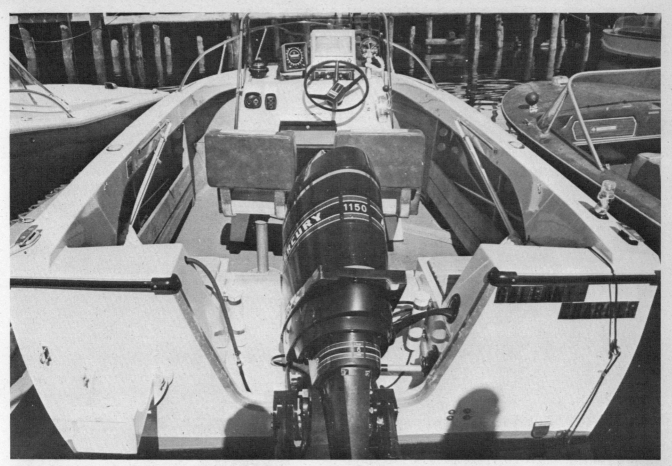

Zwirz' Fishin' Caprice is nineteen-footer with 90-inch beam and 46-inch depth. Stripped, it weighs 1500 pounds and is rated up to 160 hp. Power trim has engine tilt and is electric. It has bracket for auxiliary motor on port side of transom, plus other helpful goodies.

The console of Fishin' Caprice is fitted with Lowrance Locator/Sounder, Sona-Graf depth finder, Aqua Meter's compass, Taylor Deck-Hand spotlight, tinted windshield and grab rail. It's a fishing machine with comforts!

trailers beautifully and launches without effort from one of my trio of heavy-duty Holsclaw boat trailers.

Both boats were chosen for maximum comfort afloat and to provide me with all the safety and stability I can place under my feet. Both boats have been through exceptionally rough weather. In several cases, it was their combination of seaworthiness and speed that allowed me to make it to a safe port before Mother Nature really turned everything to froth and curses. Each boat carries aboard every safety item the Coast Guard requires, then a dozen

more of my own. Compasses and maps are always handy, though rarely do I move into alien waters before I've asked the locals for all the advice they'd care to give me. I have learned all about what each craft will tolerate, and try never to subject them to conditions under which they never were designed to perform.

There are many super-bass boats available to the public. Some have features similar to those found on my boat, others have design features which suit another school of anglers perfectly. As a good example, quite a few boats

Ouachita Convincer trailers easily on single-axle Holsclaw trailer. The fishing chairs swivel a full 360-degrees, and even will rock.

feature throne-style fishing chairs which I feel are too high above the deck. I much prefer the lower center of gravity found with the Ouachita design. Some fishermen still prefer the forward stick steering control. I like the added safety of a near-center console arrangement.

The Model M-P Convincer from Ouachita (right) has many of the features of Zwirz' boat, along with built-in rod storage box, lockable bow storage, gunwale tray and others. MFG's pair of nineteen-footers, the Super Caprice (outboard, below) and Fishin' Caprice can fill many a fisherman's dream. The Super Caprice features a brand new stern drive unit.

For power, I have been using a sixty-horsepower Evinrude on the Ouachita, and a 135-horsepower Mercury for my primary power on the MFG. This coming season, I'm going to heed staff advice from Ouachita and utilize their newer UT's ability to handle an eighty-five-horsepower with ease; for a change of pace, as well as for testing purposes, this year's motor will be a Johnson. As for the MFG, the Mercury has been exceptionally reliable. Al-though it has had hard use, often at flank speed, it continues to deliver speed and power, with sound not over a whisper. However, this coming year I will be conducting tests with an Evinrude.

The fishing boats and their accessories in the accompanying photos will, I hope, give you helpful ideas about rigging your own. These ideas have made my fishing far more productive, my hours afloat enjoyable.

While Zwirz' MFG is no small boat, it still can get anglers into tight, shallow areas in pursuit of monster fish, like this quest for largemouth bass. The big Mercury doesn't make noise to alarm fish.

Ouachita's "J" Model Convincer is a sixteen-footer designed with the fisherman in mind.
It's a lot of boat that weighs only 602 pounds. It will handle up to a 75 hp engine. Some
optional features are side console with glove box, horn, bilge pump, live well with pump and cushion.

MFG's Challenger comes in two sizes, twelve-foot (top, below) and fourteen-foot. Either will easily
fit atop a car or on a light trailer and should prove an excellent, low-cost fishing or utility boat.
Once fitted with a small outboard, the Challengers can get you into prime waters away from banks.

152

The modern-rigged fishing boats put all of the necessary controls at the angler's fingertips, along with controls for electric motor near right foot. With a boat so outfitted, an angler spends more time fishing and less time moving about to correct position of boat for casting to the big fish.

Many anglers who presently own small boats cannot afford the expense of purchasing a new model. Yet, with a little thought, planning and imagination, that old relic can become a fun and functional piece of equipment, as this boat of Zwirz' has. And it doesn't need to cost you a fortune, either!

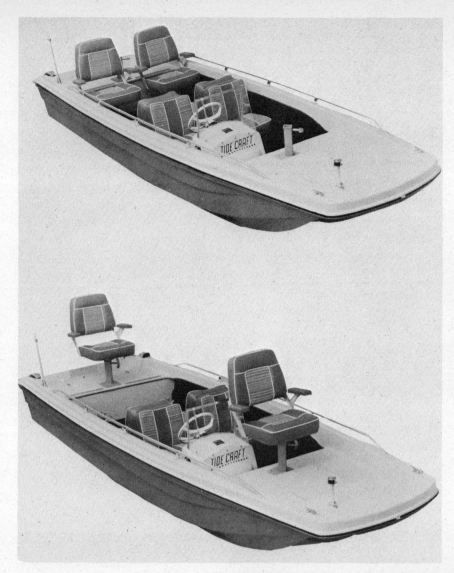

Miss Pro, from Tide Craft, is quickly changed as the photos depict, from a ski to bass rig. Miss Pro is BIA-rated to 85 hp, sixteen feet in length and 68 inches wide. Standard equipment includes mechanical steering, hand rails, rod holders, running lights, deluxe padded seats, lounge seats, drink holders and plenty more.

The folks at Rebel, already famous for their lures, are adding four models of Rebel Rambler Trolling Motors to their product line. The bow-mounted motors draw only 17 amps on full power, are quiet and sturdily constructed for anglers.

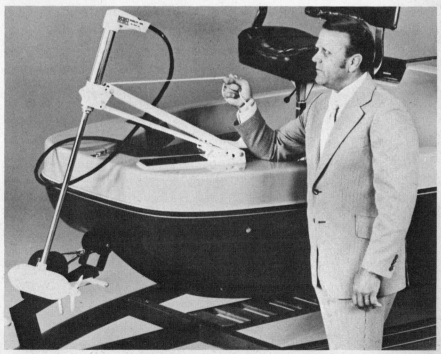

There is a special bracket for positioning Hi-Riser fishing seat on MFG's Super Fishin' Gypsy.

Johnson Outboards broke 51 years of internal combustion tradition with the introduction of this quarter-horsepower electric motor (right). It weighs 20 pounds and has all controls in foot-operated pedal. It is corrosion-protected.

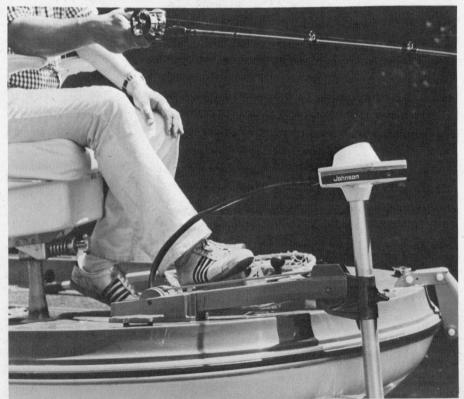

Evinrude has supplied the power for John Meyers and Yul Rhodes in the fourteen-foot Ouachita Convincer bass boat on Toledo Bend Reservoir, Texas. Up front is the new electric Scout, equipped with miracle polycarbonate LEXAN propeller. At the stern is Evinrude's 50 hp Lark — fast performance for little gas.

Author Zwirz describes the MFG Super Fishin' Gypsy as a fine, compact fishing machine. The fourteen-foot boat has foamed-in-place flotation, twin padded chairs, side-mounted console, rod holders and a host of other goodies. This one is mounted with a Mercury 800, an 80 hp engine of top quality.

Tide Craft's Tournament Special provides comfort and convenience without bulk. Measuring just an inch over sixteen feet, the Tournament Special is 57 inches wide and rated for up to 70 hp. Standard on the list of features are turf carpet, two live wells, padded seats, Pro Pedestal mounts and other goodies.

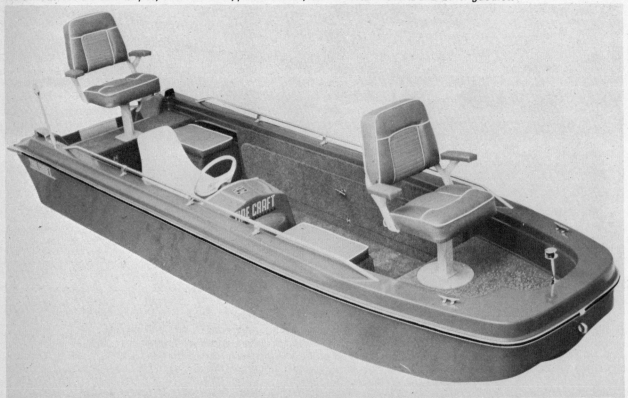

Another in the Convincer line of fishing boats is the "JT" Model. A sixteen-footer with upright flotation, it is BIA-rated for up to 75 hp. It has raised casting foredeck, a host of features.

Evinrude's new Scout draws power through permanent magnet motor. Operated through foot pedal, it offers 360-degree steering.

Three new outboards from Evinrude feature exotic names. At left is Sizzler 50 hp, center is Hustler 70 and right is Strangler 135. Color is red, white and blue. A stainless steel cupped propeller is optional. Power trim is standard, as is breakerless CD ignition.

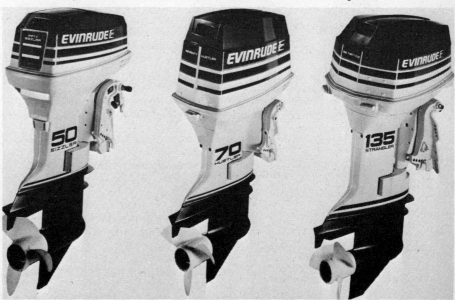

Chapter 10

BASICS OF FLY TYING

Unending Learning Is Required For Expertise, But This Introduction May Get You Hooked!

FAR TOO MANY guys and gals have taken a cursory look at fly tying, then backed off with the erroneous conviction that the manual dexterity required is beyond their skills. This simply isn't so. When you come to realize that, as a good example, I'm a relic of the football fields of yesteryear, built like the biggest of the linebackers, it's a good bet that the finer graces are not a particularly big part of my life style. But, I'm not entirely unknown in a number of books dealing with famous fly patterns. In the same breath let me say that Glad, my wife, has become far more renowned for her tying than I'd ever hope to be. Where I've sometimes been the innovator of a new pattern, Glad is the persevering one who works out the exacting details, then skillfully ties the master patterns.

Essentially, only a small number of tying tools is required. First, buy a good quality vise. With this all-important item in your possession, start accumulating such items as fly tying scissors — preferably a lightweight pair, plus a heavier model; hackle pliers; wax; tying silk; tweezers; dubbing needle; lacquer, and special fly tying hooks. If you do not have a tackle dealer in your area who specializes in fly tying materials and equipment, then I'd suggest you deal with mail order houses such as Herter's, Netcraft, Reed Tackle, Worth's and similar well known suppliers.

You will find that specific furs, feathers, materials and hook styles are required for different types of flies. As you add to the list of patterns you wish to tie, your materials will grow in proportion.

You'll find your initiation into fly tying far more enjoyable and simpler if you first make certain that you have purchased one of the better books devoted to the art of fly tying. Most any of these will take you step by step — with

These are the tools and materials for tying the stonefly nymph: (from right) vise, scissors, bobbin, bodkin, hooks, moose mane or peccary, 6/0 black silk thread, white floss, striped peacock eye, brown hackle, mallard wing.

photos — and show you the little tricks that make a tie easier and, just as important, the most durable when put to actual use.

For this chapter, I have chosen the three basic types of flies: a nymph (a wet fly variety); a dry fly, and finally a streamer pattern. Each will introduce you to the basics of tying that type of pattern. In other words, once you've mastered the tying of an Adams dry fly, there will be little standing in your way, if you wish to tie, as examples, a hairwing coachman, a light Cahill, or possibly a black gnat. It will be simply a matter of substituting the required materials for that pattern.

THE STONEFLY NYMPH

The stonefly nymph represents one of the more basic, natural foods in the diet of trout, as well as many other species of fish.

Although there are a number of recognized ties and variations for imitating the natural stonefly, the pattern developed by Charles Krom long has been my favorite.

To imitate as closely as possible, one ties this pattern on a large size hook when fishing Western streams and rivers. Actual Western stoneflies run larger and are more plentiful than in the Eastern U.S. Stoneflies (plecoptera) are found most often in waters with stony or gravel beds. Since these

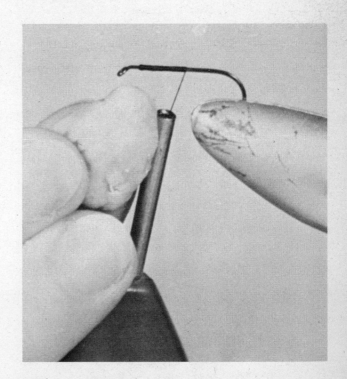

Place Mustad-Viking No. 9762 hook in vise, conceal the barb of hook, wax 6/0 black silk thread and cover shank of hook starting at eye to the bend of the hook. Use size 10 or 12 hook in Eastern waters, 6 or 8 in Western.

161

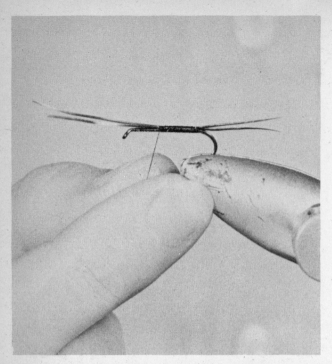

For tail, tie in two strands of peccary or moose mane
To keep strands apart in V-shape, make figure-8 wrap
around tail. Wrap thread over shank and strands to cover
three-fourths of shank; clip excess strands. (Below)
Cut 20-inch strip of white floss and begin to wrap this
floss where those excess strands were clipped away.

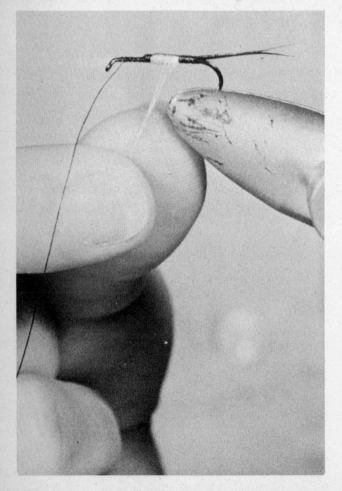

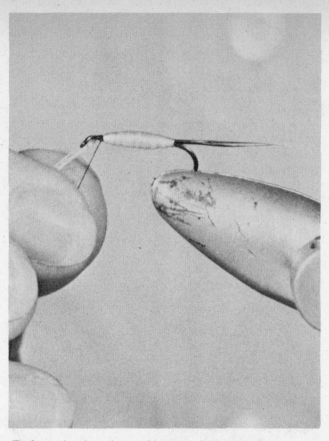

To form the cigar shape of body, build up at center
wrap floss back to tail, forward toward eye. Secure
floss with two half-hitches, cut off excess floss,
then cover entire floss section with a clear lacquer.

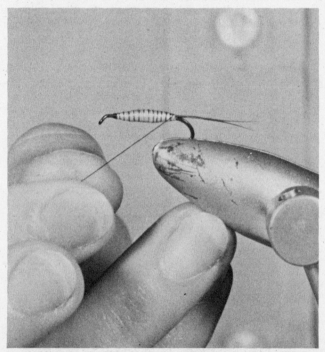

While the lacquered body is still damp, pick up 6/0
thread from eye of hook and wrap the body toward the
tail, making certain that your spacing is done evenly.

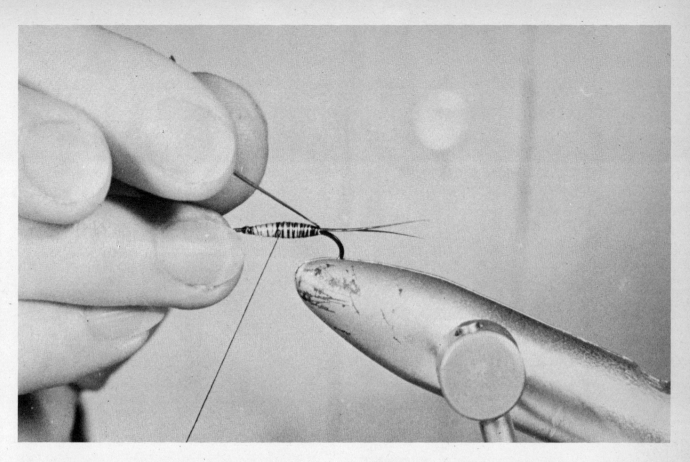

Two strands of the striped peacock eye are tied in now, using two half-hitches. The thread is wrapped back to about the center of the body, again spacing it evenly.

Wrap the quills together, each turn of quill meeting the other, ending slightly past mid-shank, tying off with two half-hitches. Lacquer the quill body twice, allowing each coat to dry after application. Clip excess quill.

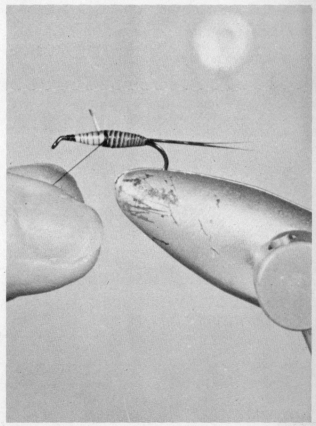

usually are upland rivers, they will produce relatively fast flows.

The stonefly is the oldest known nymph in angling. In the five-hundred-year-old "Treatise On Fishing With An Angle" by Dame Juliana Berner, the yellowed pages hold a description of a dressing for the artificial.

When fished to match the particular phase occurring, this nymph takes better than its share of trout. When one is fortunate enough to be present during the adult stage and they skate across the surface, he can expect to see the river's larger trout gorging on them, along with the normal size trout population. Western anglers know this adult form as the willow fly or, in some areas, the salmon fly.

Tie in brown hackle, three peacock herls, secondary wing quill from mallard. Wrap three herls toward hook's eye. Two half-hitches to secure herls completed this step.

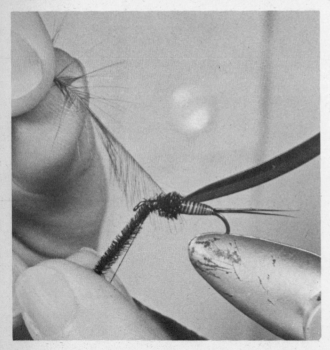

Pull hackle to one side, but do not strip or cut. Wrap hackle palmer style toward eye with two half-hitches to secure. Clip off only top section of the hackle, then clip off the excess herls as well as protruding hackle.

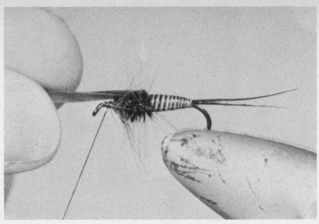

Lay secondary mallard quill flat over top of thorax. Add two half-hitches, after which excess quill is cut off.

Complete the head with whip finish knot. Lacquer thread three times with clear lacquer; allow coats to dry.

When completed, it would be tough for stonefly nymph's own brother to tell this fly from the real insect!

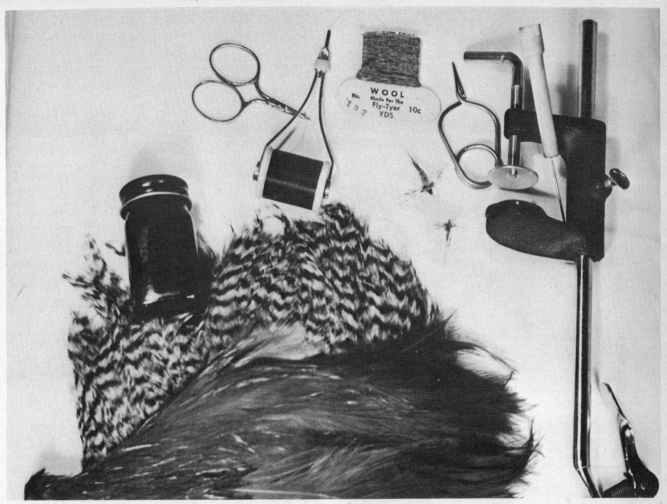

THE ADAMS DRY FLY

A popular imitation of the adult caddis fly is the Adams, which was originated by Len Halladay. Good reason for this pattern's popularity is its effectiveness on virtually all the trout waters of the world.

Although tied and fished primarily as a dry pattern, the Adams can also be tied sparsely for a presentation in the surface film when circumstances require a change in streamside strategy. I have found it difficult to choose between the Adams and Don Martinez's equally excellent whitcraft caddis pattern. I carry both in my fly boxes.

However, since it seems to me that more anglers know of the Adams, and since it is one of my personal favorites, I will show how to tie this pattern both as an adult dry imitation and as a spent-wing.

There are times when the spent-wing is more effective. On several trout rivers that I fish, there is an abundance of caddis flies. When they ride the surface, the Adams works like a charm with wings in the traditional upright position. But one day, when we were out at the crack of dawn along a particularly fine stretch of water on the East Branch of the Delaware River, it was nearly impossible to see through an unusually heavy early morning mist. Just the same, we could hear trout moving and occasionally managed to see the rings as a fish broke the surface. We found that the water was covered with many of the previous day's caddis

For tying Adams dry fly, needed are vise, bobbin, hackle pliers, bodkin, fine-tipped scissors, grizzly dry fly hackles, medium-brown dry fly hackles, gray wool or dubbed muskrat fur, 5/0 waxed black thread, wax, dry fly hooks, black or clear head cement. (Below) Set No. 84849 or 94833 Mustad-Viking hook in vise, cover shank of hook with waxed thread as shown, ending behind the hook's bend. Secure the thread with two half-hitches.

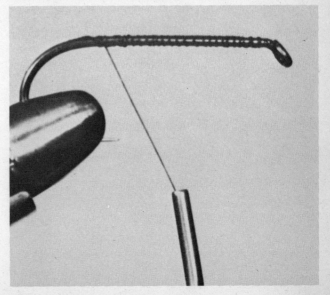

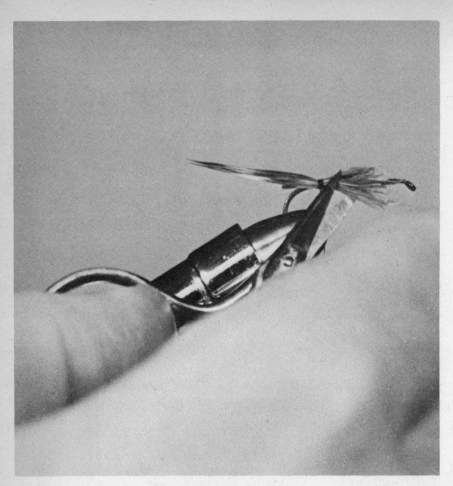

Using one brown, one grizzly hackle, pull a few strands of each for the tail of the fly. Tie in by wrapping two or three turns of waxed thread. Make one turn under the tail to prevent drooping, then secure with two half-hitches, clip excess hackle.

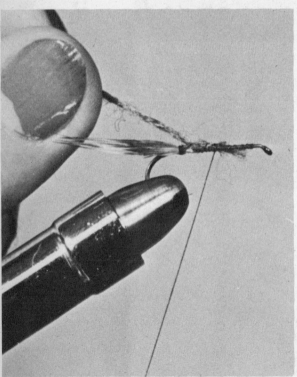

For the body, cut a small section of wool or, for a more bouyant dry fly, the muskrat fur. With heavily waxed thread, tie in at tail with half-hitch. Then wrap the thread toward eye of hook; stop short of bend in eye.

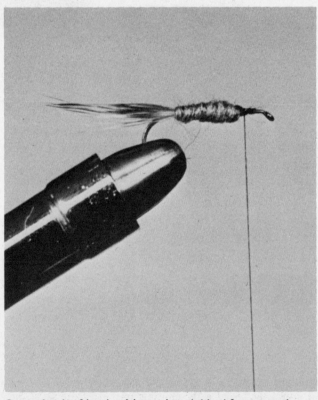

Cover shank of hook with wool or dubbed fur; taper the body slightly. End body short of the bend of the eye. Secure with two half-hitches, trim excess body material.

Upright wing: Use two grizzly hackle tips for each wing. Place hackles over eye of hook (forward). Tie in wing on hook with three turns of the thread. Lift hackles straight up and over hook shank. Wrap three turns in front of wing to keep wing upright. To separate wings, use a figure-8 knot, finishing with two half-hitches. Touch knot with head cement, then clip off any of the excess material.

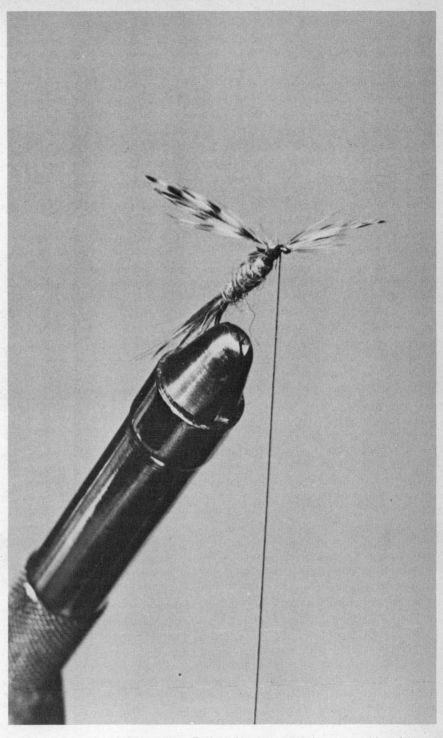

Spent-wing: Follow the same procedure as used in tying upright wing, but wind thread — using figure-8 knot — between wings, while holding wings in downward position.

hatch floating downstream. Their wings were now lying limp — spent — in the surface film.

It was a waste of time trying to fool the big trout that were rising with out-of-place upright wing patterns. The flies we were using were floating too high and the wings were simply not set correctly. As soon as we switched to spent-wings, we began to connect.

Since that day, I always carry both the standard and the spent-wing ties. Quite often, I will not fully dress the spent-

Left: For hooks larger than No. 12, choose two grizzly and one brown hackle. Smaller hooks take one hackle of each color. Strip soft fluff from hackle butts and tie in the hackle behind the wing, dull side facing tail. Pull hackles through wings after making a couple of turns in back of wing. Finish with one or two turns forward of wing. Secure with a few turns of the thread, then use two half-hitches to tie down these additions.

Adams hackle usually is tied more bushy than most dry flies. Below is finished Adams fly with upright wing.

Cut off excess material and complete head with a whip-finish knot. Snip off thread, then coat head with head cement two or three times, allowing each coat to dry.

wing with floatant just so it will ride lower in the film. Each pattern, fished at the correct time, will take trout.

Although there are other excellent caddis patterns, the two Adams types should be in every angler's box. The upright, I might add, also imitates the "trichoptera" during flight time. To suit whatever part of the country you're fishing, you should have the Adams in sizes No. 10 through No. 16.

THE MIRACLE MARABOU STREAMER

There are five imitative patterns in this series of flies, as all fresh waters — as well as some brackish waters — both in the United States and Canada, contain one or more of the baitfish represented by these streamers.

They were developed over a period of three years, then introduced to anglers in the Spring of 1963. Working with Kani Evans of Hawaii, I originated the five patterns after testing numerous new materials and designs in an effort to achieve a truly lifelike artificial. The ties for the miracle marabou were worked out, based upon realistic, quantity tying, after nearly a year of working with materials and dyes. Several of the national awards for yearly fly fishing

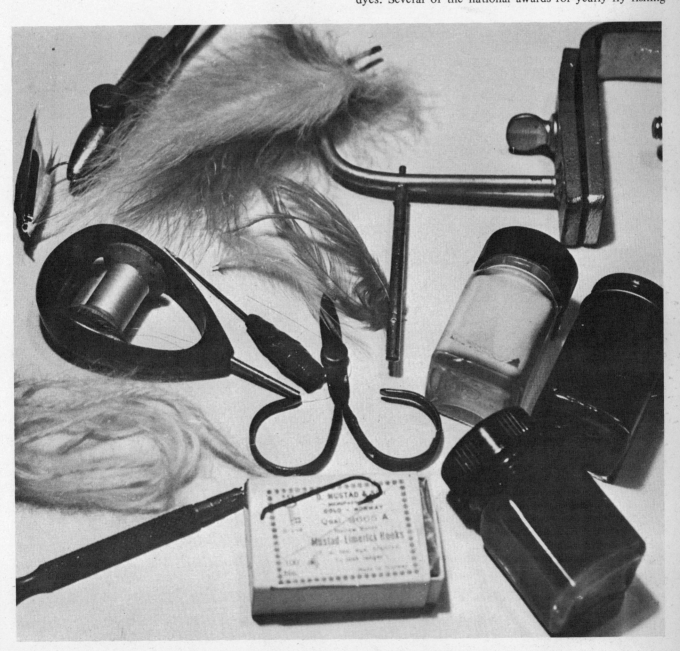

Materials and equipment required to tie the longnose dace include 3/0 silk thread; cream and orange-colored hackles; spun angora fur in pale green or pale yellow; pale yellow and olive marabou; mylar, 3/16-inch wide, as well as quick-drying lacquers in white, black and olive colors, all of which should make a colorful lure!

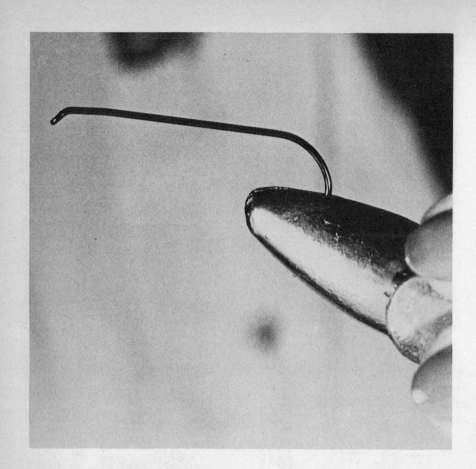

Using tools listed, insert Mustad-Limerick No. 3665A (sizes 4, 6, 8 or 10) or Mustad-Viking No. 79580 (sizes 2 and 1) hook into jaws of the vise, carefully concealing barb.

Hook shank is covered with 3/0 white silk thread; end it at the bend of the hook. After the half-hitch has been made, the shank is coated with clear lacquer.

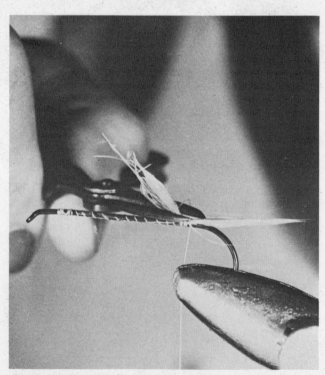

For fly's tail, strip a few strands of the dark cream hackle and tie it at the end of the thread. Another half-hitch is used here, then excess material is cut.

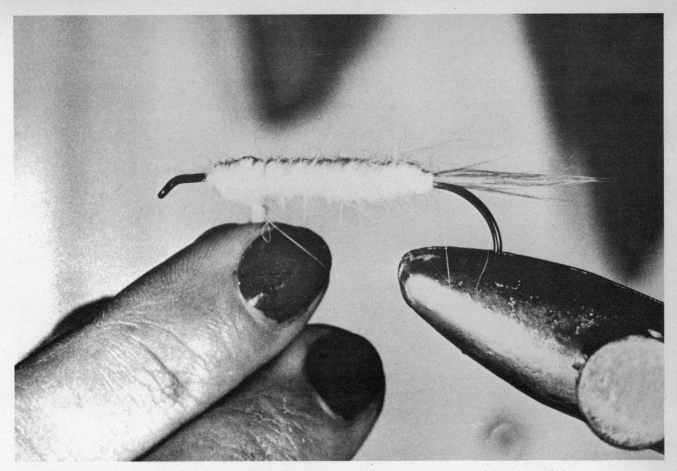

For a No. 6 hook, cut five inches of angora. Begin at tail, wrap body around eye, leaving quarter inch of the shank bare from eye. Taper, twist fur for firmer body. With the bodkin, pick out sides, stroke hair to tail.

Insert fly upside down in vise for neater tie of beard; choose short orange hackles, tying them with two half-hitches, then dab the thread with clear lacquer. The beard represents the pectoral fins of the fish.

records have gone to both casters and trollers who were using the miracle marabous.

Of the five patterns, the longnose dace is one of the most important baitfish native to the North American continent. Called a rock minnow in some sections of the country, this member of the dace family is brownish-olive on the back, shading off to a yellowish dusty-white or greenish-white on the belly. A rather broad, definite black stripe running from the eye to base of the caudal fin distinguishes this minnow as being of the dace family.

A lover of fast water, the longnose can grow to a length of six inches, though most are under four. Throughout the month of May and most of June this vigorous fish spawns the snout and fins becoming a bright reddish-orange hue. A true relative of the blacknose dace, it prefers faster water than the blacknose. It's one of the most widely distributed

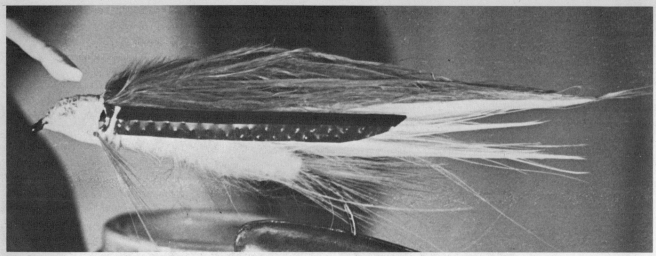

Use two pale yellow marabou feathers to shape the first layer of wing, dampening thoroughly. It should be thicker toward the eye. Cut off excess wing at an angle. Then use three half-hitches, two coats of clear lacquer.

Lay two olive feathers on top of yellow marabou; start to form back of minnow, using procedure for the wings. Tie in, coat marabou with lacquer. When it's dry, clip off the excess marabou, again making certain of angle.

Lay three-inch strip of flat gold mylar on board and paint black median strip on upper part. Roll a round file over it to give scale finish. Cut mylar and tie a strip on each side of minnow, tapering to bend in hook.

After building up the head with silk thread, complete head with whip-finish, coat with clear lacquer. When dry, coat head with white lacquer and paint the top half with a medium olive lacquer, ending it at the black median.

172

The miracle marabou is tied in several configurations, including (from top and left): salt water pattern, the blacknose dace, silver shiner, gold shiner, longnose dace and blueback shiner. All of these were hand-tied.

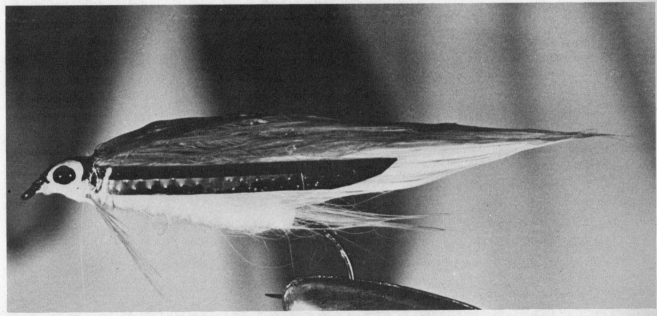

With the eye of white lacquer and a black pupil, the fly seems to come to life. The entire head now has been coated with clear lacquer and you have the so-called Miracle Marabou Longnose Dace — and luck to match it.

minnows, ranging from coast to coast in the latitude of the Great Lakes, then southward through North Carolina, thence down to the Northern tier of Mexico.

Though it's not a great problem to cast this mylar-winged fly, its greatest effectiveness lies in its use as a trolling fly for both fresh and salt water. In larger sizes, it is a proven killer on big tarpon, sailfish and similar gamefish

species. Other fly-tyers, using the mylar principle, have worked out mylar bodies which do not require the wide strips that we used originally.

Many of these special purpose ties, some commercially available, are far more effective to cast than our pioneer models. Nonetheless, patternwise, as imitations of the naturals, they are as deadly as any patterns yet conceived.

SHALLOW WATER STRATEGY FOR LARGEMOUTH BASS

Chapter 11

*Lunkers like this granddaddy largemouth are welcome
additions to any stringer. Taken in shallow water,
bass fell for a Silver Minnow made by Louis Johnson.*

NOT SURPRISING, THERE are at least two winning
ways of taking bass when they are in relatively shallow
areas or are present in a shallow strata of water. One
method calls for a slow, patient approach; the other
requires the angler to kick up all kinds of fuss and bother,
practically driving the bass up their figurative walls.

Since there is so much that can be written regarding
winning techniques for taking ol' funnelmouth, we will
stick pretty much to the art of surface and just below surface methods. At some other time we'll go into detail about
the bottom-bouncing tricks that take trophy bass. And
that, of course, will include the use of rubber and plastic
worms, and all the other go-deep devils that account for so
many heavy fish that are taken from our larger lakes and
impoundments.

But for now let's look at the still-deadly slow approach
to taking largemouth bass:

Though what I am about to say now may seem overly
basic, it is still a fact that many anglers fail to keep in mind.
Namely, that the wisest approach when presenting a sur-
face-like bass lure is to see to it that a lure or plug should
resemble in looks and action something of known interest
to bass. By and large, consistent success with any of the top
water baits lies in creating the same performance the bass
would expect to see from a crippled bait fish or the various
terrestrials, if that is the lure approach you have chosen.

And to putting on a realistic performance, the bass
fisherman should gauge the speed on his retrieve and the
action imparted to the lure based upon the conditions to be
found in the specific waters he is fishing. This will include
water temperature, air temperature and the area's natural
surroundings. Experience has taught me that, while using
surface lures on bass, greater success will be experienced if
the general tempo of fishing is slowed down to somewhere
in the vicinity of half the speed with which many anglers
insist on working. Some years ago, oldtime bass fisherman
and author, Robert Page Lincoln, told me several things
which patience could do to reward me in taking more,
larger bass.

One day that expert plug caster caught twelve fat ol' hog
bass during a morning session, while I caught just one
decent one, plus five small critters. I had been using a favorite surface plug that required some manipulation to make it
gurgle and leave a teasing, bubbling wake behind it. No
variations in my sad score. At this point, my famous companion suggested that I carefully watch what he was doing.

Once he spotted a likely looking bass hangout, he would
drop his surface lure, accurately, right on target. One of his
favorites was a well seasoned 5/8-ounce Arbogast Hula
Popper. Most of the time he would allow several moments
to pass; certainly time enough for every ripple caused by
the plug's entrance to completely disappear. He then would
transmit a shuddering quiver to his lure. At this instant the
lure's rubber tail would writhe suggestively and a series of
rings would again circle out from his lure. It looked for all
the world like some stunned critter quivering with life, but
still unable to move or fly away.

It wasn't at all uncommon for this expert angler to

175

Spinnerbaits, when buzzed before a largemouth, often will bring a strike. Taken in Illinois, bass rivals his Southern cousins for size, fight.

repeat this long wait and quiver, four, five, even six times, without actually moving the plug more than a few inches from the spot where it first landed. On occasion he would toss in a short, fast maneuver, making the popper go "glurp"! It was often at this point that some trophy size bass, almost out of his skull with frustration and fury would rear up out of his diggings and tear blazes out of Bob's plug.

Nowadays there are so many surface plugs from which anglers can choose, but many of the old time-tested favorites are as hot today as they were thirty years ago. The final effect created by most any plug will depend on the imagination and finesse of the caster who puts it to work. And, to a varying degree on his patience. Lures such as the long famous Heddon Dying Quiver and Dying Flutter were so balanced that it was possible for the angler to impart a deadly action by simply giving the lure short, quick jerks

with the rod tip. This slight nodding of the lure made it resemble a faintly struggling bait fish. There is something very special about any such item, particularly when fished with such an unhurried retrieve. At least to a largemouth bass who is so prone to be finessed into losing his cool.

Bass bugs are also among those bass lures that should be fished slowly and carefully. Have you ever watched a grasshopper vibrating after falling onto the surface of the water? Or a big, juicy moth stuggling along through the surface film? Their ruckus creates small rings on the water, and their legs and feelers move to and fro erratically. It is this very appearance and action that you should strive to simulate with your own artificial offerings.

I have a particular friend who mostly fishes bass, both smallmouth and largemouth, but he also specializes in stringing trophy-size rainbow trout. What he has shown me takes great toll on cruising bass in shallower areas. Seems

These South Dakotans, using tubes to float near bass hangouts, show success of their methods. They are using conventional bait-casting rigs and medium-sized, stout fiberglass rods in their quest.

that he had trolled a lake, used live bait, and even jigged for fish. He indeed caught fish, but not with anything bordering on satisfactory regularity. Then one day, he came to realize that the large trout he had been seeing were rarely in very deep water areas, at least not when he noted them rising to naturals morning and evenings. He then began experimenting with everything from a spinning outfit with a plastic bubble and dry flies, to a floating fly line and various dries, bugs, and even streamer flies.

Still he had no increase in his catches until one day he tied on a Muddler Minnow. He then fished it with the deadly dry/wet method, where you allow the Muddler to float a couple of feet, put it under, then allow the dressed fly to bounce back up to the surface again. Some fish

smashed it solidly; others came up to look it over, then refused it.

Finally, quite by accident, my friend stumbled into a method that really paid off. On breezy or windy days he casts his Muddler and lets it sit on the surface and blow about pretty much as nature chooses. As he tells it, "You have to watch closely or you might miss the fact that one second the fly is there in front of you, the next it isn't. Apparently the fish study this absurd stick of feathers and hair for some time before coming up and sucking it in." Depending on his choice of area this imaginative angler has found himself playing trout or bass, several of which have been of indisputable trophy size.

Some seasons back when down South, in the heart of

Once hooked, this Tennessee largemouth breaks the surface trying to rid surface-disturbing popper from his hard mouth. When used in stickups, big poppers and bugs take their toll on bass population.

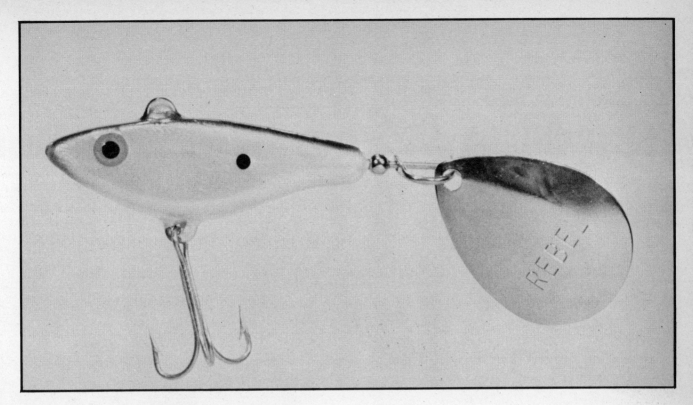

The shad is one of the favorite bass foods, so Rebel has turned out a lure which resembles the action of a dying baitfish, termed the Rocket Squid. Designed for casting long distances, the lure sinks straight while its spinner turns. When bass are busting shad, it's a deadly lure!

hog bass country, I put this technique to work one breezy day while working a stump-filled shallow lake, with my bass-bugging rod. Not surprising, it worked real well on bass of all sizes. Unfortunately I found it difficult to hook several of the bass that sucked it in. The trouble related to slack in my fly line plus slack and S-shapes in my long leader. I simply couldn't react fast enough to gather in line and sink the hook. The majority of bass I did take with this method hooked themselves against the drag of the floating fly line.

For purposes of classification, surface plugs can be placed roughly in several sub-divisions. There are the traditional poppers, while others are worked more effectively as swimmers. A third type, the torpedo or cigar-shaped variety, usually comes with either a tail propeller or both head and tail propellers. Properly worked by the caster, each plug causes some kind of surface disturbance that attracts fish by both sound and motion. In addition to the plugs that imitate bait fish, there are a number of surface disturbers that imitate frogs, mice, large bugs, birds and other terrestrials that bass find appetizing.

Possibly the one most important factor, when relying on a surface lure for bass, is the caster's accuracy in placing it where it will bring results. There are frequent times when a hog bass will make a pass at a popper that lands within inches of his station, but will totally ignore the same lure if it lands only a few feet away. Stories you hear about sliding that plug right in under overhanging branches or cover at the very edge of tangled roots or a rotting stump are, I assure you, true.

There will be times when a big fish will actually chase a plug, but why gamble on careless presentations? With a little practice and patience anyone can become adept enough to drop a plug exactly where he wants it — at a good hundred paces. The difference can and will be measured in more than one way; you will find enjoyment in becoming a skillful caster, while at the same time your stringers of fish will multiply proportionately.

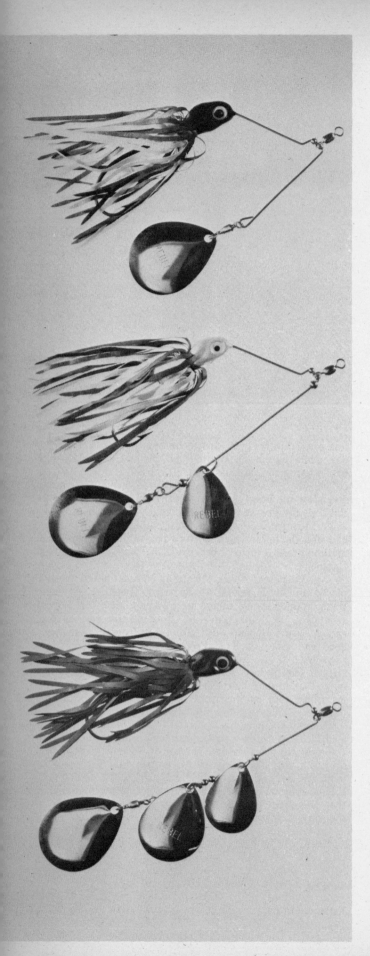

Rebel's new Destroyer series (top to bottom) I, II and III spinnerbaits are single, double and triple spin, as indicated by their flashing blades. They are easy to retrieve from brushy areas, rarely hang-up and are tough on bass. Many professional bassers use them.

At times of the year when bass are in the shallows by choice, it isn't too great a problem to take them on surface lures, nor will it matter if you choose spinning, bait-casting, or a bass-bugging rod. Farther along during the season, when the bass leave the shallows during the day — where geographically possible — they return to those shallower areas as the waters cool just before dark and often remain feeding until nearly an hour following sun-up.

While fishing from one hour before dawn until an hour after, it is not unusual to hook a day's limit of good size bass even during the hottest time of the year. The same will hold true normally late in the day as the bass move back into the shallows along their routes leading to favorite weed beds and shorelines.

During these periods bass fishermen never should forget "fish psychology." With the number of anglers throwing all the hardware they own at our bass population, the fish have, in many cases, become lure shy. It's little surprise that such bass soon learn to pass up the average offering as it tears along overhead.

Fish can thus be counted on to react in certain ways to particular stimuli. No greater example can be found than in the largemouth bass. These fish can be irritated and excited into doing things that more often than not result in their appearance on some wise old bass fisherman's stringer.

Simply remember that all-important business of accu-

Combining two proven winners results in a third, a jig-spinner with a grub-like tail. While Rebel made this example, similar types are produced by Zorro and Mann Bait Companies, among others.

racy in placing your cast where you suspect a good size bass may be lurking: under and around all deadfalls, close to stumps, gravel bars and weed beds, large rocks, and under overhanging bushes, trees and other foliage. These are but a few of their favorite hangouts. Particularly during Summer heat, bass have periods when they become lethargic and are simply not all that interested in feeding. If that favorite popper or bass bug suddenly races off away from its quarry, one of three things is bound to happen: The bass figures that just one more character has cast a lure, like all the other lures that have come before or the lure is in so great a hurry, the blazes with it. In one out of a couple of dozen cases the bass just might surmise it's just too tasty looking to get away. However, experience on a number of the country's better bass waters has shown that the larger and smarter bass will rarely buy such a performance.

Frankly stated, all it would take to improve your average is some self-control, a fair helping of that ingredient known as patience, plus a few of those psychological tricks to which bass are prone to react. When it comes down to actual lures, I find that those which incorporate a hollow head and some sort of rubber skirt work well for me.

When using those other lures that imitate to some degree everything from wounded minnows, swimming frogs and water-logged insects, analyze first the habits and reactions of the natural, then present and work your lures according-

ly. Most of the time this means imparting action a good deal slower than all too many bass fishermen believe makes sense for a surface lure. Lastly, remember to vary your retrieve and lure motion when such strategy is deemed necessary.

Though dyed-in-the-wool Southern bass fishermen are fully familiar with commotion spinner lures, lead drop lures and spinner-jig combos, they are not as widely known or accepted in other parts of the country. This is a sad state of affairs. Such commotion-type lures are real super-killers of largemouth. Firms such as Zorro, Mann, Bassbusters, Rebel, Burke, Smithwick, plus more than a dozen others, produce a fantastic line of bass lures that are producing results.

A number of these special-purpose lures are designed to drive the bass to a frenzy, whether the lures are raced along the surface, whipped along just sub-surface, or actually dragged right through the densest weeds or deadfalls. Wherever stick-ups are present the spinner jobs can be pulled through with almost no worry about hanging up in them. In essence there are simply no such things as deadfalls, foliage, bushes or fallen trees that can't be fished these days.

These lures have changed once pessimistic casters into anglers who are certain that a cast to the worst of clutter produces big bass and more bass. Here again the experienced anglers have learned that color can be important and

Bass boats, like other fishing equipment, have come a long way. Zwirz' own Ouachita hull is fitted with a Lowrance fish finder, Vexilar Model 155 Sona-Graf depth finder, padded chairs, mushroom anchors and electric trolling motor from Motor Guide. Quite a package!

so too is the matter of retrieve. This latter business can call for changes in speed, techniques in manipulation and, of course, in the areas over which they are to be fished most successfully. This takes experimentation in any given bass waters, plus research relating to where the bass are lurking at the time you are present.

Such situations call for either a first-hand knowledge of the geography of the area, or the assistance offered through the use of a good topographical map of that body of water. It is just as important to have along a good Lowrance, Vexilar or other electronic magic box. Without them, especially when fishing the really big waters, a man could find himself fishing blind.

The bass are still there in good numbers. To catch them, it requires that the fisherman know what it takes to locate bass, then go about his sport with a degree of efficiency than proves he has reason for each and every cast, each manipulation of his lure.

Fishing his own Jelly Worms and Little George lures, bait manufacturer Tom Mann (left) and David Lockhart boated 25 bass weighing 155 pounds from Lake Eufala, Georgia. The biggest largemouth weighed 13 pounds!

CHANNEL BASS - CHECK THE CHANNELS

Chapter 12

Surf And Trolling Tactics For This Fish Of Many Names Are Similar Throughout His Range, And Here Are Just A Few!

While called a variety of names, channel bass along the Southern Atlantic Coast provide the same top sports as the striped bass farther North. Averaging only 12 to 15 pounds, channel bass are tough fighters until beached.

IF I HAD to choose two super-hotspots for catching channel bass, they would have to be in the areas of North Carolina's Outer Banks or around Virginia's Barries Islands. This is not to say that they are not present in coastal waters stretching from New York to Texas. It is, however, a species confined to the Southwestern area of the North American continent.

Some anglers, particularly those residing around the Gulf region, will not know for certain which species we are discussing, unless we admit that the name, redfish, can be applied to this species. For that matter, Sciaenops ocellatus often goes under any of the following names, depending on just where you happen to hang your hat: red drum, bull redfish, redfin, pez colorado, pescado colorado, reef bass, bar bass and spottail. They are essentially school fish and, when in residence, catches of surf fishermen, trollers and casters can be phenomenal. A record rod and reel catch, made in 1949 at Cape Charles, Virginia, weighed a solid eighty-three pounds.

For a rule of thumb you can expect to find your action from June through October, North of the Carolinas. During October you can look for schools of channel bass working close to shore in the Gulf of Mexico. They are in this general area to carry on spawning, a rite which takes place in the mouths of the passes.

Average weight of channel bass would be twelve to fifteen pounds, with the more recent heavyweights tipping

the scales at near seventy-five pounds. The commercial interests catch and market what they refer to as puppy drum. These fish usually weigh four to five pounds, dressed.

Channel bass/redfish have strong cravings for crabs, mullet, menhaden, shrimp, clams and smaller fish. From the angler's viewpoint, he strongly prefers to seek out those channels, between bars, around inlets, and in the general region of sandy beaches and shorelines. Accurate commercial records and state fisheries' records point to the fact September is the top month for taking larger channel bass in the area of New Jersey, while I'd concentrate during June if fishing the waters from Virginia to Florida. In the Hatteras area my own experience has shown that anglers on the scene during November will stand a good chance of taking the year's trophy fish.

Though most channel bass are caught on bait, it is possible to cast or troll to these fish while using a two or three-ounce Hopkins. Barracuda spoons as well as the large Huntington Drone will also take a share of these school species when you concentrate on the inlet waters or just beyond the breaking of the surf.

Frankly, though I much prefer the role of lure slinger to bait slinger, this is one case where you will find the natural baits will beat most anything you'd care to name. In the surf, it is a must if you are to enjoy any appreciable success.

While fishing the Outer Banks of North Carolina with Gary Dillon, my angling associate, we found that nothing would beat a hefty surf rod as a work tool. The rod can be of either the conventional or spinning type; if the conventional stick is your choice for casting four ounces of lead, plus a fully baited fish-finder rig, then I'd recommend you saddle it with a Penn Squidder spooled with 25-pound test Dacron. Such an outfit will handle even heavier sinkers if and when the surf is found to be running high.

My own rig calls for an eleven-foot spinning rod, and a Penn Model 700, Zebco Cardinal 7 or a Daiwa 8600. Though some surf buffs will spool monofilament as heavy as twenty pounds or more, I for one content myself with a top quality line such as Perlene or Daiwa's new high-quality monofilament, in 15 or 17-pound test.

Many of the beach aficionados swear by either dead low water or the first few hours of an incoming tide for the most consistent fishing action. As to whether they bait with strip mullet or chunk mullet, it is up to personal whim, though some of these experts often prefer to bait-up with just the head section of either a spot or a medium-size mullet. This type of head bait does serve well to resist the gnawings of the ubiquitous blue or calico crabs, at the same time serving well as an acceptable bait for big channel bass.

When you are ready to put the hook to a red, you will score best if you allow time between when he seizes the bait and the point where you sock the barb into your fish. He is slow as a rule in mouthing the bait and the time it actually takes him to swallow it. Don't be over-eager.

As previously pointed out, be on the alert for cuts in the bar. This is a game fish that utilizes those passes as you and I would stick to a well worn path. All the science of reading the water, as it pertains to stripers, will pay off handsomely in this case.

A few seasons ago, while trolling off Chincoteague, Virginia, and not actually fishing for channel bass, we still caught several heavyweights on our yellow feathered spoons as well as on black and white Jap feather lures. It would appear to me that, if this species is present and within range

Fishing the Outer Banks of North Carolina, the author drags in a gaffed channel bass taken from high surf. Note the heavy-duty rig he uses when shore-casting for bass.

In the shallows of Pamlico, this fly fisherman has decided to stalk his channel bass with streamer flies.

Left: Light tackle used in open water resulted in this channel bass caught in Pamlico Sound, North Carolina. Opposite page: Showing that first effort at left wasn't a fluke, angler boats another channel bass from the same general location. Good sport!

At Cape Hatteras National Seashore, Joel Arrington of the North Carolina Conservation Department hand-gaffs a channel bass for a lucky Long Island visitor. Fishing can be excellent in Fall storms if the water doesn't get too off-color, making it tough for the quarry to see baits presented.

of your trolled or cast lure, they will hit it more often than not.

If you are craving for a most rewarding session on channel bass/reds, I'll personally recommend the areas around Ocrachoke, Oregon, Hatteras or Nags Head. This includes boaters and the shore-bound. In fact, the entire area of Cape Hatteras National Seashore is beautiful, clean, well run and beckoning to the sand-jockey set. You'll find ample parking, ramps for the four-wheelers, plus a number of camping spots, all of which makes this scene a natural for visiting sportsmen with a yen to fish amidst unspoiled, non-commercial surroundings. I can practically promise you that fish of at least fifty pounds are taken hereabouts each year. Remember, North Carolina has a limit of two large (over thirty-two inches) channel bass per angler. When the schools are in, the inlet's boat parties have no problem filling that limit.

During the 1968 season several knowledgeable fishermen demonstrated conclusively that channel bass could be taken on certain shoals in Pamlico Sound throughout the Summer months. As a greater number of the curious look into this new fishery, it is likely that fishing for these trophy-size fish will no longer be confined to the Spring and Fall months.

If there was any single word of advice on the subject of fishing for channel bass it would relate to the tackle an angler chooses. If the natural surroundings, especially bottom conditions, allow it, keep your tackle as light and sporting as possible. This is the answer to fully enjoying this conservative fighter.

Ben Hardesty used Shakespeare tackle to take this dorado from Argentina's Rio Parana recently. Caramba!

HOW WOULD YOU like to tangle with a fish that can weigh up to forty pounds, has both the teeth and savage disposition of a bluefish, the tenacity of an Atlantic salmon fresh from the sea, plus the lightning-fast aerial acrobatics of a hooked tarpon?

If this account sounds challenging, then you should become one of the few who have pitted their skill and tackle against fresh water's most savage fighter, the dorado; the trophy fish to beat all trophy fish — the golden giant of the Parana.

As luck would have it, dorado fishing is not just around the corner, not unless you happen to live somewhere in the vicinity of the Rio Parana. This great river, heralded in legends and ballads of Latin America, has its headwaters far up in the jungles of Brazil not far south of the new inland capital of this nation, Brazilia. It then runs South by Southeast through Brazil, finally becoming the legal dividing line separating the countries of Paraguay and Argentina. It is big water from any man's view and abounds in amazingly deep, turbulent pools, white-flecked rapids and long flats that twist and turn through hundreds of miles of gorgeous country.

The dorado is not unlike our rainbow trout when it comes to seeking out the fast water of a river, taking cover behind boulders in the big rapids and preferring the more turbulent stretches rather than the peaceful flats. While we are speaking of this river it would not be out of place to put an end to an untruth as reported by an American outdoor writer in a well-known outdoor magazine.

There are no schools of the dreaded piranha present in the river in the area between Argentina and Paraguay. It is only beyond the massive Falls of Iguazu, well up into the tropical regions of Brazil that these demons make their home in this river. They require warm water and actually seem to prefer the smaller, shallower streams and rivers of the true tropic regions.

At the request of the Argentine government and their national airline, Aerolineas Argentinas, I returned to Argentina to report upon and evaluate this republic's fishing and hunting. In this instance, I was in their Northernmost state — Misiones. It was my eighth trip into the more remote sectors of Argentina and, like a number of previous ones, lasted several months. Over the years there has been precious little I've not seen and experienced in this still unspoiled land. Thanks to my long-time fishing amigo, Argentine General Garcia Baltar, retired president of Aerolineas, and once Chief of the Argentine Air Force, I had access to one of the finest guides available in South

Take All The Qualities You See In A Gamefish, Then Seek This Beauty In Latin Climes!

Spotlight On An Exotic Gamefish: the Dorado

Chapter 13

America. This is Hugo Pesce, top South American professional hunter and a most congenial fishing companion.

It was Pesce who personally took care to see that accommodations and vehicles, as well as the numerous other necessities of a long stay, were all in order no matter where we journeyed or how far we traveled from our headquarters in the friendly river town of Monte Carlo.

Before the many weeks of this trip were over, our party had fished and hunted in Argentina, Paraguay and Brazil. Every minute of those days afield brought new experiences, though nothing could top those days spent fishing for the dorado. When it comes to hair-raising excitement, that never to be forgotten challenge of taking big fish in fast water, it would be difficult to think of a tougher adversary than the dorado.

Any who have fished the largest, brawling Western rivers for rainbow would take the typical dorado water in stride. As mentioned, these big fish show a strong preference for the edges of fast water runs, the hollowed-out depressions behind large boulders and usually can be found wherever you locate rapids or pocket water in a heavy flow, just as salmon and trout do back home.

A North American will immediately notice that the rods, reels and general tackle of the local Argentines and Paraguayans have not kept pace with the equipment available. Unfortunately, they do not have the selection of light, sporting tackle; thus, they end up settling for a typical salt water rod and reel, a basic rig that we might have aboard our boat when trolling for blues or stripers. The limitation of this rig forces the local anglers to troll, whether they like it or not.

Recently, several of the affluent Argentine sportsmen have come to the river with excellent casting tackle, most of it purchased here in the States. Now that they have light, fast-handling gear, there is no keeping them home at the ranch once the dorado season gets into full swing.

To get the feel of a dorado, I first played the game according to the local rules. This meant trolling large spoons from the comparative comfort of a small runabout with a fair-sized outboard motor providing the power. On that first morning, several miles downriver from Monte Carlo, I watched as my boatman swung the runabout at an angle so as to slide the big spoon into a large pocket just along the edge of a fast, white-water rapid. He knew what he was doing.

Just as the gleaming spoon dipped deep into the murky

pocket he winked at me and said, "Grande, senor, muy grande!" Before I could inquire whether he had talked to God on that particular morning, I found myself lifted clear out of the seat. Both of my arms and the rod were fully extended, the rod tip pointing straight down into the vicinity of the strike.

Before I could collect my dignity, I found myself looking up at one of the most beautiful fish I have ever seen. Weighing around twenty-five pounds he seemed to radiate a brilliant golden hue. His fins and tail were tinted a deep red, giving him the appearance of a violent flash of light silhouetted against the shoreline.

There was nothing else for me to do but watch him, for in that single instant he leaped seven or eight feet above the surface. While he thrashed in the air, there were three distinct times when his jaws came down on the spoon, and with such force, that it sounded like someone striking a metal gong. He then disappeared in a shower of spray and was off on a downriver run that stripped 150 yards before I realized just how fast everything was happening.

My boatman, an Argentine with a well-honed sense of humor, was chuckling and repeating over and over, in Spanish, "This you like, eh?"

I had found a species of fish that I hadn't even heard of

One of these golden dorado was taken with a large spoon on spinning tackle, the other on a fly rod using a Miracle Marabou of author's design. A top fighter, the dorado more than surprised Zwirz.

ten years ago. And, it was plain to see that dorado had all the manners of a bull in a bedroom, plus the general disposition of a Sumo wrestler with a bad case of gout. I was soon to realize he could add to these characteristics the ability to hang on and fight it out, even when I put the full power of that powerful rod against him and tried to horse him out of the deep current where he finally decided to hug the river bottom. Before it was over, he had jumped seven times and shown me the power and elusiveness rarely found with any game fish in either fresh or salt water.

Speaking for members of my party and myself, we strongly prefer casting for our fish, no matter where we are or how tough it seems getting into position to reach fish. This was no exception. We found two methods that worked, although I must admit we took more than one bath over the days that followed. Easier of the two methods called for anchoring the boat above or alongside a likely rapid, on a long line, and casting to all the water we could reach. In this manner we were able to handle the fly rod, spinning gear or bait casting outfits pretty much as our personal whims dictated.

To handle the large plugs, spoons and jigs that paid off

Happy with his catch, author Zwirz hoists two of the testy gamefish taken while wading the shores of the Rio Parana (right). The golden battlers look ferocious even in defeat! Senora Adela F. de Paz (below), wife of Monte Carlo's mayor, poses with six dorado she and her husband caught while trolling. Note the chewed tails.

Ejecting this average-size dorado from shallow water, Zwirz takes a big chance. Had he missed the gills, he might have lost his fingers to its many sharp teeth.

Struggling to rid itself of the heavy trolling spoon in its jaws, this dorado bends local angler's heavy tackle (above). Zwirz found little light tackle available in Argentina. Angling partner Eric Gornek (right) beaches a fine dorado taken with a fly rod using wire leader.

best, it was necessary to use fairly heavy line. The bait casting outfits spooled anywhere from 15 to 25-pound test line. The spinning outfits were loaded with the same test mono that you and I would use fishing the North Bar at Montauk Point during the night when the big stripers lie just over the dropoff. No matter which type of tackle you choose, bend on several inches of wire between line and lure. Without wire you do not even feel the strike as a general rule. The dorado's sharp teeth cut you off that fast and that clean.

Having learned a little more about the general behavior of the dorado, two of us decided to don our waders and hobnails and wade the edges of the less treacherous rapids. With the same basic fly rod and Scientific Anglers fly line I use on big tarpon, we cast large streamers, tied especially for this trip. They were five inches in length, with a four-inch wire leader pre-connected to the eye. On several I had rigged a propeller for added flash when the water was off-color due to heavy rain. The brighter patterns paid off most successfully with yellows, whites, and blue and white sharing the honors. Large Zwirz Miracle Marabou streamers tied on 1/0 and 3/0 hooks worked extremely well while they lasted.

During some of those fantastic days of fly fishing on the Rio Parana, or up along the Brazilian border, practically under the Cataratas del Iguazu, I found that it's impossible to build a streamer that will last through more than one or two sessions with an enraged dorado. The vast majority of the conventional salt water flies I had brought along were stripped of most of their fur and feathers within a few minutes of hooking the fish.

Below: Zwriz gets close look at dorado which rivals him in size. It was taken on bait-casting tackle and a large spoon, connected to a length of wire leader.

Once your cast starts moving through likely looking holding-water it is not at all unlikely that you will be jolted clear down to your hobnails by the sheer savagery of the initial strike. If your reflexes are satisfactory and you set the hook with enough power to sink its needle sharp point through those armor-thick jaws, then it won't be more than a fraction of a second before you come eye to eye with your dorado.

The instant he feels the steel, he is ready to do battle. Invariably his first move will be straight up. I've noted times, however, when he changes the rules to suit his mood and instead of settling for one jump, on the strike, continues to leap and roll while taking line downriver with a speed that is nothing short of amazing. More dorado throw the hook during the first moments of the contest than at any other time. And it is not unlikely that an inexperienced angler will find his hooks straightening out and plugs snapping in half. Or, too much drag and the game is over muy pronto.

There are two incidents that are fresh in my mind; incidents which will give you some idea of the bluefish-like aggressiveness of these golden brutes of the river. First, there was a lure I had with me, a lure that I couldn't replace even though it held a special magic for the fish. It happened to be an old, beat up Kautsky Musky Ike, the largest model they make and painted a flashing orange with dark spots running the length of it.

Those dorado simply went berserk when the thing tried scooting past them. After four or five fish there was practically no finish left on it and only an oversize single tail hook that we wired to the tail-end, rather than retire it. The last big fish tore the hook loose as I was attempting to beach it. All that remained was something that looked like a clothespin that a puppy had used as a teething bone.

The second incident was not without its moment of humor. Argentines have an excellent sense of humor, by the way, and you can be certain of receiving a share of good-natured kidding and clowning about the time when you are working your best fish of the day. It was next to my last week on the river and we were sitting along the shore relaxing, when suddenly Angel Paz, the mayor of Monte Carlo, hooked a tremendous dorado. We all saw it in the air and agreed it might be a record fish. He played his fish through jump after jump, as well as twenty minutes of greyhounding, then bulldogging the bottom. The fish finally moved into comparatively calm water.

At this moment the dorado spotted Paz, put on full power toward the boat, not away, then ripped out of the river in a great shower of spray. This golden goliath whipped himself clear over the amazed angler, not only scaring him half to death, but also managing to deposit the spoon with its 6/0 hook right in the shoulder of the gentleman's jacket. That, amigo, is how trophy fish do not get over the mantel.

The national airline of Argentina has the entire trip to the State of Misiones worked out so that there is no delay, no wasted motion. After leaving Buenos Aires they set you down at the border town of Posadas, a town within a few hours, by jeep, of the Monte Carlo headquarters.

Posadas, I might mention, has the envied reputation of having some of the best looking dolls in all of Latin

The great falls of Iguazu (above) are headwaters of Rio Parana, which flows between Argentina and Paraguay. The falls are located in Brazil, which Zwirz found to be beautiful country. Miracle Marabou streamers proved effective on dorado, and a selection is laid before the jaws of one of the golden battlers. Razor-sharp, the numerous teeth will quickly sever a finger, if proffered.

America. It takes an awful lot of will power to get yourself out of Posadas and into the river with those dorado.

The Club de Pescadores at Monte Carlo is the kind of place where the accommodations, food and wine are so superb that no man could find a thing to complain about, unless he simply hates good living.

The trouble with countries like Argentina, Paraguay and Brazil is that few of us have the time, within a single lifetime, to sample all the great fishing and hunting that they can offer. You always leave reluctantly, feeling you should wait to see just one more great fish lunge for the sky, listen just one more time to the coughing sounds of el tigre as he hunts his dinner along the lonely, up-country rivers; rivers with names like music, watering mile upon mile of fertile land that man has not yet spoiled.

The golden giants of the Rio Parana are but one reason to see this part of our world, but there is so much more. Take the time, if you can, and a massive supply of lures while you're about it.

The truly expert fisherman, working with either live or rigged baitfish, consistently takes his quota of trophy-size trout — like the beauty pictured above — regardless of the season.

Chapter 14

YEAR-ROUND TIPS
FOR TAKING
TROUT

Where Legal, This Favorite Of Anglers Can Be A 365-Day-A-Year Challenge.

Excellent results are possible when fishing the deep pockets of water found alongside boulder-strewn runs. It's here, in this natural cover, that the big trout congregate.

DESPITE THE INSISTENCE of some poorly informed individuals that the arrival of Summer's lazy, hazy days spell the end of trout fishing, there's really no valid reason for trout fishermen to store their rods away until the following Spring.

Trout fishing is just too challenging and enjoyable to limit it to a paltry thirty or forty-day season. I know for a fact that these fine gamefish can be taken from the opening day of the season right on up through the entire Summer and Fall. In fact, in those states where you can fish for trout throughout the year, it can be a 365-day-a-year season.

It's simply a matter of knowing where the fish are going to be at a given time. Knowledge of their feeding needs, based upon the time of the year and temperature of the water, won't hurt your chances, either.

So, if you want to get your licks in on trout anytime — from ice out up until the hunting bug bites and you decide to give your rods a rest — here is my view of the trout picture. And, since I work out my own schedules and methods, it really won't matter where you fish. Assuming there's a trout population in the state where you live, my recommendations are nearly universal, since they are based on natural conditions present in almost all trout waters and upon climatic conditions.

In the early Spring, trout fishing actually is a double-barreled kind of sport. On the one hand, it's no secret that a large percentage of the trout caught during the first few weeks of the season are recent plantings, fresh from the hatchery. These fish haven't had the time to become fully streamwise or develop any degree of trout sophistication. They haven't truly adapted to natural feeding

The late Joe Brooks with the kind of trout that can be taken during the hours of darkness by the thoroughly knowledgeable and expert angler.

conditions. Compared to a native, hold-over trout, the hatchery trout is a bumbling newcomer, lacking the elementary knowledge to survive even the most amateurish offerings of bait and lure. Those who manage to learn, survive. Or should I say survive and learn? The majority, not being wild and cautious, wind up in a frying pan.

These put-and-take trout, as I like to call them, are an entirely different breed than the elder, native trout that have learned the ways of the stream and natural feeding, and most important, the ways of fishermen and the bag of tricks used to move a trout from the stream to the skillet.

I might mention here, while on the subject of hold-over or trophy-size trout, that conservation crews in various states have collected volumes of data proving that the country's better rivers and streams still have excellent populations of trout year-round. The modern stocking devices used to compile this data show that an amazing proportion of this natural trout population is comprised of fish over twelve inches long, with a high share weighing in at trophy, or near-trophy size.

These trout feed several times during each twenty-four-hour period once the springtime waters warm up to around

During early season cold-water periods, best results are obtained when fishing flies, baits or lures deep and slow. When water temperatures drop, fish become less active.

forty-eight degrees Fahrenheit. They continue to feed without any serious discomfort until the water temperature reaches seventy-one degrees for brown trout, sixty-nine degrees for rainbows and sixty-eight degrees for brook trout.

Life for a trout is a deadly serious business, marked by an unending search for food. As the trout grows larger, this search becomes more demanding. It is this need that is at the root of a trout's willingness to take your offerings. Since this is the case, let's get down to the basics that will answer your questions as to what, when and where. Correct seasonal evaluations and proper fishing techniques on your part will turn you into a winner, from one month to the next.

You must consider trout as being a cold water species until the water temperature drops below forty degrees. Then it becomes a different story. At forty degrees or below, trout can do little but exist in a veritable state of lethargy. From an angler's viewpoint, any activity is practically useless. Feeding is close to non-existent, as compared to early Summer.

If this turns out to be the condition on your trout waters this Spring, don't jump to the conclusion that you

won't get any trout until the weather warms up a bit. This is the time wise, old fishermen start thinking in terms of the usual favorite trout baits or deepest working lures and plugs. They scout out the deepest pools and cuts where the water runs the deepest or areas where underground drainage and spring holes offer enough of a temperature variation to maintain a minimum reading of forty degrees.

Over most of the United States, Winter, with its low air temperature and snow, generally will result in a water temperature ranging from thirty-four degrees to what might be considered a balmy forty-eight degrees. If you want to fish under these conditions, remember that you have to find those warmer areas that will hold the fish population until conditions improve and warrant their moving out more widely.

Once you do find one of those warmer spots it still is necessary for you to fish your bait or lure considerably slower than you would under normal conditions. Deep, slow and accurate are the magic ingredients when you cast for trout in extreme cold.

In terms of fish caught, you'll probably get your best results by relying on natural baits. Garden worms, California red wigglers, small minnows or the larvae of

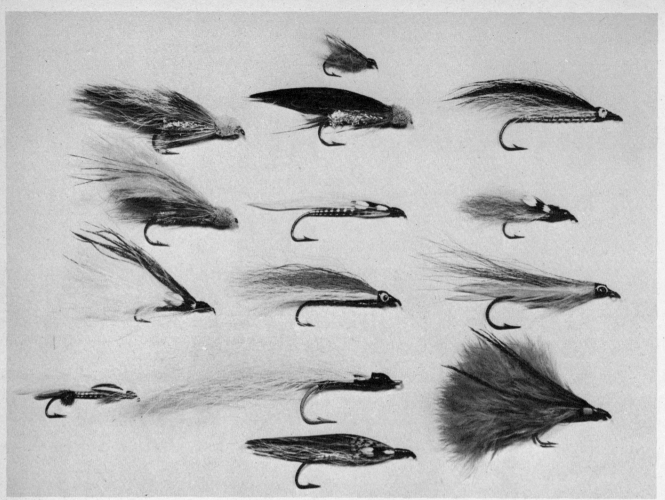

A small selection of the author's favorite streamers and bucktails. When properly used deep and slow, they prove deadly on big trout.

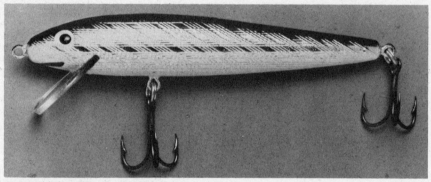

Imitation baitfish plugs can be particularly effective where big trout are involved. This Rebel represents an excellent imitation.

nymphs common to the stream being fished (where legal), usually will produce results.

If you prefer artificials, then stick to small, minnow-type plugs or other hardware made for the same purpose. The minnow-type plugs are especially good on bigger trout.

No matter whether you prefer natural baits or artificials, remember to work them slow and deep. Most early season bait and lure fishermen are rarely fishing as deep as they think they are — or as deep as they should be.

While you've been busy looking for and fishing those warm spots, the weeks have been passing and the sun has begun to warm the land and Spring has turned into Summer. The fact that it's now June, July or August doesn't change a trout's needs one bit. And, this being the case, there's no reason on earth why you shouldn't be able to take an even larger share of fish — probably far better fish than you'd be able to take during that Spring period when streamsides are packed tackle box to tackle box with anglers frothing the water with their casts.

There are quite a few ways of taking early, mid and late-Summer fish — rainbows, brookies and brown trout included. May and June aren't difficult months at all and when I talk about late season, low water conditions, I'm referring specifically to the months of July and August.

September and the first part of October I consider the best time for Fall fishing. It's a time that many anglers

Curt Gowdy, Jr., nets a good brown trout while fishing Wyoming's North Platte River. With know-how, action like this is possible year-round.

consider tops, for they can take fish from the slowly cooling rivers, streams and impoundments without haste, as most of their fellow fishermen have long since called it a season. The trout are on the prowl, continuously feeding as they get ready for the lean, hard months of Winter. Fall is a season apart with refreshing, crisp evenings and cooperative fish — fish that relish large streamers, big wet flies and deep probing nymphs. Bait and minnow lures come into their own again.

Not as cooperative and rarely as careless are the trout of Summer. To take them requires both imagination and a degree of finesse, if you are going to find the kind of action that all of us are looking for. There are several avenues of

approach, each requiring a different set of tactics. If one method or timetable doesn't appeal to you, perhaps one of the alternate solutions will.

For openers, you can try to beat the fish at his own game — deception. This can be done during any time of day over any prime stretch of trout water. All the caster has to do is probe likely looking water with careful cast after careful cast, trying to entice a worthwhile fish into action even if up to then he hasn't been reacting within any definite feeding cycle. You can use spinning lures, bait or flies.

Unless a welcome Summer shower comes along, the chances are that worms aren't going to produce with any degree of consistency. Of course, a highly skilled live-bait fisherman who knows the lay of big rainbows or brown trout in a given area of water would be an exception. Such an expert, especially if he's a live-minnow fisherman, is a threat to even the wiliest trophy trout at any time of the season.

For the fly fisherman, it must be a patient game of fine casts and of utilizing cover before attempting each presentation. You must carefully consider the effectiveness of a deeply worked nymph against a wet fly; or using a streamer in fast water against the possible acceptance by a trout of a high floating dry pattern dancing along a shadowed run.

Dapping along alder-lined streams, coupled with every conceivable sneak tactic you can think of, goes hand-in-hand with long, gossamer tippets, with rod and temperament to match.

But, when it comes to catching fish, it is far more rewarding to be on the trout waters during those hours that coincide with the trout's natural Summer feeding schedules — especially at dusk when lengthening shadows bring a general cooling of both air and water. At this time, brook trout ponds spring to life in a pattern of surface dimples and flashing rises. The rainbow feeds more openly in runs and riffles high in oxygen content, while the more cautious brown begins his hours of nocturnal foraging that will, in his case, last until the approach of dawn.

It's during these peak periods that the fly fisherman can really connect. For those quiet beaver ponds that hold brook trout, try number 18 or 20 black gnats, the effective Hornberg pattern or one of the spiders for the streams. For rainbows, a flashing bucktail or a number 10 or 12 dry

When water conditions are low, extreme care must be taken in making your presentation; but, it's prudent to remember that whatever the particular water conditions, trout feed within every twenty-four-hour period.

Western rivers and streams very often offer fast running pocket water, in which the high oxygen content is especially attractive to rainbows. The wise fisherman seeks areas like these, particularly in Summer.

hairwing coachman fished at the head of a fast run or over a promising pool should get results. And, during July and August, even the most cautious brown trout is apt to fall for a delicately cast pale evening dun. Most rivers and streams of any consequence still produce this hatch, children of the Potamanthus nymph.

On a warm July evening, my own favorite for browns is the dun of the Potamanthus with the best dry fly pattern being a sparsely dressed number 12 cream variant.

From mid-July through August, fly fishermen are fortunate to have some excellent hatches of light yellow mayfly (Ephemers), that usually show up about an hour or two before dark. Again, you'll find that the cream variant

pattern works wonders, even on larger fish. When using the Ephemers, I'd suggest moving up to the slightly larger pattern that is called for and try using a number 10 hook.

Over the years I've been singing the praises of using large wet patterns for brown trout and with good reason. Over a period of many seasons during the months of June, July and August, I have been able to put my pet theories on night fishing for brown trout to test. Some monster browns have come my way after dark and some of these huge cannibals I have beaten. Many others have beaten me in fair battles known only to the fish, myself and the night.

If you're the type who prefers to use spinning tackle exclusively, you probably have your own line of top

Certainly one of the most effective offerings to trout is the nymph, which also can be fished with a bubble. Whether your choice fishing hole is located East or West, the Caddis nymph can be a real winner.

Deep-running lures of relatively short length, like the Rebel, are the ticket for enticing big, cannibal trout when casting into deep runs and/or pools.

producing lures. Here are a few deadly and efficient lures that I will not be without when I'm fishing trout in rivers, streams or lakes.

The deadliest lure on my list would still have to be Rebel's minnow. This trout killer, the model F-49, is a shallow runner measuring just 1½ inches in length and weighing one-sixth of an ounce. It comes in just about any color combination necessary to imitate the baitfish prevalent in different parts of the country.

The Rebel firm also has a sinking model that is 2½ inches long and weighs one-quarter-ounce. It is especially effective in deep running streams and rivers and when used for casting or slow trolling in lakes. The model number of this sinking lure is S-1050. To give you some idea of its effectiveness, my wife, Glad, and I hooked over 170 trout with this fine baitfish imitation.

We've also had great results when using various Panther Martin lures, including the standard spinner and more recently the spinner with the baitfish imitation riding behind the blade. Rounding out my list of favorites would be such all-time winners as the Mepps, with or without squirrel tail, the C.P. Swing or Garcia's Abu series.

Just remember that warm water conditions make it a natural time for you to spend sufficient time probing fast water pockets. No matter where you live, East or West, pocket water spells trout.

Remember, too, that the heads and tails of large pools will hold more than their share of trophy size trout.

What this all boils down to is that trout fishing is an enjoyable business whether it's Spring, Summer or Fall. All it takes is some commonsensicial schedule to match the season and the temperature of the water. With the exception of difficult Winter conditions, when trout become lethargic, the feeding of this species is continuous throughout every twenty-four-hour period.

Rock and boulder-strewn North Carolina stream illustrates importance of "reading water" before casting.

Chapter 15
PANFISH:
HOW AND WHERE
TO FIND THEM

I DON'T KNOW who first made the observation that "variety is the spice of life," but if he was a fisherman, he must have been referring to the fabulous mixed-bags that come out of our Southern states.

When it comes to taking stringers of panfish and bass, not only are your opportunities great, but few places in the country will allow one to use a wider variety of methods to do so.

And, when it comes to fishing down South, you'll soon find that variety also extends to language. Most Southern fishermen I know have come up with so many unofficial names for various species that an honest ichthyologist would feel like a fish out of water.

My angling pals, especially those living in Florida and in the Gulf states, look at me with wonder when, for example, I ask about local fishing conditions for spotted sunfish.

Most panfish fall into the species of school fish. Once located, there is good reason to believe the action will continue. When schooling, stringers like this are common.

They agree that there just ain't no such fish in their waters. But, if I had asked about it under the popular Southern name — stumpknocker — it would be an entirely different story. I'd receive more advice than any one fisherman could use on the whereabouts, habits and eating qualities of this species.

So, if you're a Yankee planning to fish the Carolinas, Georgia, Florida or the Gulf states, you'd better do your homework before crossing the Mason-Dixon line. You can't talk about panfish in general, but have to refer to specific fish. Thus, questions concerning the local bream fishing will get you started in the right direction for bluegill.

Along these same lines, the green sunfish becomes a rubbertail and common sunfish are shellcrackers. Crappies, known to Northerners as either black or white depending on the sub-species, become specks down South. Black crappies are called calico or speckled perch. White crappies, on the other hand, have a dozen or so local names, the most surprising of which is strawberry bass. Down Florida way, the white crappie becomes a papermouth. In Dixie, red-breasts become yellow breasts, rock bass are called redeyes or goggle-eyes and one that never ceases to amaze me is the name for largemouth bass. Try green trout!

If you're thoroughly confused about fishing down South by now, take heart. Fish are fish, whether you find them North or South, East or West and the tackle, methods and other general information we're going to talk about will hold true anywhere and under most conditions. While each of the different panfish have habits that require some individual discussion, learning a little of their general behavior will result in mixed bags much of the time, along with a bass or two as frosting on the cake.

If bass are present and striking, it's fairly safe to assume that most of us will be going after them. But if the funnel-mouths are sulking or just simply refusing to try anything you have in your tackle box, that's the time to scale down your tackle and try your hand with the local panfish.

The results can be delightful, if you remember to match your tackle to the job at hand. If you show up with a stiff bait-casting outfit or a medium-action spinning rig, you're not going to have too much fun. What gets you a trophy bass from weed-tangled cover or a tough shoreline isn't going to hack it for panfish.

Go light is the word, when concentrating on panfish, and take a chance that, if you do hook a solitary bass, luck will be a lady. A day spent fishing for crappies, rock bass, blue-

Panfish offer great sport and are particularly vulnerable to small bass bugs and popping lures.

When it's crappie time in Kentucky, you'll find the young and old alike out on the water with their special rigs — even during rainy weather.

gill or our old friend, the stumpknocker, can be mighty enjoyable when you limit yourself to an ultra-light spinning outfit or a light-action fly rod.

As I said earlier, it makes no difference where you are fishing, since certain behavior patterns of these fish are the same North or South. Panfish generally are school fish by nature.

As a group, panfish don't go for fast currents or turbulent water. Try farm ponds, lakes of all sizes, backwaters

Hundreds of thousands of ponds throughout the United States contain trout, such as New York State's Eldred Preserve (below), but many also hold panfish and warm water species.

and slow-moving river eddies. Probe around weed beds and areas with brush or underwater deadfalls.

Temperature of the water is as important to panfish as to the more finicky bass. Where possible, panfish will move according to the thermometer. They are on a changing schedule that will vary little from season to season. They'll stay deep during the Winter and early Spring. Up North, when the temperature drops below 45 degrees F, panfish schools will go as deep as possible. In farm ponds and larger waters, they'll seek out a stratum of ten to twelve feet on down to twenty to thirty feet in some areas I've fished.

When you can locate them during cold weather, they respond well to a small hook with a worm. They also can be coaxed into going for an extra-small ice-fishing jig and can be taken on the smaller, slowly trolled or retrieved fly and spinner combination.

When the water warms to between forty-five and sixty degrees, panfish will begin to move out of their winter hideaways and look more actively in medium depths for food. This is the time when weed beds lying in seven to twelve feet of water will produce consistently. The story will be the same wherever deadfalls and other underwater debris have collected and provide cover and food to both baitfish and nymphal life. When this natural food is present, it doesn't take long for panfish to arrive on the scene.

Drifting and still-fishing with natural baits will get you your share of fish at this time. Tops on the bait list everywhere is the common angleworm, white grubs and other small preserved baits and very small minnows are equally effective on most panfish.

This is also the time of year when well-handled flies begin to produce. Wet fly patterns, miniature bucktails and streamers, along with natural or imitations of prevalent nymphs, snails and crustaceans will fill your stringer nine times out of ten. It's also a peak time for using all sorts of small imitation bugs and the like, known to be favored by panfish and, for that matter, bass. Spinner and fly combinations are great, as are such ultra-light spinning lures as Mepps, C. P. Swing or Panther Martins. Ultra-light jointed plugs also are good, especially on crappie.

When Summer and its long, hot days arrives on the scene and the water has warmed up sixty to eighty degrees, arm yourself with a light-action fly rod and have a ball. Small wet or dry flies, when presented anywhere from a couple of inches of water cover down to depths of five or six feet, will give you fine results.

Hairbugs and small panfish poppers, like the larger ones used for bass, will give you all the action you can handle. Often a mean-tempered old bass will take your offering to add an extra thrill and keep you on your toes.

As indicated earlier, it would be almost impossible to spell out all the rules for taking each and every member of the panfish families. Instead, I'll try to put them into a couple of major groups. And, while it's true that each of the panfish feeds according to the availability of certain local foods, they also follow a somewhat general tendency toward a natural routine. This allows one to make a few generalizations.

For example, the yellow perch, which is indeed panfish, will tend to avoid those areas used by its smaller brethren. He's fooled many an angler by frequenting waters from twenty to thirty-two feet deep. Wherever I've found the bottom twenty-five or thirty-five feet below the surface, the chances of locating a concentration of these scrappers have been excellent. Yellow perch have a strong preference for minnows, so concentrate on using minnow type plugs or lures, if you don't want to fish the real thing.

Bluegills, crappies, rock bass and white perch of the landlocked variety all usually hold to the general depth, temperature and feeding habits already outlined.

I want to explain why I defined the white perch as landlocked. What we have here are two distinct fish, but not different species and the difference is in their travels.

The landlocked white perch obviously is limited to those waters in which he is present. His migrating brother, on the other hand, can be found in salt, brackish and fresh water. This sea-run panfish makes a great showing and is sought after when he makes his spawning run in the Spring. That's the time many tributaries run heavy with these fish which are in their prime. Throughout the South, bridges are lined with anglers, while still others wade the shores looking for hard-fighting whites. Minnows are the top bait with float fishermen, while in the Gulf states, shrimp register a close favorite.

With all of the various panfish, no matter what their local name or where you are fishing for them, there always are favorite natural baits that are preferred in each locality. On this score it pays to check with the natives. And, while you're chatting, cover the subjects of top spots and methods as well as baits.

Now, when it comes to taking these rascals with a fly, let me offer you some suggestions that will pay off almost anywhere. First of all, don't tie on a fly larger than a size No. 10. Personally, I put my faith in No. 12 or No. 14 sizes. This makes it easier for these fish to get their small mouths into the pattern. If you find yourself handling the larger schools of white bass, though, I'll change my advice a little.

For those who don't mind cold feet, there is still plenty of action after the waters freeze up. This New Jersey ice-fisherman proves the point with catch of yellow perch.

Although these particular white bass were taken in North Carolina's Lake Fontana, they are not unlike others of their species elsewhere and will quite readily take to baitfish and baitfish imitations.

These fish can swallow a three-inch minnow with ease, so it's just as easy for one to gulp a three-inch bucktail.

Nearly all panfish will go for a small, light-colored dry fly pattern once they're inshore or have made a home in the shallows. In this case, the light Cahill and the hair wing coachman tied on a No. 14 dry fly hook are winners. If you'd rather fish natural and drift or still fish, try a No. 6 bait holder hook. If you are after migrating perch or big

Probably more youngsters have been "started out" on bluegills than any other species in the United States.

Favorite outing for many Tennessee families is fishing the "stick-ups" during the early season.

white bass, I'd recommend substituting a No. 6.

There are numerous ultra-light reels such as the Quick Micro-Life and Alcedo Micron. Rods such as Fenwick's Feralite FS-60, Heddon, Shakespeare and Wright-McGill among others, will give you a suitable light outfit for panfish. Fly rods and lines of No. 5 or No. 6 class provide the most thrills for fishermen of the long rod fraternity. Spin fishermen and fly-casters will find four-pound test all that's necessary in the way of terminal gear. It's perfect for spinning with 1/16 to 1/4-ounce lures and plugs.

My friends down in Dixie never cease to amaze and educate me. The top anglers I've fished with have their individual preferences in all phases of their fishing, baits included. Worms are their day-to-day fish-getter, but they don't stop there. When they finesse a high score or find themselves on an off day, nothing makes up the difference better than manure worms. Crickets are the thing for bream and grasshoppers aren't too bad.

Some guys will put a light up against a screen at night, then go out each hour and collect the harvest of miller moths, beetles and other night flying beasts. Others rate grubs, catalpa worms and cornborers high on the list. I even know a few who advocate the use of cockroaches.

The wide range of panfish, along with the simple tackle and perseverence needed, make them naturals for anyone who wants to fish. They offer a great opportunity for you to teach your youngsters the basics of fishing.

As one ol' Georgia boy told me years ago, "Never heard tell of a fellow knocking a stumpknocker once he caught himself a stringer full."

215

Chapter 16

PICKING A PLACE FOR PIKE

If You Troll, You're In; If You Want To Cast, Here Is How — And Where

IF SPRING IS the time of the year when a young man's fancy turns to thoughts of love, it's also the time a wise fisherman knows is the best opportunity to produce a catch of Northerns.

These fish not only are voracious feeders, but they concentrate in shallow waters. Usually these are areas known to local guides and other fishermen familiar with the waters.

In much of the Northern pike country, these fish will be located in the acres of weed beds normally spotted throughout the big lakes. This type of cover also is available to the Northern in rivers and creeks where it grows heavily along slow water flats and in backwaters and natural eddies.

Now, many fishermen will argue when I say that the largest percentage of Northern pike are caught by casters, far more than can be taken by trolling methods. Trollers tend to work their boats around the weed beds and bars. Rarely, if ever, do they present their lures through them or over them.

If you consider that the Northern strongly prefers to be right in among the cover, then it's a fair bet that anglers working their lures within, or just above the growth will

Voracious and cannibalistic best describe the Northern pike; a temperament augmented by savage countenance.

One of author's fishing companions, Cap Anderson of Cranberry Portage, Manitoba, boats a fat Northern pike that latched onto a cast Rebel.

score best. If you run your boat and lure over the Northern's sanctuary continuously, all you can expect to do is spook the fish you are trying to catch.

As important as knowing the specific locations in which these fish are likely to be found is the matter of knowing, with some certainty, that you'll be doing your fishing in prime areas. That's the only way you'll take trophy-size Northerns.

In the United States there's generally average quality fishing for the Northern in Wisconsin, Michigan, Minnesota, Nebraska and North Dakota. Minnesota probably is the best when it comes to naming the top U.S. hotspot. However, most of the suitable habitat has been heavily fished for a number of years. When I crave some top-quality Northern pike fishing, I make tracks for one of the Canadian provinces. Manitoba, Saskatchewan, Quebec and Ontario long have been at the top of my list.

Most fishermen agree with me that Northern pike fishing is best in those waters that have remained remote. Northerns are simply so voracious that they can be practically fished out of a region, if and when fishing pressures become too concentrated for the region. The sad fact is that the old cannibal is just too anxious to strike a lure or take a bait.

Some Northwest sections of Ontario, though, are still far enough from well traveled roads. But in the Southern tier of the province, where one finds easy access, you'll also find that the waters are fished heavily throughout the season. Fortunately, Manitoba and Saskatchewan can provide one with some truly fast fishing with an appreciable number of big fish available.

Manitoba offers some 28,000 square miles of lakes and streams. Most of these contain Northern pike, as well as trophy-size lake trout, brookies and walleye. In the area

Taken on a trolled spoon, fished in a deep channel area, this is one Quebec trophy that didn't get away.

between the Manitoba-Ontario border and Lake Winnepeg, there are literally hundreds of fly-in lakes. Many of them are virgin fishing waters.

There are other promising lakes waiting to be fished in the extreme sector between The Pas, in the Northern part of the province, and the town of Churchill. It's an area of five hundred miles of wilderness between these two stops on the Canadian National Railway.

My latest trip to Manitoba centered around Cranberry Portage. I stayed at the Caribou Lodge which lies between The Pas and Flin Flon.

In taking a look at Saskatchewan's Northern pike fishing, one will find that the Northernmost reaches of this beautiful province contain some of the least fished lakes in all of Canada. To reach many of them, one needs a bush pilot to put him down where the fish are, but this is a relatively inexpensive part of your trip. The town of Prince Albert offers all types of package deals for visiting anglers and boasts enough float planes to take care of a sportsman's schedule without too much prior notice.

All of these provinces, along with the other provinces that contain Northern pike among their many other species of fish, have numerous commercial camps that are set up to handle individuals, groups or a typical family excursion. The choice is whether you want to rough it or stick to the comforts of a well-run commercial camp.

Methods, lures and tackle are dictated by the type of water you'll be fishing and the average size of Northerns in the area. But, no matter what type lure and tackle you prefer, it is important to work the typical hotspots carefully.

Areas such as weed beds, lily pads, reeds and underwater deadfalls are the typical locations where Northerns will generally congregate. These are also the spots where large, trophy-size loners are likely to be stationed. If they aren't actually lying within the openings in these covers, it's even money they are showing little more than eyes and snout at the very edge of it.

This strong habit of the Northern's, hiding in heavy cover, brings us to the subject of which tackle is best under these conditions that will almost guarantee snagged lines and hooks.

There's no reason why you shouldn't use a light, sporty rod and a correspondingly light line, at least from the viewpoint of pound test as opposed to the weight of average Northerns.

The only trouble is that this isn't the crux of the problem. Not only must you consider the bugaboos of a snagged lure from time to time, but the mess of vegetation a hooked pike is liable to gather on your line during a knock-down, drag-out battle.

These two reasons alone practically force you to use a stiffer action rod along with a line capable of taking the weight when you have to lay into your fish. During the first

A line-up of some of Zwirz's favorite Mepps fly and spinner combinations, and spinner and bead combinations. These large sizes are considered tops for just about any and all of the monster-size, fighting gamefish.

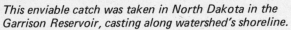

These Rebel Hot-Spins are not only tops for bass, they are killers on Northerns, muskies and walleyes as well.

This enviable catch was taken in North Dakota in the Garrison Reservoir, casting along watershed's shoreline.

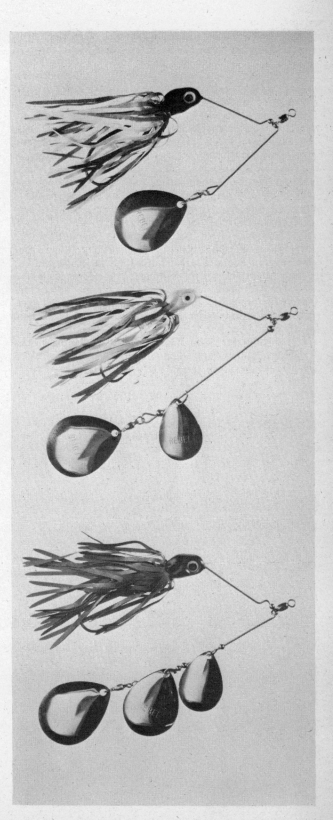

few moments of hooking a big Northern, it's not a bad idea, when possible, to put the pressure on him immediately, simply to turn him and force him to the outer edge of his cabbage patch. This is where the combination of a rod and line with built-in backbone will help you bring the fish into the open water.

There is another consideration, also. Lures, spoons and even the larger spinner and bucktail lures are of a size that make your typical bass bugs look skimpy. The average pike spoon is anywhere from three to five inches long. Not only are they heavier, but because of their size, they frequently catch the wind and cast like a winged saucer. So, seventeen-pound test line is none too heavy and many skilled pike fishermen won't consider anything lighter than twenty-five-pound test. And don't forget the rule that the heavier and bulkier your lure, the heavier the line you need to cast it. If your line is too light for the lure it not only will belly during the cast, but will control poorly when you retrieve.

A heavy oval spoon with a nickel finish on one side and red and white on the other seems to score exceptionally well for me. Adding a red bucktail onto its tail hooks makes it more effective. Remember to keep spinners, spoons and other lures glistening. The flash and erratic movement are important, if you're trying to persuade a particularly lazy fish to strike, especially on an overcast day.

If you want to hold onto that pike throughout a battle of any duration, don't forget to use a section of wire leader between your line and lure. This is the exact same kind of rig used for fishing for muskellunge. You can get leaders of six to twelve inches at tackle shops. Some are nylon-covered for flexibility and others are made of braided wire. They have a built-in swivel and snap so you can fasten them directly onto your line.

Just casting the large pike-muskie spinners or spoons into likely holding water, then retrieving, isn't enough. You have to impart some finesse to your presentation. As it strikes the water, give it a twitch. Lurch along for a few inches like a baitfish breaking the surface. Concentrate on making your lure look like a real, live fish trying to swim off and escape. The more realism you impart, the better your chances of enticing the big one, no matter what you hear to the contrary.

Most of the time, you'll find the Northern along the inshore waters and around cover that holds baitfish, frogs and similar fish fare. It's the same basic cover we described earlier as holding the most fish. At times, though, pike will seek deep holes, if the weather is extremely hot during the daytime, and again as Winter sets in. But, even hot Summer fish can be found along the shoreline in the hours just prior to sunup and for an hour or two afterwards.

At times, you are going to find that certain waters that hold pike do not have all the types of cover we've described. If that's the case, look for your fish in channel areas, drop-offs and especially where brooks and streams empty into the lake. Pike often will be lying there in anywhere from eight to twelve feet of water. They can be even deeper in some parts of the country.

Areas such as these often call for the use of live bait. Suckers are an excellent pike bait. They should be at least six to eight inches long. Large pike prefer baitfish as long as twelve inches. Yellow perch, dogfish and bullheads with the spines clipped off are deadly when still-fishing.

These can be used in any of the special trolling rigs that are favored by fishermen scouting the deeper runs and coves while trolling bait and spinner behind their runabouts and being careful not to spook the fish.

A good number of rivers will hold trophy-size pike. These are great for those of you who want to stick with slightly lighter lures than the ones used on the big lakes. Fly and spinner combinations can be handled on a good, stout bass-bugging fly rod. Remember, too, that a weight-forward line will help your casting.

If you present this combination or a large bucktail into those likely looking openings along the shore, around deadfalls or into pockets in the weed beds and lily pad growths, you're bound to have rewarding results.

Proof of the broad distribution of Northern pike are these three taken by Zwirz while casting near harbor located at Helsinki, Finland.

Tom Pierce, owner of Sportsman's Lodge, fighting a twenty-three-pound Northern pike caught near McIntosh Lake, Saskatchewan.

Chapter 17

IT'S STILL A fact that confusion often runs rampant when anglers in various parts of the country begin discussing the heavyweight among fresh water gamefish, Salvelinus mamaycush.

It's also a fact that too many people consider any of the trouts or char caught within the confines of a lake to be — you guessed it — a lake trout. Not so.

The term, "laker," is its most popular designation, although there most certainly are regions where referring to it by this name won't win you any cigars. Anglers living in the Eastern Canadian provinces, as well as in Maine and parts of

New Hampshire, rarely refer to it as anything but a togue, or possibly a gray trout. But when the same species makes its appearance in regions of the Midwest, all of the Far West and Alaska, ol' mamaycush has but one name and that is mackinaw. No matter which of its eight or nine names you may use, it is an impressive gamefish. And it's of growing importance throughout its distribution, no matter how strongly some anglers feel about its piscivorous leanings.

In this chapter, I'll concentrate on practical fishing methods for the species as they apply to the Midwest, West and Northwest distributions. For this reason, more than

Winning Ways with Mackinaw and Cutthroat

Under Whatever Local Name You Prefer, These Fish Present A Challenge That Is Met With Info Outlined Here!

any other, it will be referred to as a mackinaw. However, don't believe that the methods mentioned here will not work just as well in all areas in which this fish is to be found.

Basically, we'll be discussing two general approaches for mackinaw; the latter utilizing all three of our most popular types of tackle, spinning, bait-casting and the fly rod. And since cutthroat trout are practically synonymous with the term Western, we also can take a brief look at ways and means of fishing for these.

The cutthroat, by the way, makes his home in both lakes and streams, and there are numerous methods which can be used when fishing for him.

During all but the hotter months it becomes just a matter of proper timing on the part of the angler. There is a pre-Fall period when the mackinaw prefers to remain deep in his cold water sanctuaries, and for that matter there are large lakes where he even conducts spawning at depths of up to one hundred feet. However, he usually is on his shoreward move by October. The mackinaw's major preoccupation at this time will be, firstly, on spawning and, secondly, on feeding heavily before Winter.

Let's examine a few of the methods for taking these gamefish while they are still living and feeding beyond the practical reach of normal casting tackle; while they are still holding out in deep areas.

The mackinaw is a fish which you must seek out with water temperature clearly imprinted in your planning. Over the years I've found a marked difference between my fishing success in perfect water as against water slightly below or above the optimum temperature for the species. When I check and find readings of from forty-two to forty-eight degrees Fahrenheit, I'm fairly certain of being on the right track.

It may be due to the spawning schedule of the species, but Fall is the one time of year when they will tolerate a water temperature of up to fifty-five degrees F. During their early Spring frolic in relatively shallower waters you normally will note that they will slowly disappear into their deep, cold hideaways once temperatures build up to the fifty-degree mark. Let's simply say the fifty-degree variation becomes, no matter the reason, a bonus set aside just for Fall anglers.

Basically, the mackinaw is a school fish. Once you locate the prime conditions to attract one, it's a reasonable assumption that others are in residence. Further, when you

do locate them, mark the spot. Not unlike the case with Summer largemouth or smallmouth bass, you have found a preferred area; a sanctuary offering both optimum temperature and oxygen, plus a close proximity to food.

Prior to the cooler Fall periods when they sense the time to move out, the angler is, on occasion, forced to troll at a depth of anywhere from sixty to two hundred or more feet. Unfortunately this calls for the less-than-satisfactory business of wire line. In my opinion the tackle, plus the extreme depth, go a long way toward defeating the fighting ability of this gamefish.

And here I might add that I am well aware of most of the deep-fishing techniques calling for break-away weights, self-releasing planers, et al. The mackinaw never performs as well as when the angler is fortunate enough to make the contact with light tackle and at a reasonable depth.

For those who wish to get in a few licks while they are still lying deep, here are a few tips which put mackinaw in the boat. Since it's my belief that these fish move more slowly and less distance than their nearer-to-the-surface cousins, due to environmental conditions, those who have come to know of a number of possible hangouts in their waters will score best when still-fishing. This method of fishing, coupled with the use of ciscoes or smelt for bait, has proved to be a deadly combination; so much so that it is banned in certain waters containing the mackinaw.

When you couple the still-fishing method to a properly used electronic depth-finder/fish-locater, an angler has the mackinaw dead in his sights. Again, for anglers not possessing prior knowledge about hot spots or temperatures at various depths, items such as battery-operated thermometers are a great assist. I have found the Vexilar Zonar to be well worth carrying. This particular unit serves as both a temperature and depth indicator. Such modern assists, put to work in conjunction with deep trolling techniques, will find fish.

The use of "cowbells," fished in front of lake trout spoons, or plugs imitating the mackinaw's favorite coarse fish (again used with the cowbells, or chain-of-lights as they are sometimes referred to) account for all sizes of fish. Live bait also can be trolled slowly and it is a proven fact that the flashing hardware does help attract this gamefish for a closer look, particularly when the mackinaw is beyond the sixty to eighty-foot depth.

The ciscoes, large smelt, alewives, whitefish, suckers or yellow perch are good choices for this type of fishing. No

Author coaxed this prize specimen into a solid strike and eventual landing with large wobbling spoon.

Zwirz, companion and foursome landed in less than one hour of casting with medium action spinning equipment.

matter whether you fish with natural bait or artificials, one factor remains the same: When baits are presented at precisely the correct depth, success will be most consistent.

In deep water you can anticipate a savage strike, especially from the larger fish; so savage that there could be little doubt of it being anything but a mackinaw.

There is a third school of deep water mackinaw fishermen. These carry-overs from the salt water scene prefer to jig weighted spoons and flashy squids. It's not unusual to find them working their heavy lures at depths from two hundred to three hundred feet.

The mature mackinaws, though apt to eat almost anything, strongly prefer a diet of fish. That is why knowledgeable anglers use large wobbing-type spoons, which act as veritable look-alikes, when trying for those trophy-size fish you hear about. The following are just a few of the all-time favorite trolling lures: Northwest's Super Flash (all sizes),

Lucky-Strike, Williams Wobbler, Len Thompson No. 4 (and larger sizes), L&W Half Wave, L&W Full Wave, Pflueger Chum and Record spoons, Tony Acetta Pet spoons, Huntington Drone spoons, Dardevles (larger sizes) and the large Trix-Oreno.

As waters cool and the first of the males begin cruising, generally over rocky shoal areas, these same artificials will produce well. But now, since you will be able to switch to lighter trolling and casting equipment, there's good reason for you to rule out those lures which are either too large or too difficult to troll with ease, while using the more standard class of spinning or bait-casting tackle. A fair number of anglers experience good results while using this type of tackle and when combined with a slightly weighted spinner and fly combo.

For the record, I've personally tried this arrangement during late September, while fishing one of the larger lakes

227

Regardless of what they are commercially called, big lakers/mackinaws will take any of this selection of the author's favorites, which include Mepps, Rebels and other varieties of wobbling spoons.

in Manitoba. It didn't seem to matter whether I fished it with mono or trolled it behind a sinking fly line, it worked. For that matter, so did a medium-size Mepps with a squirrel tail.

All of the baitfish-type lures which work on landlocked salmon will produce on mackinaw. However, I still believe in the old saying, "big fish, big lures." That goes for the streamer flies I cast to rocky shoal areas, especially to those spots situated closely adjacent to the deep water areas. Fast, sloping, rocky dropoffs that lead to the deep, cold strata of a lake are prime targets for the fly fisherman who will cast or troll his streamers during this time of renewed, near-surface action. Streamers measuring anywhere from four to even six inches will fill the bill nicely. If necessary, and in order to gain length and extra hooking power, tandem streamers may prove a necessity.

If you're one of those fortunate enough to join battle with a real brute of a mackinaw on his terms, and while fishing with reasonably light tackle, you'll never again doubt his fighting abilities. But if not, remember one last, parting thought: Until you have hooked and fought this fine gamefish in the shallower waters — you haven't yet come to know him.

Although my statement may expose me to correction, it would seem true that the cutthroat enjoys a vaster range than any other of our true trout species. You'll find them in residence from the Western Dakotas into Montana, Idaho, Wyoming and Washington to the Pacific shores. Their southerly distribution includes Colorado and Northern New Mexico. It also includes Nevada, Utah, Oregon and a northerly section of California. In the Northwest, it can be found in British Columbia, Alberta and well into Southern Alaska and the Yukon.

Back in the days when population wasn't our problem and fish and game departments were not the necessity they are today, there were for all practical purposes of indentification two important divisions of trout in the West. Local anglers generally could tell them apart, but insisted on referring to both species as natives. Those "natives" were the cutthroat and the rainbow.

One more fact should be discussed before we take a look at known methods for taking cutthroat. And this relates to the unavoidable truth that the coloring and even the markings differ greatly from one locality to another. I've personally seen cutthroat so dark, yet so predominantly marked with yellow spots, that for comparison, these are direct opposites to those fish in some other area which boast light sides and black spots. Others look so similar to sea-run rainbows that more than a few anglers on the West Coast are fooled.

Don't think for a second that you may presume there will be the famous red slash under the lower jaw. Again, depending on environmental conditions, you may face a fifty-fifty chance of finding no such dominant feature. Often, there is a marked difference between cutthroats caught in one type of stream flow as opposed to another, and similar variations from one lake to another. Often, the slash is almost hidden by the fish's lower jaw, or it is so faint it's not easy to see.

An angler fishing for cutthroat usually can guess the approximate weight of the average fish he will take, based upon the water he is fishing. Most of the rocky, smaller, fast-moving streams will offer fish under fourteen inches. Still, this does not rule out the fact that you may latch onto a rare specimen of eighteen to twenty inches. Fish taken from coastal areas most often exceed the length and weight of those taken from their upland flows, and by comparison, cutthroats caught in a number of lakes will be the trophies.

Although I must go all the way back to 1925 to impress the reader with possibilities, it's still interesting to know Johnny Skimmerhorn's record cutthroat, weighing forty-one pounds and measuring thirty-nine inches, was taken on rod and reel from Pyramid Lake, Nevada. This gives you a pretty fair idea of the possible spread in size, although, frankly, I'd be very surprised to ever again see a cutthroat which would approach that old Nevada record.

In both streams and lakes the cutthroat is justly acclaimed to be one of our best fly rod species. He's a perfect adversary for anglers who prefer to use light spinning equip-

Priest Lake in Idaho yielded this forty-six-pound mackinaw taken in deep water on baitfish imitation plug.

ment, and it's not unheard of for big water fishermen to handle small plugs and lures while utilizing one of our modern bait-casting reels with matched rod.

From a seasonal viewpoint I strongly prefer the period from late Summer into Fall. In this statement I'm including the high country inlanders, both in streams and lakes, as well as those migrant cutthroats which have access to the sea.

During late Summer and early Fall, many West Coast fishermen with access to Oregon or Washington flows wait impatiently for grapevine news that the seasonal appearance of flying ants has begun. Usually, this signals the beginning of great fly fishing action as the cutthroats move back from salt water to upstream, fresh water areas. At this time the fly fisherman is wise to try various of the ant patterns, as well as most of the popular ties of terrestrial insects.

Keep in mind throughout the season, over most all of their distribution, cutthroat show great interest in terrestrial food. Mayflies, midges, caddis flies and typical aquatic larvae make up a great part of the remaining needs. Although the larger fish feed on minnows and other of the forage fish, this is one species of trout which seems never to swing predominantly to cannibalism. Even larger cutthroats still rely on aquatic and terrestrial food to an extent. As said earlier, this makes them a perfect target for the fly fisherman using dries, wets and nymphs. Streamers or buck-tails will account for a percentage of the larger, adult fish.

No matter the type of tackle an angler chooses, when fishing in waters normally offering average-size trout, he'll do best when he keeps his bait and lures on the small size. Colorado spinners, assorted varieties of small spoons and small plugs imitating natural baitfish will prove deadly. Particularly when fishing the lakes, you'll do well casting or trolling such items as the two smallest sizes of Rebels (both the floating and sinking models) or the same basic sizes in Rapalas. It's also wise to carry a supply of fly and spinner combos, such as the Mepps, Anglias or C-P Swings, plus most of the popular lineup of trout lures used for spinning.

You'll find early morning and evening periods are tops for the fly fisherman using any of the popular wets or dries. And since cutthroats tend to feed along the shoal areas, even in the largest lakes they inhabit, they're within practical reach of any type of light tackle. During the day, especially in the Summer months, trollers can take cutthroat from the deeper waters of lakes; again, the best producing baits and lures will be those imitating natural foods available. Worms, salmon eggs and small minnows can account for heavy catches. So too will a combination of a minnow used behind a flashing spinner. And while speaking of lakes, I'll bet eighty-five percent of my fish, taken on a fly rod, were attracted to wet fly patterns.

Sitting here in New England, I find myself remembering gorgeous days spent on such great cutthroat waters as the Madison, Firehole and Yellowstone. Conjuring such

Flanking patterns are Miracle Marabous designed by Zwirz, with which he has recorded good success on big mackinaws in shallow waters. Fly pattern shown in center has been tied with special mylar body.

Fishing at sunset in a coastal area — where fish run larger than in smaller streams — this angler has hooked a fine cutthroat.

memories brought me to a realization that readers who have not fished the species may be interested in knowing the names of fly patterns which have worked well for me and a number of my angling friends. And, they are just as effective on most other trout and char. Hook sizes should be based on type of water and assumed average size of fish in each geographical area.

Patterns: (W — wet, D — dry)
Gray Hackle (yellow) — W or D
Brown Hackle — W or D
Hair-Wing Royal Coachman — W or D
Silver Doctor — W
Fly Caddis (Kalzer Firefly w/Gantron)
Ginger Quill — W or D
Rat-faced McDougall — D
Queen Of The Waters — W
Whit Gray Nymph — W
Grizzly King — W
Black Gnat — W or D

Big Hole Demon — W
Spruce Fly (lt. or dk.) — W
B. Woolly Worm (red tail) — W
Lady Mite — W
Black Nose Dace — W
Renegade — W
Zug Bug — W
Silver Darter — W
Montana Nymph — W
Red Ant — W
Flying Black Ant — W or D
Bucktail Caddis — W
Cow Dung — W
Pink Lady — W
Rio Grande King — W
The Cutthroat — W
Gray Bi-Visible — W or D
Gold-ribbed Hare's Ear — W
Bird's Stone Fly — W

Chapter 18

CATCHING STRIPERS AROUND THE CLOCK

Here Is An All-Season Fish Off Both Coasts That Is Always Available With The Right Techniques!

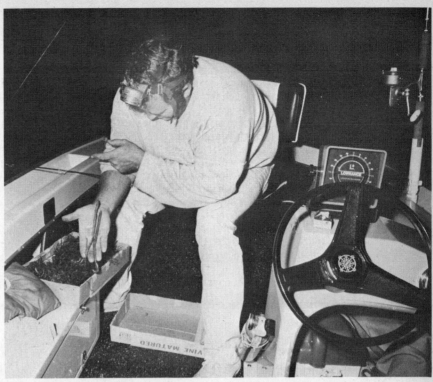

Gary Dillon, one of author's fishing compadres, examines a double sandworm setup, as used for stripers. They ride naturally in the water, yet hide the double Eagle Claw hooks most effectively.

THERE ARE A number of fishermen who will be quick to point out that deep trolling accounts for more and larger fish than are taken by any other method. This is a point not worth arguing. But I will go so far as to state that there are far more challenging, sporty ways to catch them.

First, let's look at the distribution of the striper, then at the several techniques that can make him available to the sportsman at various times during any twenty-four-hour period.

Striped bass (Roccus saxatilis), also known as rockfish or linesides, are to be found on both the West and East Coasts. Along the Atlantic they range from Florida all the way North to Nova Scotia. They appear in greatest quantity in the waters lying roughly between North Carolina and Cape Cod, Massachusetts. During May and June, stripers are a feature attraction in the Chesapeake Bay area, while at about the same time the species makes a first seasonal appearance around Cape Cod and Cuttyhunk. The striper run stays with us throughout the Summer months, reaching a peak of activity during September and October. Possibly the top brand of striper fishing becomes available during the Fall months as the big schools work back along their southerly route.

In addition to this mass movement pattern there also are fair numbers of stripers that Winter in many of our coastal rivers and creeks. They too are available to early season anglers as they work their way seaward from their Wintering sites. Once they clear the tributaries, they quickly join up with the main force of stripers moving northward along the shores.

Striped bass also are present to some degree in the Gulf of Mexico, though for some unknown reason they offer themselves as targets for anglers only when present in coastal rivers. From a seasonal viewpoint, they present peak activity through the months of June and early July.

West Coast lure and bait-slingers have good reason to show growing interest in the striper as an important gamefish. Though the striped bass currently inhabiting Pacific coastal waters is indeed a transplant, the species has made massive strides during the ninety-one years since being planted in San Francisco Bay. The transplants, by the way, had been collected from New Jersey waters for this experiment.

Fortunately for sportsmen, the striper rapidly took hold from clear up on the Columbia River in Washington, southerly to Monterey, California. The Pacific fraternity will find their periods of greatest activity during the Spring and Fall months, although the striper is available throughout the entire year.

It does not matter on which coast you fish for stripers, he is predominantly what is referred to as an inshore species. It is also true that ol' linesides is the surf-caster's favorite gamefish. This does not, however, preclude the fact that many a striper (and many a trophy) goes to the various trolling methods, and other special techniques, such as fishing live bunkers, or cut-bait from this species.

The methods for catching these fish are so numerous that it becomes a necessity that we limit ourselves to a selected few which will serve the greatest number of fishermen. It is all-important that before we talk of actual fishing, we accept the fact that we are now discussing a fish which shows strong preferences as to habitation. Remember, he is very much at home in our bays, inlets, and sandy or rocky shorelines, particularly where the movement of water, such as surf, churns up a supply of food. You can add to this such hotspots as tidal areas, brackish waters, and even fresh water rivers where the brackish mixture almost gives way to fresh, inland flows.

There is one method that generally pays off more readily than any other, and it doesn't take all the savvy in the world to make this method work. Also, it proves a winner whether the angler puts it to use during the hours of daylight or darkness. It is probably most deadly during the early weeks of any season though a number of us who often fish in this manner find it a killer over extensive periods of any season. The magic is in the offering itself: Seaworms, a natural food that plays an important part in every striper's feeding spree, following the fish's long, hard Winter of near inactivity.

Bloodworms and sandworms are not only top striper fare, but are usually not difficult to obtain. On numerous occasions when I've found it impossible to get a strike on a cast or trolled lure or fly, a quiet presentation of a seaworm has almost immediately turned the trick.

To get yourself close to the most productive areas, and getting the bait in front of your fish, you'll find it hard to

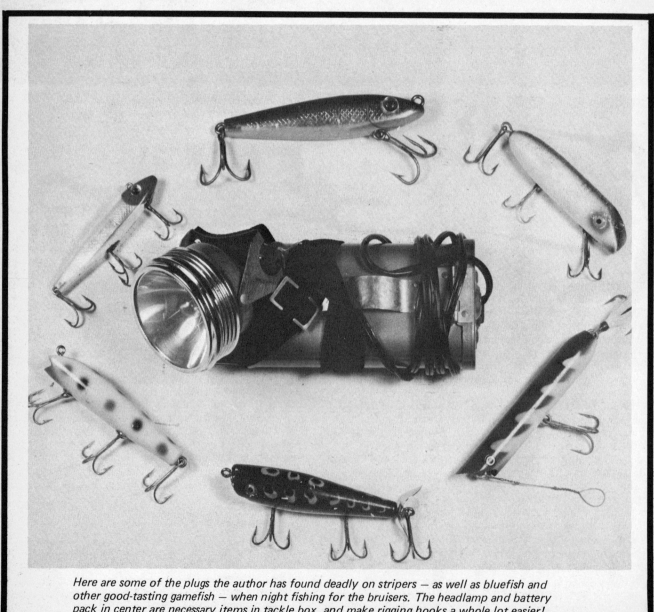

Here are some of the plugs the author has found deadly on stripers — as well as bluefish and other good-tasting gamefish — when night fishing for the bruisers. The headlamp and battery pack in center are necessary items in tackle box, and make rigging hooks a whole lot easier!

Gary Dillon and Jerry DeRosa grimace gleefully as they hoist a brace of stripers in forty-pound class. When the stripers make their appearance, the action gets fast and furious — and fun!

beat the assist of a small run-about or skiff. At night, particularly when probing shallow, rocky shorelines or grassy banks, you will also find that an electric trolling motor helps tremendously in working an area while sparing the noise and commotion of a typical gas engine.

Bass, like most all gamefish, tend to be easily spooked by such items as noise, light and visual movement. Possibly that's why my fishing companions and I refer to my "Mindy II," or Ouachita Super-Fishing boat as a "super sneak-boat." With such a craft you probe every eddy, contour-caused rip, channel edges, shoreline banks and rocky shallows, along with all bridge foundations, pilings or

other types of bulkhead structures. Never neglect any area that appears to be a holding spot for baitfish or any complex section of current that might stir up natural foods. These all represent possible hotspots.

There are several techniques favored for presenting sea-worms. Variation depends mostly on regional preferences and conditions. The one specific rig we find most dependable has worked nicely all along the Carolinas, Virginia, New Jersey and throughout New England. While on the Pacific scene some time ago, it paid off in more than a dozen stripers while practically in sight of 'Frisco's Golden Gate Bridge.

The setup calls for a terminal rig consisting of a June bug spinner and two seaworms when the water is at all off-color or deeper than average. At all other times, the worms are slow-trolled or drifted without the spinner. This simple-to-use rig requires little more than a supply of Eagle Claw offset hooks, in sizes from 2/0 to 4/0. In the rocky shallows or when working close by the grass, no weight need be used. The hook and fairly heavy worms have no trouble skimming along through the bottom cover unaided.

In cases where depth, speed of tide and local current conditions necessitate added weight, it is not unusual to find an angler using bank sinkers running in weight from one ounce to possibly five, in order to work the bait right down along the bottom.

The most practical way of rigging this outfit is to tie a three-way swivel to your line; next, tie in a thirty-six-inch section of leader material, testing anywhere from twelve to fifteen pounds, then bend on an Eagle Claw at the end of the leader. To the side-projecting section of the three-way swivel, you simply tie in a six-inch piece of monofilament for looping into the sinker. Normally, I rely on eight-pound test mono. That way, if the sinker fouls under some obstruction, it will break off rather than hang up the entire works.

At those times when I'm fishing really shallow areas, I dispense with this special rig and instead, simply tie the Eagle Claw to the spinning line itself. If for some reason slight weight is required, I can always bend on any of a number of sizes of split-shot, or better yet, a Gremlin-sinker of appropriate weight.

As far as rod and reel are concerned, I tend to use either of the following: a 6½ or seven-foot spinning rod, saddled with a reel such as Zebco's Cardinal 6 or their number 7, or a Daiwa Model 8300. Mono is usually twelve-pound test, although at night I'll often go to fifteen-pound test when I have reason to believe that stripers of over twenty pounds are lurking in the murky, black depths.

I'm also prone to reach for a favorite popping rod and one of the highly dependable level-wind reels. Popping rods, as offered by Garcia or Fenwick, are excellent choices. So too are Garcia's Ambassadeur 5000A or 6000 series of reels. Rarely do I spool anything heavier than fifteen or twenty-pound test mono since there is simply no problem when using reels of this quality.

In the past I had firmly believed that the best presentation of any of the seaworms was a presentation that seemed most natural and realistic. My thought related to the idea that when a live worm is dislodged and moves freely in a

It's all over but the shouting for this striper, being gaffed for Gary Dillon by Bill Schmidt. Inhaling a live bunker bait proved striper's downfall. Other baits work as well.

Gary Dillon watches as Bill Schmidt hauls in a good striper gaffed seconds earlier. Using live mossbunker, the striper was taken near Zwirz' dock in afternoon.

typical flow, it goes along much in the direction of that flow. For this reason I always made certain that boat and worm drifted as naturally as possible and at the same rate as the flow — at all times controlling the boat with an electric motor guide, working it into each and every likely area.

However, during the past couple of seasons, particularly when working the islands in Long Island Sound, I have come to realize that just as long as speed is kept to a minimum it doesn't seem to be all that important which way the boat or bait moves. Even when moved slowly into the flow it doesn't seem to affect the ratio of success. Frankly, this came as something of a surprise, considering that for years I have been so careful to avoid such a presentation.

While on the subject of using seaworms, note that they lose little of their magic when used in the surf, in typical striper holes, and along the surf line. They can be handled with any of the standard fish-finder terminal rigs, or drifted from a boat positioned just beyond the breaking waves.

For those who may not wish to stick with seaworms during mid and late-season activity, there is no reason why they cannot have excellent results while using light casting tackle with lures and plugs. And of course, there is always the specialized and challenging business of fishing stripers from the surf. Either way, it's a game that calls for lots of casting; it can be a sport that is just as rewarding for spin-fishermen, bait-casters, or the steadily growing number of fly rod addicts. The bass, surprisingly enough, will run anywhere from five or six pounds right on up to those forty and fifty-pounders that can easily straighten a hook on their first hard run.

All along our East Coast there are hundreds of miles of salt and brackish waters, some of these areas lying inside the general coastline. Small boats are the winning ticket for such waters, although some of the tidal areas can be handled by carefully walking the shorelines, banks and narrow sandy strips. It's a good time for using one-handed rods, such as you might use for fishing Southern "hog" bass under tough natural conditions. The deep-working Rebels seem to be about tops for enticing the hard-feeding stripers. So too are the lipless, sinking Mirro-Lures and Alou Eels, to name but two of our effective artificials.

Early morning, evening and the hours of darkness seem best for heavy catches of stripers — especially if larger fish are the angler's target. Hotspots are around bridge foundations, wherever drainage canals or creeks empty into the waterways and bays, and along rocky shorelines where baitfish tend to school up. All, as I've pointed out, are natural stations for feeding striped bass.

Bob Zwirz and Neal Mason have their hands full of heavyweight stripers after a most fruitful fishing day. Two other biggies lay on the deck.

One night Gary Dillon and I beached my Ouachita sneak-boat on a narrow strip of sand that bordered an area of rocky, island shoreline. To make it even more promising, there were two different flows coming together just in front of our casting position. Baitfish and other natural foods were in evidence all around us. Our first inkling of what the night was to hold came as first one striper, then another, slashed into the masses of bait. In minutes, stripers of all sizes were feeding, slashing and rolling within a few feet of our casting positions. At times they were literally sneaking around in a foot or so of water, between us and the shoreline.

The fracas lasted long enough for both of us to take fish running from four or five pounds to several that weighed in at better than twenty — all taken on that fresh water/salt water tackle that allowed each fish to perform at its dogged best. On two occasions exceptionally large fish tore off line, then cut it off on the sharply encrusted rocks lying somewhere out in the darkness. Moments later another Rebel, Mirro-Lure or Creek Chub would be bent on and our action would start all over again. Keep it in mind that anything we can do here in the East, as far as casting is concerned, can easily be duplicated on Pacific striper waters.

And for that matter, West Coast trolling techniques do not differ greatly from those used in the East; bloodworms are deadly behind a Cape Cod spinner or the Northern-type spinner, which also works well. A slow troll is best here, too, especially where larger stripers are concerned and Spring is the best of all times for the worm tactics. Rigged eels, utilizing a two-hook setup, are also an excellent answer. Again, they are deadliest when fished close to the bottom as slowly as possible.

Eel skins are great, but seemingly even better are the remarkably effective eels and worms produced by Garcia/Alou. These artificials continue to score high on both coasts for trollers and casters. The same is true of the latex line of lures created by Don Bingler of Creative Sportsmen.

Barracuda jigs, many models of Rebels and the Mirro-Lures are not to be forgotten — they are just as deadly on the Pacific side when baitfish are on the scene. Top-water plugs (for either coast) would include the Atom, Striper Swiper, Gibbs Popper, Sylvester Blue Mullet, Rebel Surface Popper and Creek Chub Darters. Jigs such as the Hopkins, Montauk and Sand Eel are also a must; tipped with a strip of pork rind, cut bait or squid, they have even stronger striper appeal. A Drone or Acetta spoon is a good idea when trolling for really heavy bass.

When you become truly serious about "dredging up" those trophy specimens, I've found that my top producer has consistently been Rebel's long-lip, deep-running salt water plugs. Results have been exceptional with these plugs and, for that matter, with the same type of plug as produced by Rapala. Pflueger's Mustang, Ballerina, Creek Chub's Striper, the weighted Alou Eels or the weighted eel-skin rigs are also a must for the dyed-in-the-wool striper fisherman.

The bait fisherman will find whole squid a terrific bait for large fish. It works well in the surf or on any bottom offering sandy composition. In addition to bloodworms and seaworms, shrimp, small live eels or whole crabs are good producers along both coasts. In fact, shrimp used in conjunction with a chum line is a top baiting method in California waters. Strip mullet or bunker (cut or live) are other good baits and neither are difficult to obtain in their areas.

While mentioning the subject of fishing with moss-bunkers, it should be noted that during the fast-cooling Autumn months, my fishing companion, Gary Dillon, and I spend any free time we can manage fishing either live or "chunk" bunker in our section of Long Island Sound. The results are, to say the least, phenomenal. In the period from late September through early November, our small group accounts for several dozen stripers weighing anywhere from fifteen or eighteen pounds to the fifty-pound mark. If there is a secret to the technique, it would relate to the difficulty of getting the bait to the bass before a big bluefish grabs it.

If it's big stripers you crave for, get out and snag a supply of bunkers, then swim them around your most likely local hotspots.

Meat on the table! Neal Mason, on lobster platform of Gary Dillon's boat, hefts striper hooked by Jerry DeRosa. They're tough fighters.

Gary Dillon stands at the ready with net as Glad Zwirz coaxes a striper toward the boat during night action. Trolling sandworms from behind Zwirz' Ouachita bass boat proved deadly on this noctural feeder, as does slowly drifting the rigged sandworms. True action around the clock!

Chapter 19

FLY FISHING FOR ATLANTIC SALMON

Canada's Pinware River In Labrador Is An Unspoiled Paradise For The Serious Fisherman.

NOT MORE THAN fifteen yards from the rock on which I was standing, well positioned to observe the drift of my sparsely dressed fly, there appeared the unmistakable silvery side of a fine salmon. In the flash of an instant he had the Blue Charm firmly in his jaws, and leader and fly line were now tightening as he half-rolled back toward the boulder-strewn cover of the great holding pool.

The mound of rock upon which I was balanced precariously overlooked one of the largest and most productive pools on Labrador's brawling Pinware River. Due to the presence of a powerful waterfall, it is a pool that tends to hold a concentration of salmon as they rest momentarily from the rigors of their upriver fight.

Now the line had become taut between fish and angler. With a firm roll of my wrist, the sharply honed hook was made to sink more firmly into the tough sidewall of his jaw. Immediately his course reversed and now he could be seen by my companions, as he smashed upward through the surface and high into the air.

If there was a best way to play and land this fish successfully, it was, at the same time, the only way. He had to be kept within the confines of this deep and tremendously wide pool. If he managed to fight his way downriver, chances were he would be lost in the raging rapids.

The combination of a buggered leg, a memento of a long ago war, and the rain-soaked, slick boulders lining every foot of the Pinware's bank certainly would join forces to see that I would not be able to move quickly enough to play him by his own rules.

This is a fact of life that I learned many years ago and, because of it, I have come to know the exact limits of the tackle I use. My philosophy now is based upon the premise

Winning combination of a floating fly line and a smattering of patience resulted in this fine Atlantic salmon being displayed by the beaming fisherman, Jim Stark, and his equally enthusiastic guide (left).

Author plays a leaping, twisting Atlantic salmon during period of high water on Labrador's Pinware River.

that, if I cannot whip a strong fish with the excellent equipment available to me, coupled with a skill sharpened over thirty years of angling, then that fish deserves to defeat me. Anyway, those fast-as-lightning salmon never will have to worry that I will attempt to match one of their downstream dashes with a shore-bound foot race.

As this magnificent gamefish tried run after run, punctuated with wild leaps and rolls, there was little doubt in my mind that he soon would find the powerful flex of the bamboo fly rod too great to resist for long. If the fly held in his jaw — and the leader hadn't frayed as he brushed past underwater rocks — experience dictated that he soon would be within reach of my guide's net. Within relatively few minutes the salmon was, indeed, fighting against a fairly short line. Even those who had been watching from the rocky walls behind me now could see him as he sacrificed his last strength to resist. Then, as he angled toward our position, fins moving with less determination, Stuart Pike signaled me to be ready. Seconds later the net slid quickly under the fish and this game was over; at least until further probing casts located yet another Atlantic salmon for me. Then the duel between angler and fish would be repeated, as a contest that rarely guarantees positive success for the fisherman. This, of course, is the reason why fly fishing for the heavier gamefish species can be classified as a gentleman's sport that can offer all the challenge a sportsman is willing to accept.

My coming to Canada's Pinware River had been long planned. Just a few seasons back I had traveled far into the Northwest Territories to Snowbird Lake, with Gene Burden of Air Canada. Gene, an executive based in the Halifax, Nova Scotia, offices of this Canadian airline, had told me stories of the top-quality fishing which he had enjoyed earlier while fishing Labrador's Pinware.

During those fantastic days on Snowbird, it was difficult for me to think of anything but lake trout; particularly since my second day of fly fishing had brought me a twenty-six-pound, three-ounce lake trout on a cast fly. Caught on an eight-pound test tippet, this fish, although I didn't know it then, won first place for fly-casting in the 1969 Field & Stream contest.

It was later that I again heard from Gene Burden. How would I like to spend a week or so fishing salmon in Labrador? The river he spoke about was the Pinware, the great, fast flowing river about which Burden had told me so much.

So it was that I found myself climbing into one of Gene Manion's Newfoundland-Labrador Air Transport planes, ready to make the last leg of the journey from Deer Lake to the Labrador shore. With the party was Jim Stark, a long-time friend, Monsieur Burden and his son.

Gene couldn't resist putting the lad into the kind of action he had already experienced on the Pinware. Needless to say, he was not being unmindful of himself as well; as Gene said to me during an earlier part of the trip, on Air Canada, "...once you see the river, Bob, you'll know why I could hardly wait to see it again."

The first person I met, as we unloaded our gear along the Labrador airstrip, was a stranger. Within a single hour he was no longer a stranger but, instead, the kind of warm host that you feel you've known most of your life. This man was Elmer Lovett, owner and operator of Pinware Lodge.

During the days that followed, he gave freely of his extensive knowledge of the river, his hospitality and his complete time and assistance. Not only did Elmer and his chief guide, Stuart Pike, point out the "lie" of the river's salmon, but they went so far as to take me to a number of beautiful, remote streams and ponds that held trout. Just a special bonus. One spot located by Lovett, which he shared with me, produced results that are enough to bring tears to a grown man's eyes.

Three casts were made as I watched; the end result of these three short and simple casts added up to one trout of 6½ pounds. Almost unbelievable in this day and age, although, of course, Labrador has yet to feel any real fishing pressure as we know it. Dragging a fisherman out of that trout paradise almost requires a team of horses.

There is a wild, bleak-but-beautiful spot where the mighty Pinware empties into salt water. It's a place of diving birds and waves that pound endlessly across the sandy spits of land. As you stand here, even in mid-Summer, great numbers of massive icebergs are drifting and grinding their way through the frigid waters. Possibly more important than all this untouched beauty, at least to a visiting angler, is the fact that the sea in front of you — and especially the river, considerably brackish at this point — plays host to sea-run trout as they too begin moving upriver.

These are heavy trout filled with the strength and stamina gained during their long months of feeding voraciously on the ample food available in their salt water haunts. The trout take flies readily and are not at all unwilling to strike minnow-like plugs and lures.

During the time we were on the Pinware, there was a good deal more rain than you'd wish to see. It surprised no one that the river, always a tough adversary, became tougher due to the unusually high water. Though reading the water became more difficult, and casting required greater skill, every one of the fly-casters continued to take salmon. On more than one occasion an angler would lose line control, and in an instant the salmon would be in command.

When this became the case, it wasn't rare to see the startled fisherman running as fast as he could over the slippery, wet boulders, ofttimes with more than a hundred yards of fly line and backing already gone from their screaming fly reels. Many such games ended in defeat for the breathless sport.

And that is why fly fishing is the fascinating sport that it is. Fresh water gamefish such as salmon, sea-run trout, lakers or char, to name a few champions, are never duck-soup for even the most skilled. Neither are tarpon, sails, whites and any of dozens of other species available to anglers with imagination.

The Pinware is not a river for old ladies; perhaps not even for young ones. It is tough to wade and not terribly easy to travel along, but it is a great salmon river. It demands much of the caster's ability, plus a fair amount of stamina. It cannot and should not be waded carelessly. In its fast, whitewater stretches it would not be kind to anyone careless enough to find himself in it and fighting it.

Silvery-sided salmon finally is brought to net after author's successful bid to keep the fast-as-lightning fighter confined to the deep and tremendously wide, boulder-strewn holding pool created by small waterfall.

When at day's end you wend your way back to Elmer's Pinware Lodge, you have the distinct feeling that you are ready to sit and relax. It's that good kind of tired feeling; where you know all the frustrations of living have been left behind and that you will sleep soundly. Dreaming only of fine, strong salmon and how good the river will be to you come dawn.

But before sleep there are lobsters to be eaten, relaxed drinking to be done, and many lies to each other concerning the reasons this fish or that fish broke off. You cannot help but wish the time was not so short; that there was far more opportunity to visit with the quiet, pioneer-type people who live in the several fishing villages along the coast. You wish there were more daylight hours for further exploring the Pinware and other of Labrador's rivers and streams, their wild coastline and the miles of uninhabited land which seems to hold promise of hidden beauty to those who take the time to explore it.

Like the Northwest Territory, Labrador has not yet felt too much of man's encroachment. Some of Canada's truly great scenery is still untarnished, waiting to be enjoyed by those who love the out-of-doors. I know I shall go back, and when I do it will be with my wife, Glad. Maybe the river will know she's a gal, and because of it make the boulders less slippery, its waters less turbulent. But this she must someday share with me.

Those who wish to see the mighty Pinware for themselves should not hesitate to talk to the Air Canada people about it. For that matter, John Harrison of the Canadian Travel Bureau, in New York City, could offer suggestions. So too could Gene Manion, the man who can provide the wings on the final lap to the Pinware. Gene can be contacted through Box 3, Cornerbrook, Newfoundland.

Needless to say perhaps, but anglers craving to tangle with those salmon, trout, or sea-runs should write or call the Master of the Pinware himself — Elmer Lovett. Off-season, his stateside address is as follows — 4527 DuBois Boulevard, Brookfield, Illinois 60513. The area code is 312, and his personal number: 485-6209

Tell him an angler full of fond memories told you to call him.

Guide tails another of the author's trophies taken from the fabulous Pinware River. To get fly in main current's pocket of water, Zwirz used stern of boat as a casting platform.

Thoroughly contented Zwirz (standing on rock in stream) and guide admire Atlantic salmon referred to in text. Although the Pinware is tough to wade and not easy to travel along, author is planning another visit...soon!

Few fish can match the Atlantic salmon, in beauty or fighting ability, as it enters the coastal rivers on its return to the place of its birth. Taken with a fly rod in fast water, they are the ultimate challenge.

LIGHT TACKLE
in the BAHAMAS

Dolphin offer the salt water angler terrific sport; and never better than when caught on light tackle!

THIS IS ONE angler who has made a blood oath relating to the sticky business of taking along great quantities of expensive tackle when traveling on commercial airlines to distant fishing hotspots.

During this past year I've gone off on a number of fishing trips with nary a valuable bamboo fly rod or one-of-a-kind rod in my possession. Instead, I've been taking only factory-produced glass rods that can be replaced normally with minimum effort. Basically, the same has been true of all other manner of allied equipment. Everything possible is chosen so that it can be duplicated. Just as important, all tackle is kept to an absolute minimum.

Assuming the outdoor fraternity takes the time to carefully pack their valuable rods in one of the better quality rod containers, such as the Imperial Oceanic No. 202 from NuPack, Incorporated, of Chicago, Illinois, it is still possible to experience a disaster. Apparently there are airline personnel handling luggage these days who have found a way to telescope even this hard-to-punish rod-caddy.

Over the past year I've added up the chances of breakage and retaliated by really traveling light. Fortunately, this is compatible with my own yen for fishing the lightest tackle common sense permits. However, even if it didn't my nerves wouldn't allow me to load aboard more tackle than I

could stand to lose. Admittedly I travel by air far more than average, but does this fact give the airlines the right to break a total of seven rods over a three-year period or to lose an entire rod case containing four rods?

Similar frustrations have been heaped upon a number of my fishing amigos, all of which tends to guarantee badly buggered fishing jaunts. Need I tell you about the reactions of some disinterested airline personnel when you attempt to convince them that items such as Payne's, Gillum's and other such rods are not just fishing poles and cannot be replaced adequately? And, that such quality custom equipment did cost top dollar?

As many have come to realize, some fishing trips are simple as apple pie to pack for and plan. This is particularly true in cases where only one species of fish will be on the angler's agenda or where the individual has decided to rely solely on but one type of tackle. On the other hand, it's far more difficult to arrive adequately equipped in an area where several species are present, some requiring vastly different methods, all running the gamut in both weights and fighting ability.

When there also is a definite requirement or simply a strong wish on the part of the fisherman to use more than one type of fishing equipment while on the scene, then he

Under Rigorous Travel Conditions, One Should Choose Carefully On This Weighty Problem.

Chapter 20

Bonefish are real fighters any way you catch them, but caught on a light spinning outfit or fly rod they are even a greater fishing challenge, requiring the consummate of angling skills.

truly must plan with care.

Recently, my wife, Glad, and I had ample opportunity to find out if just such careful and thorough planning could prove satisfactory in a situation where about anything could occur as we fished our way, out-island to out-island, throughout the Bahamas group.

Long before we left on the trip itself, it had been pointed out by our Bahamian friends that we would have ample opportunities for fishing offshore waters, reefs and several possible productive flats during our island-hopping spree. The inclusion of these three vastly different types of water makes for tackle requirements that, possibly needless to explain, are anything but simple.

What all of this adds up to is simply this: An angler could find himself in the presence of such popular species as white marlin, sailfish, blue marlin, blue, black and yellowfin tuna, dolphin, wahoo, kings, grouper, amberjack, barracuda, and cero mackerel, plus that much sought-after ghost of the flats — the bonefish.

Bob and Glad Zwirz used a variety of lures in their quests for the scrappy bonefish. Yellow and white bonefish lures — in this case, bonefish jigs — usually produce the best results. Majority of these lures feature splay-wing hackle feathers, although some are fashioned utilizing multi-colored bucktails.

Naturally, the presence of several of the listed species would depend on the time of the year chosen for a particular fishing jaunt. Now, would you consider there to be any problems relating to fishing for the species just named? Yes sir, namely — can anyone carry a sensible lineup of tackle to handle them all, short of carrying it in a jumbo-size steamer trunk?

Here is a report on the tackle we packed along, with our personal opinions relating to how it performed under the actual field conditions we encountered. However, it is important for other anglers to realize that both Glad and I are confirmed fly fishing practitioners. Although we are well aware that this equipment possesses limitations for the so-called offshore gamefish species, we still tend to put our salt water fly rods to work whenever and wherever reasonably possible. Often, this is in situations where local experts swear they are of no use and will not take fish. Happily, in the case of more gamefish species than you might guess, they are proved incorrect.

When a traveling angler has decided to cut down his tackle in numbers, weight, bulk and monetary value, he will not be far wrong if he chooses to leave behind almost all big game tackle. This certainly would include both eighty and fifty-pound class outfits.

Fishing out of a number of South American, Central American and Mexican ports specializing in big game species, I have rarely found their charter boats poorly equipped. In the Bahamas I have yet to be aboard a boat that couldn't furnish adequate tackle. For the most part it would only be the highly skilled specialist in search of a "class" record that would be best advised to fish with his own familiar tackle. In most cases, it's spooled with fresh line before each important fishing trip.

Even for such members of the finicky fraternity, they would have to go some to find finer equipment or better maintained equipment than provided on charter boats such as George Seamann's Mitchell II. He is a fantastically well outfitted sportfisherman berthed at Great Harbour Cay, Bahamas. To step aboard George and Kate Seamann's cruiser with a FinNor would be like bringing coals to Newcastle.

If a sportsman were to take just one conventional outfit along, I would strongly suggest he choose a favorite thirty-pound class trolling rod and a 4/0 reel well filled with fresh thirty-pound test line. And, since it doesn't weigh much or take up all that much packing space, I'd further suggest he take along his personal gimbal-belt. The larger charter boats do carry such items aboard, but you rarely will find them available on the smaller guide boats.

If and when an experienced fisherman wishes to try his hand with lighter than thirty-pound test, while working waters touted for populations of such species as wahoo, dolphin, white marlin or sails, this could well be the time to try one of the highly efficient salt water spinning combos; a rig where the reel is capable of spooling 15, 17 or, preferably, 20-pound-test mono. Such an outfit can serve for casting plugs, spoons or bucktail jigs, and when a situation presents itself for drifting bait.

Obviously the reel should be of dependable quality, offering adequate line capacity (at least 250 yards); the rod we prefer for this special brand of mayhem measures 7½ feet, features two-handed cork grips and does a fine job

This shrimp-fly pattern proved to be a real winner for the Zwirz'. Bonefish usually are vulnerable to this type of artificial or when presented a natural bait such as shrimp.

Author's wife, Glad, displays typical day's catch from the out-islands of the Bahama group. With a catch like this it's almost impossible not to smile. Correct angling techniques and equipment can guarantee happy faces.

with any line from a minimum of twelve-pound test and on through to twenty-pound, which, by the way, was the line it was designed specifically to handle. It is the kind of outfit that provides great sport when dolphin are around the boat, or when it becomes possible to cast a bait to any of the other pelagic species, whether they be whites, wahoo or you-name-it.

Somehow we managed to cram all our rods into the largest size rod-caddy produced by Oceanic. All of our reels, extra spools, ball bearing swivels, wire leader material, hooks and assorted artificial lures, knives and angler's pliers were carefully packed into a well made, exceptionally strong wooden tackle box that measures exactly 20x8x9 inches.

When I built it, allowances were made so that compartment separators could be adjusted to take any size lures, from typical fresh water to large salt water plugs. It also has an interior-bolted hasp made to accommodate a sturdy padlock.

The rods taken to the Bahamas were as follows: that aforementioned twenty-pound class spinning combo, which happens to be a Daiwa Model 3026; the matching number reel is their Model 8700 with ball bearings. Three spools were included, one each spooled with 15, 17 and 20-pound-test mono.

There were two other open face spinning rigs included, for use on the bonefish flats. The reels were, again, Daiwa's, in this case their Model 8300 (also with ball bearings). One extra spool was packed for each of these outfits; one spool contained ten-pound test, the other, a top-quality, fine diameter twelve-pound test.

Finally, there was a nine-foot Fenwick, Model 109F, and a FinNor No. 3 fly reel. This reel was carried with two extra spools of fly line. Though the rod can handle either No. 9, 10 or 11 weight fly lines, I tend to rely on weight forward No. 10s for most situations. Spool 1 carries a salt water fly line featuring a floating body/sinking tip; spool 2 carries a salt water floating line; and 3 carries a shooting head, plus all the mono backing it will hold.

If it weren't for the need to keep equipment simple and in lesser numbers, you can bet that I would prefer to have an 8½-foot fly rod for working those bonefish flats, while a 9½-foot heavy-duty fly rod would be my choice for whites, sail and larger dolphin, the same rod classification that I normally would use when taming giant tarpon. It's impossible, however, with those new, protect-yourself-from-the-airlines rules of mine.

As it turned out, Glad and I shared the Fenwick/FinNor combo and found that it wasn't all that bad in the case of the bonefish, although both of us agreed it could have been more sporting if we had used a lighter action 8½-foot rod. Wind conditions on the Bahamas flats weren't all that difficult, so fly lines of lighter weight wouldn't have presented much of a handicap.

The Model 109F also was put to use on the numerous schools of dolphin that frequent the waters off Cat Island. Here, in a fairly tight area called the Tartar Banks, it is possible to hang most all the species we have named previously. It usually is a particularly good spot for white marlin, although this time accounting only for dolphin, barracuda, a few allison tuna and a variety of jacks.

Possibly the hottest session occurred when I dropped a four-inch bucktail in front of a following form and immediately found myself fully involved with a forty-six-pound wahoo. The assist from the No. 3 FinNor came in mighty handy. The same assist came in handy when a grouper left his reef cover and rushed up some fifteen feet to grab a large streamer that I had been casting to the general area. He had to weigh thirty pounds at least. Once he hit his coral retreat I held onto this fellow for all of three minutes.

Although we had excellent mixed-bag fishing while working out of Cat Island's Hawks Nest Fishing & Yachting Club and while fishing the waters around Eleuthera, there can be no doubt that the high point of this tour of the Bahamas out-islands had to be while sampling the goodies abounding in and around Great Harbour Cay, one of the Berry Islands group. Loving the light tackle concept as dearly as we do, there is little wonder that we couldn't get enough of those miles upon miles of flats that rim one full side of the cay.

Each dawn, as we left the Great Harbour Club burdened down with sun screening lotions, Polaroids, visored hats and our carefully chosen fishing gear, we would make bets as to whether that day could be as fruitful as the last. Amazingly enough there was no let-up to the action provided by the hordes of bones that frequent that close-by flat. We took all sizes of bones using our guide's frozen shrimp, casting our own bonefish lures, (1/8, 3/16 and 1/4 ounce) or using the fly rod and a large-pattern shrimp fly. A pattern that almost smelled like the real McCoy, it was that good an imitation.

Among the spinning lures that produced best were those colored yellow, white, pink or subtle combinations. The same was true of other bonefish streamer flies we experimented with when not using the shrimp pattern. All such foolishness was uncalled for, seeing that it was almost impossible to miss with the shrimp fly, just as long as the cast was in line with their into-the-tide wanderings, and didn't spook them by a too-close presentation.

Before watching the magic produced by our guide and his bag of shrimp, there is good reason to believe that I'd still be an advocate of conch for bones. He had conch along, plus the shrimp, but preferred it, he said, only for use as a chum line, when and if necessary. It never was. Not for a minute.

For those who may wish to stick solely with the deadly, natural shrimp, they will find any of the Eagle Claw-type hooks to be ideal, and 1/0 or 2/0 sizes to be just the ticket.

By relying on the better than adequate conventional tackle available aboard the charter boats we were well armed for blue marlin or bluefin tuna, if they were willing to give us a look. Actually, we did rather poorly on the larger billfish, while faring far better than average on bones, wahoo, dolphin and a variety of other Caribbean critters, including three species of sharks.

We also learned that with twenty-pound-test mono for the heavy spinning rod, ten-pound test for the flats, the various weights of fly lines, plus the salt water sinking-tip fly line for the Fenwick/FinNor outfit, plus leaders of various tippet strengths, we could have managed nicely. Even the abnormally meager supply (at least for this writer) of plugs, spoons, jigs and other assorted lures, proved adequate.

So it was that with one tackle box between us, plus one crammed rod carrier, the two of us never encountered a single serious deficiency. In fact, over-simplified though we may have been, we somehow managed to boat no less a number of gamefish than if we had carried along three times the amount of gear.

An angler brings in a big one in the mouth of the Columbia River near Astoria, Oregon. This salmon was not a record breaker, but is typical of those brought in during fall salmon run in Oregon streams. Chinook will weigh up to sixty pounds, according to author. August and September are considered the best fishing times.

Chapter 21
WESTWARD THE SALMON!

The Chinook And His Close Relatives Rate High Among Anglers Seeking A Demanding Challenge.

Using conventional tackle, these fishermen troll for king salmon in the coastal waters off Sitka, Alaska.

FROM THE STATE of Alaska to midway down the coast of California the chinook or king salmon, as it is often called, wins the popularity polls of thousands of devout rod and reelers.

This fine gamefish rates by far as the largest of the true salmon family. In fact, its average weight overshadows that of the Atlantic salmon by a considerable margin. It is not unusual for an average chinook to weigh twenty pounds and these salmon have been taken, in the commercial nets, weighing up to 125 pounds. For those who wish to set their sights high, the existing rod and reel record stands at a whopping eighty-three pounds.

Westerners have, along with chinook, a cousin of slightly lesser popularity — the silver salmon. The East Coast angling fraternity, who must limit themselves to the fly rod only when fishing for Atlantic salmon, may find it surpris-

ing that West Coast laws allow for most any type of tackle or methods.

Possibly the finest fishing for either the chinook or silver is available in Puget Sound. Top periods run from May well into October. Along with the large concentration of silvers, which are most always present in Puget Sound, add the adult king salmon that pass through on their routes to the various spawning rivers such as the Fraser, Skagit and the famed Columbia River.

Silver salmon are fine fly rod fish and take a cast fly without much hesitancy. Patterns should be monochromatic and bucktails seemingly work best. Bucktails of four or five inches are just the ticket, especially when tied to resemble candlefish or herring. Hook sizes run from 2/0 to 5/0. It takes a rod with power and a caster with good timing to cast these wind catchers.

255

A salmon, fresh from the sea, is being played on a conventional rod and reel with plenty of exciting action. When caught, this one was proved to be in 60-pound class.

The vast majority of all the Western salmon species are taken on lures and bait. This is certainly the case with the kings. Lures such as the Lucky Louie and baits cut from the side of a large herring produce best.

Some years ago, I found that these fish can be taken on large, trolled bucktails. With a shiny brass No. 2 spinner revolving ahead of it results were even better.

The more conventional methods for taking the large chinooks call for either bottom fishing techniques or typical open water trolling. Depths favored by these big-water salmon run anywhere from thirty to better than two hundred feet. At the deeper depths, the troller requires more weight than most would wish to use. It also is important that trolling speed be kept within the three-knot limit.

Rods for this type of fishing lean toward what is commonly termed a boat rod. Reels should be capable of spooling lines testing at least thirty pounds. Many oldtimers fishing prime Northwest waters will not hesitate to jack this up to fifty-pound test when looking to boat the forty and fifty-pounders that aren't all that uncommon.

Almost every area has its own peculiarities as to lures or baits that are preferred, and the depths most commonly fished. When the visiting angler finds himself confronted with a choice of varied techniques, such as mooching with cut bait, trolling artificials and a good dozen other possibilities, it's time for him to stop wasting his time with wrong guesses. If he doesn't have an experienced local angler holding him by the hand, then it's time to seek the services of a professional guide, at least until he learns the basics.

Correspondence reaching me has once and for all convinced me that it is possible to do what this angler and my West Coast correspondents always had believed was possible: namely, to take kings of over thirty pounds on a cast fly and, though it is far less of a trick, taking a fair share with various trolling methods while using fly fishing tackle.

For some reason, possibly the abundance of shallow water feeding areas, Alaska's west coast has been proving itself as the perfect set-up for taking the king salmon on cast or trolled flies.

Actor Glenn Ford (right) can smile over this catch at the end of a good day on the Campbell River, one of the better known salmon spots in British Columbia.

For those not familiar with fly fishing for Pacific salmon, there is little reluctance on the part of anglers to agree that silver salmon, long a favorite target of West Coast fly fishermen, can be taken quite effectively on a cast fly and, of course, in greater number on a trolled fly. However, not that many of the brotherhood buy the idea that the mighty king salmon can be taken on the cast, except by something bordering on accidental means.

Well, I know for a fact of three fly fishermen, living in three different locales, who have managed to take a number of kings over the past four years. They use the same basic outfits that I favor using on giant tarpon, although they of necessity find need of more specialized fly line lashups than I would need ordinarily.

The kings that they have taken on a cast fly have been attracted to their patterns at depths ranging from fourteen

Fishing the surf, this angler has taken his 36-pound Chinook salmon at mouth of Rogue River in southwest Oregon.

feet to an extreme of sixty feet. The solution to this latter depth calls for a special lead core shooting head, along with a large fly pattern that will show up in this deep water strata.

Those anglers who went along with my suggestion and tied or bought themselves the Salminus-L patterns, possibly in candlefish (eulachon) or herring patterns for use on larger salmon species, were working in the right direction.

Up until a short while ago, few anglers figured that anyone would actually take a thirty-six-pound Pacific halibut on a fly (ten-pound test tippet), but Johnny Smart of Edmonds, Washington, did just that. For that matter, everyone stated that it would be most unlikely for me to take large lake trout from fairly deep water on a cast fly. Yet the proof would seem self-explanatory in my twenty-six-pound, three-ounce laker (eight-pound test tippet) — a fish that rated a first place fly fishing award in a Field & Stream contest.

The point I make is simple: namely, that the picture is rapidly changing for fly fishermen. Due to improvements in special purpose fly lines, rods/reels, flies and the techniques which we are continually perfecting, angling feats once thought impossible are being accomplished with greater and greater frequency. Resourcefulness and imagination are ingredients that have played their parts, as well.

December-January will find supposedly impossible-to-catch dog-salmon making the scene in Puget Sound. What's to stop some diligent fly-rodder from forgetting about cut-herring spinners or the mooching method and rigging up an outfit that will take them on a fly as they lay over around the Gig Harbor area? If nary a single, knowledgeable fly fisherman tries, we'll never know.

Essentially, the same is true of the king salmon — if more anglers don't give the game a mighty serious try, then the majority will continue to believe it's not to be in the cards.

Of this mixed catch taken off of California's famed Golden Gate, two are salmon, the others striped bass.

Chapter 22

The ART AND SCIENCE Of Bait-Egg Fishing

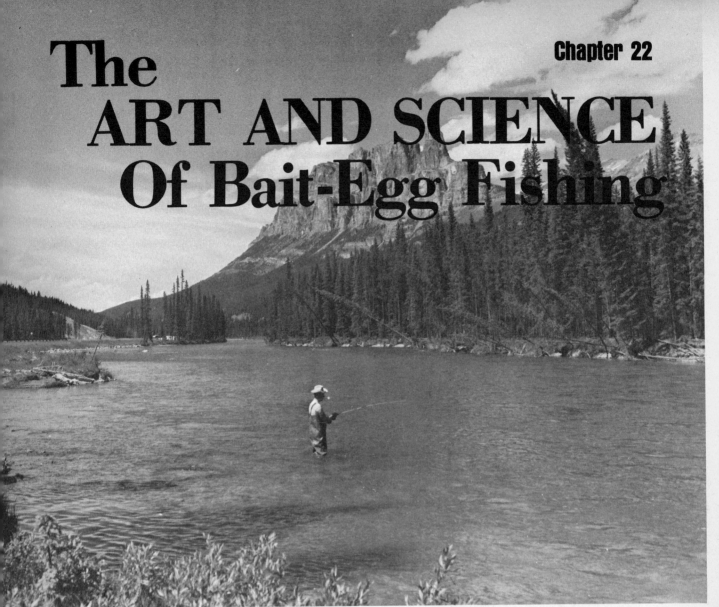

Angling for trout in Alberta, Canada's, beautiful Bow River, beneath the ramparts of 9300-foot Mt. Eisenhower.

Equipment And Techniques For
Fishing The Single Salmon Egg

IT IS THE rare day indeed when you meet an angler who has mastered a specialized method of fishing to a degree that makes him truly an expert in his field. It is far rarer when such an individual agrees to share his hard-earned skills and streamside experience with fellow sportsmen.

This, however, has been the case with Jim Akers of Tacoma, Washington. During the past year I had the pleasure of fishing with Jim on several of his favorite lakes and streams, and it became clear that here was a man who knew more about salmon egg fishing than any other dozen people.

Part of the reason for Jim's unusual wealth of knowledge is due to the fact that this manner of bait presentation has long been a favorite of his. Plus, he manages to spend sufficient time on the waters to practice his art. Further, Jim Akers actually researches bait use for Olympic Fish Products, Incorporated, one of the largest processers and packers of bait-eggs in the world, and he serves as sales manager and special consultant.

It is due to the courtesy of Jim and Olympic that I have been privileged to bring you this synopsis of a treatise Jim recently prepared for his company. It is packed with information and line drawings that can't help but start new anglers off on the right foot and, for that matter, improve the scores of even the more knowledgeable fisherman. I know that watching, listening and fishing with Jim did much to better my own fishing techniques.

Now to the all important how-to, as described by the expert himself — Jim Akers.

Successful bait-egg fishing requires the correct type of tackle. Selection should not be hit or miss. A good rod should be sensitive throughout the tip section. Have someone gently hold the tip with two fingers approximately one foot from the end of the tip. Tap on the end with a twig or wooden match — the way you would tap on a desk with a pencil. If the tapping can be easily felt, the rod is adequate for sensitivity. The length of the rod can be from six to nine feet, depending on how much all-around usage you are looking for. For lake use, Jim prefers an 8½-foot rod and for streams a 7½-foot rod. The reel is especially important, because the proper line and leader weight are determined by the reel. The better your reel, the lighter line and leader you theoretically can use. A good, smooth drag is imperative. With a good drag you could land a five-pound trout with a four-pound line and a one pound leader. If the drag hesitates at any time, it is not good enough. It is the tip of the rod that plays out the fish, not the weight of the line or leader.

In general, the type of reel used in fishing the single salmon egg may be insignificant to the angler, provided it allows him to deliver the bait easily and effectively. The popular spinning reels — both open and closed face models — allow the angler ease in casting and versatility of use. Being easy to operate, they work efficiently whether you choose to fish from an anchored boat or cast from shore.

They are readily available and reasonably inexpensive. In addition, the spinning reel may be used in many kinds of fishing, whether with the single salmon egg or other bait or lures.

Another reel used in fishing the single egg is the single-action fly reel. Its popularity stems from ease of operation and reasonable price. However, its use primarily is limited to boat fishing, since one must strip the line off of the reel by hand in order to cast. Strip casting can be particularly difficult from shore, but in boat fishing it often is possible to simply lower the bait to the fish by stripping the line out and allowing the bait to sink. In fact, this type of fishing is very popular and may be preferred regardless of the type of reel used.

The next important thing is to have the right line for the right reel. If your line gets kinks or loops and curls, get some new line that is soft and limber and will not get curls. The line cannot be too soft; the same is true for the leader. Do not be penny-wise and pound-foolish with reel, line, leader and hooks. You are better off with an inexpensive rod than a cheap reel.

A balanced outfit can be determined by placing the forward portion of the cork grip on one finger and have it balance level. Buy the rod first and then match up your reel on a balance basis. Generally speaking, the longer the rod, the larger the reel. Most sporting goods stores can show you what is best if you tell them what type of fishing you expect to do. In this day and age, unless you tell them you want a rod and reel for bait fishing, you are apt to end up with a combination geared more for spinning lure and/or fly fishing.

To check line and leader before buying, wrap six or

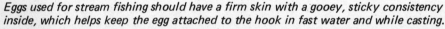
Eggs used for stream fishing should have a firm skin with a gooey, sticky consistency inside, which helps keep the egg attached to the hook in fast water and while casting.

HOOK SIZES AND TYPES

Best.

General use—single egg.

No. 16 ⎫
No. 14 ⎬ Small trout or large slow feeding trout.
No. 12　6 to 14 inch trout.
No. 10　14 to 18 inch trout, double egg.
No.　8　18 to 20 inch trout, double egg.

Not so good.　Shank too long, bend to close.

Highly sensitive rods—fish not hitting.

No. 16　1 lb. leaders must have excellent drag on proper reel.
No. 14　1 lb. leaders must have excellent drag on proper reel.

NOTE: For use when fish are mouthing bait and finning on bottom—usually larger fish.

hookups • stream fishing

LEADER AND LEAD SPLIT SHOT

1. To get bait down to rocks and hiding places, lead should be 4 to 6 inches from hook; in small streams 2 BB shot is best.

2. In large streams 6 to 8 inches between hook and lead using 2 No. 3/0 lead; possibly 2 No. 5.

3. In rivers 8 inch maximum distance from hook to lead using No. 4, 5, 7, or cannon ball size lead.

4. The current and depth of water will determine the size of lead to use.

5. Use 3 to 4 foot leaders.

BOBBER HOOKUP

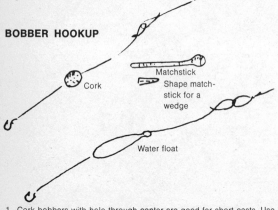

1. Cork bobbers with hole through center are good for short casts. Use a wedge to hold cork in place. Start with 6 inch spread from cork to hook and work up to length that works. A BB split shot or No. 5 can be used if necessary, 4 to 6 inches from bait depending on final length of spread on hook to bobber.

2. Torpedo water floats can be cast quite far and you can adjust the weight. Basically you follow the same procedure as No. 1 above in the use of split shot and distance of float and hook arrangement.

seven wraps of line or leader around a pencil rather tightly. If the line straightens out and is in the same condition before wrapping, you have a fairly good line or leader as far as being flexible and soft without kink or curl problems. You also can check for knot strength. Tie a knot in one piece and check breaking strength against a piece of equal length without knots. The two should have nearly the same breaking strength. If the piece with the knot breaks much easier at the knot, look to another brand. Good, flexible line does two things for you. Flexible line casts smoothly and easily; thus eliminating a lost or damaged bait on the cast. Also, your line slack is much better controlled and your hooking abilities are much improved.

Usually, in fishing the single egg, you will not need a line heavier than eight-pound test. Six-pound test will provide the best combination of strength and invisibility needed under normal conditions. Soft nylon, monofilament line perhaps is the best that can be used in fishing the single egg. It is strong, difficult for the fish to see, and is widely available. However, it is easy to tangle and almost impossible to straighten out.

When using nylon line on a spinning reel equipped with a drag, always remember to pump the rod, bringing the fish closer. Lower the tip as you reel in the line. This rhythm can be important: If the drag is too loose — when the fish is heading one way and you're reeling the other — your line is being twisted with each turn of the reel. The difficulty arises when the twisting reaches the tangling point, at which time the line will tend to wind around itself and become a colossal tangle; and with monofilament line the solution is either great practice or a sharp knife.

If your line is only kinked, it may be straightened by tying a piece of line around a tree or something similar and snapping a swivel to it. With the swivel tied to your line, walk away playing out all of the kinked line. By having someone hold your rod keeping the line taut, you walk back to the tree running the line out between your thumb and index finger. The swivel will turn and all the kinks will be squeezed out like water from a wet sock.

The leader used in fishing the single salmon egg depends on the size of the fish, but also on the probability of becoming snagged in weeds or sunken logs. The choice of leader also depends on how sensitive the fish is to heavier sizes. At times the only way to entice fish to bite is to change your leader to a smaller pound test that is very difficult for them to see. In general, you should choose a lighter leader for clear water and smaller fish. Heavier leader is recommended for larger fish. The leader material should be nylon mono and should never be heavier than that of the line; and usually lighter. A helpful scale:

Leader weight	Fish length
¾ to 1½ lbs. test	6 to 10 in.
1½ to 2	10 to 14 in.
2 to 3	14 to 16 in.
4 to 6	16 to 18 in.
6 to 8	18 to 24 in.

Learn how to tie proper knots on line to swivel, line to leader and leader to hook. The best of line and leader will break if you do not tie the proper knot. Backing is a must on hook knots and swivel knots. The one big fish you may hook will break your line or leader, even with good equipment, if your knots are not tied properly.

Any experienced fisherman ties his own hooks. How else can you try various hookups? The only ones you can buy ready-tied are snelled hooks or three-foot egg leaders.

Usually the hook size or leader weight is not what you want or the leader is too stiff. A three-foot leader may be satisfactory at times, but why use a hookup made for general use after you have spent your money on specific equipment to meet particular conditions in order to improve your fishing? Your self-tied hookup, using better quality leader and hooks, will cost about one-half the price of a ready-tied hookup. Most pre-tied leaders come from the Orient. These leaders are not as flexible and usually are thicker in diameter for their weighted breaking strength.

The hook used in fishing the single salmon egg is a small one, sometimes gold, sometimes silver in color and is called, quite naturally, an egg hook. The size of the egg hook depends largely on the size of the egg being fished and on the size of the fish you are apt to catch. The following may serve as a guide:

Hook Sizes	Fish length	Egg
No. 16	For smaller and	Single
No. 14	elusive fish	Single
No. 12	6-14 in.	Single
No. 10	14-18 in.	Double
No. 8	18-20 in.	Double

When selecting egg hooks, be sure to pick those with a short shank; so that when you bait them you will be able to roll the egg on with ease, without having part of the hook protruding. Ideally, one egg should completely cover the hook, since fish have very sensitive mouths and may drop the bait if they feel the cold steel of the hook before you feel them. Furthermore, when using No. 14 and No. 16 hooks, use a light leader, ¾ to 1½-pound test, and be sure to keep a loose drag on the reel. A sensitive-tipped rod also will help avoid broken leaders and lost fish on these small hooks.

A swivel often is used in fishing the single egg, since it tends to reduce the twisting of the leader and the line. It also serves as a connector in that both the line and leader are tied to it. The best swivel to use is the barrel type without the snap. Ninety-five percent of your fishing will call for a size 14 swivel which will handle leaders to six pounds. A No. 12 swivel may be used for eight to ten-pound test leaders.

Although just about any piece of lead will get your bait to the bottom, perhaps the best sinker for fishing the single egg is the slip sinker. It is round or oval and comes in varying sizes. The beauty of this weight is its versatility. It can be used in all styles of trout fishing and especially for the hit and run. The hit-run occurs after you have cast your bait, allowing it to settle to the bottom, and the fish takes your egg gently — a hit! He starts to move off with it, feeling no dragging — the line sliding through the lead. He then takes off like a chicken thief and you sock it to him! Any other lead will bounce along with the fish and may convince him not to fully swallow the egg. In addition, the

hookups • lake fishing

PLACING EGG ON HOOK

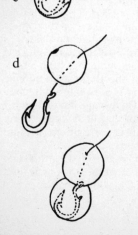

a. Oil sack. (Small dark spot.) Do not place hook through oil sack.

b. Roll egg onto hook.

c. Bury eye into egg when possible, a toothpick (round type) is very handy. Place toothpick into eye of hook and gently push. Remember direction you rolled the egg onto hook!

d. If double egg is required, thread hook and line completely through first egg. Use a twisting motion back and forth to eliminate tearing of the egg. Place second egg on as in steps b and c. Then pull first egg down to second egg.

hookups • lake fishing

PLACING EGG ON HOOK

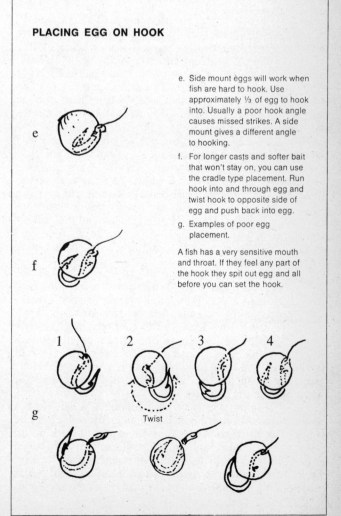

e. Side mount eggs will work when fish are hard to hook. Use approximately ⅓ of egg to hook into. Usually a poor hook angle causes missed strikes. A side mount gives a different angle to hooking.

f. For longer casts and softer bait that won't stay on, you can use the cradle type placement. Run hook into and through egg and twist hook to opposite side of egg and push back into egg.

g. Examples of poor egg placement.

A fish has a very sensitive mouth and throat. If they feel any part of the hook they spit out egg and all before you can set the hook.

oval slip sinker comes in many sizes.

The simplest way to select the correct bait-egg depends on whether you are going to fish a lake or a stream. You should look for a soft-milky (milking) egg with soft, thin skin for lake fishing. A good lake egg will milk out its oil and fluid in less than three to five minutes, leaving a much lighter colored egg 1/3 to 1/2-filled with water, but still fully round. Because a good lake egg milks out, it's wise to change your bait fairly often. You will find variables in lake eggs as to milking qualities, as some are softer than others.

First thing to do is to look for an egg that states natural or naturally cured. Second, it would be simple if it also said for lake or stream use. At this writing, the only brands on the market that Jim or I know of which definitely state for lake or for stream are the Alaska Spawner by Science Sports Products, packed in Tacoma, Washington, by Olympic Fish Products, Incorporated, and the Olympic brand. Alaska Spawner also lists the type of skin and the milking qualities on their label, as well as when and how they are to be used.

Since most stores frown on opening a jar of eggs to check it, you will probably have to ask an expert in the store what to buy — if there is one available. The sales clerk may be willing to help, but his advice likely will be limited to his own experience or hearsay. The only way to know for sure is if the label states Lake Egg, or you open the jar and check the egg itself.

Stream eggs are another ball game all over again, except for the processing. First, the egg should have a firm skin with a gooey, sticky consistency inside. The egg does not have to milk very much, since a moving bait is what is doing the trick when it comes to attracting the fish. Obviously, the skin has to be tougher than a lake egg and it must have a stiffer inner matter so the egg will stay on when casting and not come off in strong currents. If an egg is too hard, however, it will split. Also, an overly hard egg usually is not a naturally cured egg. Fish will strike and get a taste of an egg, and if the fish likes the taste, he'll be back for the second cast. The salt and sugar in naturally cured eggs are real winners in this case.

How do we know which or what egg is for stream use? We don't unless the label tells us so, so Jim and I are sticking to his own Alaska Spawners. The No. 2 stream egg is unbelievably beautiful in color and the texture is perfection! Jim cast one egg four to six times and still caught a sleek ten-inch trout. Probably the easiest way to check out an egg for stream use is to put it on a hook and then take it off by pulling it away, so that the skin tears. What you should have is a glob of the interior clinging to the hook without falling off.

There are times when you could use an egg that has lake and stream characteristics; sort of a cross between the two. A medium skin and a medium milking, semi-sticky interior. Very slow running currents in large rivers or sandy, level-bottomed streams are ideal for this type of an egg. Another situation might be the mouth of a stream entering into a lake where the current slows and fades away. When fish are hitting fast and hard in a lake, a firmer bait is desirable; especially when the fish hit the bait on the way down or when bobbers are being used.

Color is important in bait-egg fishing, as a bait-egg is a form of natural food. Fishing with an artificial bait or lure is a science of its own, and what Jim explains here is not to be applied to lures and various artificial baits. To begin with, natural bait in its natural surroundings is the key! Dark water produces dark colored food as light water produces bright colored food. On a dark, cloudy day, food,

There are numerous ways in which these brown trout could have been caught from Oregon's Wickiup Reservoir, but it's certain deeply presented bait-eggs would be a good method.

fish, water bugs, et al., are difficult to see. On bright sunny days you'll find it nearly as difficult to see the same food, bugs or fish. Why is this? Natural foods and fish are somewhat like chameleons.

Common sense would dictate using a bright bait in dark water and a dark bait in bright water. Well, common sense has dictated you a bummer. Since you are going to use a natural bait, use it just the way Mother Nature displays it. Dark days and dark water call for dark bait-eggs. Fish can feed in total darkness, a tip most beneficial in lake fishing. Gamefish have scent glands the entire length of their backbones, and feed by smell as well as sight. That's why the expert bait-egg fisherman insists on a lake egg that milks out well: The milking action attracts by smell and sight.

Red is considered a dark color. Select a dark red egg with some fluorescent color tone and you have both a dark bait and some attraction through the fluorescent toning. Just a touch of fluorescent toning is adequate; extremely bright days call for yellow tones. On average days when it's partly cloudy, slightly overcast or in shady areas, early morning and late evening, the call is for light to medium reds, oranges and natural colored baits.

You can tone down the color orange to red, natural and brown to orange tones. A good orange/brown or medium brown natural tone generally does a good job. On exceptionally bright days a near natural color is best, while on dark days a red egg may be best.

You should now know how to select an egg and when or where to use it — lake or stream — and what color. But, you still have other decisions to make if you can: What is the water condition where you are going? What is the weather going to be like? Will you fish only one lake; maybe you'll try just one stream. How about the trip after this one? What and where will you be going? At this point you probably realize that to be properly equipped for weather and water conditions, not to mention the fact you may fish lake and stream within the same day, you will need a selection of bait-eggs. Go equipped for any type water, weather or type of fishing.

Successful fishermen always carry a flavor alternate just in case. A good tackle box combination calls for light eggs, dark eggs and cheese eggs. The wise fishermen always offers the fish a choice, and changes his bait often. One reason the single egg is such an excellent fish catcher is that it milks its flavor out into the surrounding water, thoroughly attracting feeding trout. For this reason, always check your bait. If it appears light in color and partially collapsed (an egg may be fully rounded yet milked out — five minutes is about right) it's time for a new egg. A fresh, strong milking egg is a real fish-getter. Alaska Spawner and Olympic's Natural Cheese Regal, Fireballs, Surefire and Starfire are excellent single eggs specifically developed to provide the highest degree of milking quality. And, of course, they are superb fish catchers. They are especially made to milk out their flavor to attract hungry trout.

Another tip to consider: Any day you are not catching fish, and your fishing companions are, you may smell bad. Body oil secrets through all your pores including your hands and fingers. Jim has found that by smashing an egg between his two fingers, and letting it dry for a few minutes, the oil from the egg forms a coating and eliminates scent.

Most people believe you should fish early morning and late afternoon or evening and forget the middle of the day. This is not true. You can catch fish in the heat of the day and sometimes at a faster rate than morning or evening. At times you will catch fish in the heat of the day and never get a bite in the evening. Fish do not feed on a time schedule, the way you and I do.

Water temperature plays a big part. Fish are much more active when waters warm up. Along with weather is the barometric pressure. A falling barometer is a bad time to go fishing. A rising or steady barometer is good fishing time.

Bait-egg fishing can be good during the heat of the day because the fish, especially trout, lay on the bottom during

East or West, egg baits are deadly on trout, as this angler fishing Kedgie Park, Nova Scotia, has found.

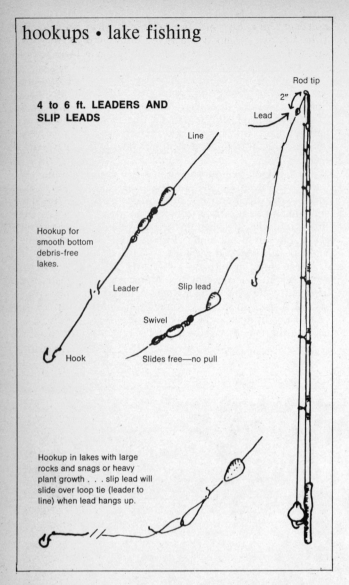

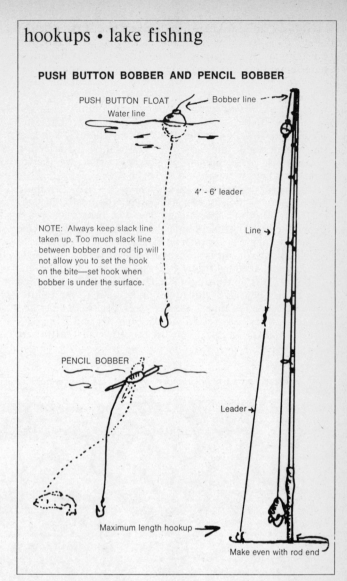

the day and rise to the surface in the evening. Bugs often are more prevalent in the morning and in the evening. Fish rise in the evening and by morning or late morning are back towards the bottom. When fish are hungry and hitting, any time of day is good. Whenever you catch a fish, clean him and see how full his stomach is. It can give you an idea when they feed and possibly the best fishing time. In case you wonder why fishermen can catch fish through ice in the Winter, the fish have very little natural food. Plus, the colder water slows them down and they require less food. The daylight hours are considerably shorter and the fish feed over a shorter span of time. Also, the ice, plus snow, allows far less light at night and they feed primarily by smell only.

Would you like to catch fish in the evening when fish are rising all over the place but won't touch your bait-egg? You can, quite easily, if you take along a weightless float or water float. Pick an area with the greatest concentration of rising fish. By casting the proper water float, without lead, you have a very slow-sinking bait-egg right among the hungry fish. By stripping in line, two to three feet at a time with rapid pulls, you will resurface your float and bait. This has a tendency to tease fish, as well as bringing your bait back up to cruising depth. A fish is in a semi-dive position when looking for food on the bottom from more than four to six feet.

When water becomes overly warm, fish will lay on the bottom near natural springs. Other than seeing bubbles it is difficult to know where underwater springs are located. About the only way to find them is to go swimming. Cold spots, three to six feet under the surface, usually indicate a natural spring. Fish the cold spots at any time, directly into or alongside. Another way to find cold spots is to take a weighted thermometer along and drop it overboard every twenty or thirty feet along a straight line. Pull the thermometer up rapidly so the surface water does not change the reading. Using a thermometer also is good for determining water temperatures at various depths. Fish prefer a certain temperature and will cruise at that temperature level. This is a good technique in deep lakes, when using water bobbers, as you can find the level the fish are cruising at and hopefully catch fish.

One of the best hookups for straight bait-egg fishing, using a slip lead, allows the fish to pick up the bait and mouth it without getting pull from the lead. Larger fish usually cruise very slowly while feeding. When picking up bait, large fish will spit the bait out two or three times before swallowing it. If the fish feels a drag when he picks up the bait, many times he will spit it out and not pick it up again. It's best to cast your bait a short distance and leave enough slack line for the bait to fall to the bottom in a natural way. After the bait and line have stopped falling,

hookups • lake fishing

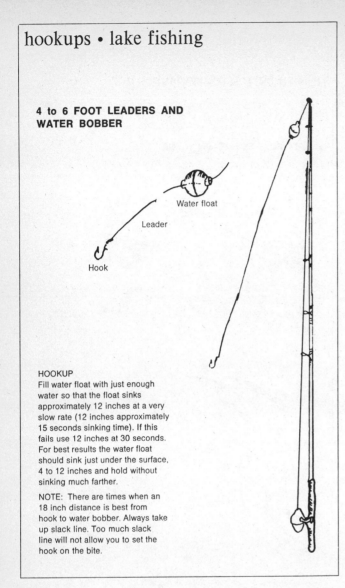

4 to 6 FOOT LEADERS AND WATER BOBBER

Water float

Leader

Hook

HOOKUP
Fill water float with just enough water so that the float sinks approximately 12 inches at a very slow rate (12 inches approximately 15 seconds sinking time). If this fails use 12 inches at 30 seconds. For best results the water float should sink just under the surface, 4 to 12 inches and hold without sinking much farther.

NOTE: There are times when an 18 inch distance is best from hook to water bobber. Always take up slack line. Too much slack line will not allow you to set the hook on the bite.

take up the slack to the point where the line is almost tight, with a slight bow in the line. Since you have a four to six-foot leader beyond the slip lead and approximately twelve inches of loose, bowed line behind the slip lead, the fish will not feel any pull until he is through playing with the bait and has really taken it.

Watch the tip of the rod and the bow in your line closely. The large fish can be deceiving since they do not hit and run normally. The large fish may take the bait and just fin along moving a few inches at a time. When you suspect this is happening, strip a little line very slowly, about one to two inches at a time. When your tip has a gentle tap, set the hook.

There also is a trick to setting a hook properly. Unless you have a very stiff rod, you should move your wrist in a downward motion while moving your arm in an upward motion. Take your rod and try it. See for yourself how the tip actually comes up as you make the downward motion with your wrist. The tougher the fishing the more important this is.

Another fish-getter tip is teasing. When fishing is slow, strip in the line two to three inches at a time, fairly slowly. Fish will pick up bait and hide it for later feeding. By teasing, you are moving a later dinner and the fish will pick up the bait and contain it or hide it somewhere. When fish are reacting to teasing, they usually are carrying

the bait in their mouth and can be difficult to hook unless you are using the best of hooks and do everything right. Jim uses a Mustad, No. 12 hook. They have the right angle for hooking, plus they are not too long in the shank. A short-shanked hook is easier to bury in the egg. Using the right hook, you will find many fish hooked in the top side of the mouth, where normally you would have come up without a fish. Jim uses a round tooth pick to bury the hook in the softest of eggs.

With a short-shanked hook you get a different angle of hooking when you pull on the line. Since the hook should be entirely buried inside the egg, the fish will swallow the egg and the fish feels no eye or barb until after it has passed through the gullet. By the time the fish feels the hook you should be aware he has your bait and start to set the hook. If you are slow, you will set the hook in the side or top of the mouth.

Unless you know the water you are going to fish, look around before starting out and try to determine the best area to fish. As a matter of fact, waters you are familiar with should be reviewed from time to time. The water level, the time of year, the natural food supply, the type of fish available, all vary during the season. A good place today may not be the best next week. You might even keep a record on each fishing trip as to what worked where, the weather conditions, water conditions, time of year and any other pertinent information you feel will help you later.

Spinning tackle turned the trick for this successful angler with a spring steelhead from Michigan's famous Platte River.

Rainbows, brook trout and small silvers are all in some lakes. One time the rainbow may be slow to strike; if so, try for the brook trout. You will find him in different type surroundings than the rainbow. Brook trout like lots of logs and cover to hide in. Silvers are deep, except at the beginning of the spawning season. These are a few reasons for keeping a log or record of your fishing trips, as well as looking over the fishable waters. One of the reasons so many of us like stream fishing is that you can move freely and find many more chances to second-guess where the fish are. Stream fishing does not become boring, because you are able to move about.

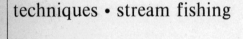

techniques • stream fishing

Water Flow

NOTE: Keep slack line taken up. Bait should barely bump bottom.

It is very difficult to fish upstream without hanging up in the rocks when you cast ahead. Eliminate hang ups. Use a cork or water bobber.

Proper eggs, line, hooks, leaders, et al., have been fairly well covered already. The only difference here is the lead and length of leaders. It is important to get the bait down to the fish. Too long a distance from bait to lead fails to get bait down to the hiding places you're attempting to reach.

Fish generally face upstream in order to stay in the current. Fish also watch for bait being washed downstream, so fish with the current. Fish often lie near large rocks just above or below pools, waterfalls, logs and logjams. Many fishermen miss fish by not fishing the top or head of pools. Slow fishing finds fish in resting pools, behind large rocks and under large logs. Use the current to entice your fish out of resting holes by working bait in a natural manner. If you get a strike, but cannot get a second strike within two casts, change your bait. If a fish takes a dislike for a bait he is not going to hit it again. Try working your bait from another angle so it takes on a new look and action. As much as possible, keep your eye on your line where it enters the water. Many times, due to current flow, you can see the line move in such a manner that you know a fish is hitting before you feel the fish. Also, you can determine about where your fish is hiding.

One of the mistakes most fishermen make is casting their shadow on the water where they are trying to catch fish. Fish are wary, and a shadow is as bad as your body coming into view. Movement frightens off the fish. If you fish downstream, the fish see you coming unless you can cast at least thirty feet or more in front of you. Downstream fishing is the easiest, in that you can control your line better and not hangup as much. Fishing upstream is difficult un-

hookups • stream fishing

BAIT PLACEMENT ON HOOK

There are times an egg and fly make a good combination bait.

Best placement of egg is cradle types shown on page.., illustration 10f.

Steelhead—summer run— hookup for very clear shallow streams. 2 eggs and strip of yarn on a No. 4 hook, (1 to 1½ inches of bright yarn with light red or yellow eggs.

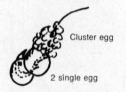

Cluster egg

2 single egg

Adds bright color and 3 or more drift casts per cluster bait. Clusters lose color rapidly and soften in 1 or 2 drifts, most clusters are not bright to begin with.

Another popular steelhead bait make up is 1 or 2 single eggs on barb end of hook with cluster eggs.

less you fish from the side of the stream. This is where your shadow can cause you problems. Try to be opposite the sun or, best of all, have the sun to the right or left of you. When all else fails, and you have to fish upstream and have to cast out past a shadow, consider using a water bobber to eliminate hangups and still use the water currents properly. The water bobber is also excellent for slow currents in wide, shallow areas, especially in the early morning or late evening when fish are after insects. When long casts are necessary and slow currents or shallow water make it difficult to avoid hangups, try a water bobber. A fast current leading into a large pool or quiet water is also water-bobber time. Fast, rough currents find cutthroat trout as well as hangups, so the bobber again can be a winner.

Another fish-getter is a fly and egg combination. At times the combination attracts fish for reasons unknown. A straight fly often does not work nor does a straight bait-egg, but used together the fish will strike.

Bait-eggs can be used to fish steelhead at specific times and under certain conditions. You usually are using lighter line and less lead. One of the better fish-getters when the water is clear and low is to use two or possibly three bait-

A pair of good-looking steelheads taken from Canada's Cooper River, located in Victoria, British Columbia.

eggs on a No. 14 hook with a strip of bright yarn. Since a bait-egg is a natural food, a steelhead can be enticed to take them. Steelhead have a habit of picking up food and hiding it for a later meal. As many know, steelhead do not always sock a bait. It takes a sensitive feel to know when a steelhead is mouthing or moving your bait.

Another use for bait-eggs in steelheading is to use a cluster with one or two single bait-eggs. Clusters can be cast only a few times before they soften up and lose their color. To get extra life out of each cluster, the single bait-egg does two things: First, the bait-egg holds color much longer, as

the color of single bait-eggs is much brighter than clusters. Second, the single bait-egg does not soften up nearly as fast as clusters. By using a few single bait-eggs you will probably cut your cost of clusters by at least half and more likely catch more fish. Cluster eggs are not cheap and most fishermen use a pretty good sized chunk for each bait-up.

As a final help to those who are interested in utilizing Jim Akers' sage advice, you'll find several special illustrations accompanying this article. They were created by Jim's wife to better show certain, all-important steps and techniques relating to this rewarding art of bait-egg fishing.

THE SAFETY FACTOR

Dᴜʀɪɴɢ ᴛʜᴇ ʏᴇᴀʀꜱ between World War II and today, no outdoor participation sport has enjoyed the phenomenal growth that has taken place in both fresh and salt water fishing. Paralleling this growth has been an increasing need to formulate clearly some basic rules, procedures, or considerations — call them what you will — that contribute to safe fishing.

In streams and rivers, respect the power of water. In wading streams or rivers, do not get in the current so deeply that you can no longer fight it. Wading technique in trout fishing is an art in itself.

Exercise extreme care and restraint when fording a stream. Realize that stream beds are usually uneven and often made up of rocks of various uneven sizes, often quite slippery.

If you do fall in, do not panic. If you can swim or walk out, do so. If you can't swim, you have no business being there to begin with.

If you should be carried downstream, always try to keep your feet in front of you. Tread water in the sitting

Once down to the business of fishing, don't leave lures and hooks on seats, as angler above is doing. When everyone is excited, playing a fish, someone is liable to put a hand down or sit quickly and bingo! Disaster.

Almost Any Action — Including Stepping Off A Curb — Has Dangers, But Here Are Tips For Minimizing The Risks In Fishing!

On charter fishing boats, lots of anglers means plenty of equipment laying around cluttering up the deck. Running — as the fish-carrying gent is — can prove painful if he slips on fish slime or trips over equipment. Also, be careful with back-casts: You might hook someone behind.

position so as to be able to fend yourself off rocks or boulders if they lie in your path.

In meadow or swamp streams, it is advisable not to walk too close along the banks; more than likely, the banks are undercut from erosion and do not provide safe footing. Also, fish sense vibration from these banks and are frightened away by the angler who walks too close to them.

Familiarize yourself with your surroundings. People who have a tendency to become easily disoriented sometimes decide they are lost when they are really not. Keep in mind the following: Streams run downhill, strangely enough, and in this day and age they usually cross some kind of road or join a larger stream that eventually reaches a town. When I go off exploring new areas here in the United States or in South America, I always carry a compass and have, through experience, learned to have complete faith in my ability to

use it effectively. No man, whether on fresh or salt water, is truly an experienced or safe outdoorsman until he is capable of operating a compass. Similarly, the ability to read limited area maps is a must for the man who decides to rough it on a fishing trip, whether it is in our Catskills or Blue Ridge Mountains or the wilds of Canada. Being lost in any of the three is far from being a joke.

During any violent storm, where there is a chance of lightning, it is urged that you stop fishing and head for inside shelter. This applies to fishing on streams or lakes. Standing in water with a metal reel in your hand is a fine way to get electrocuted. If you can't reach inside shelter, find fairly open ground to wait out the storm. Keep away from that proverbial sheltering tree.

Increasingly, youngsters are tagging along with Dad. If you're one of these dads, you should be aware of the fol-

When angling for large gamefish, with powerful jaws and sharp teeth like this muskie, use a hook remover to free the deeply-imbedded hooks.

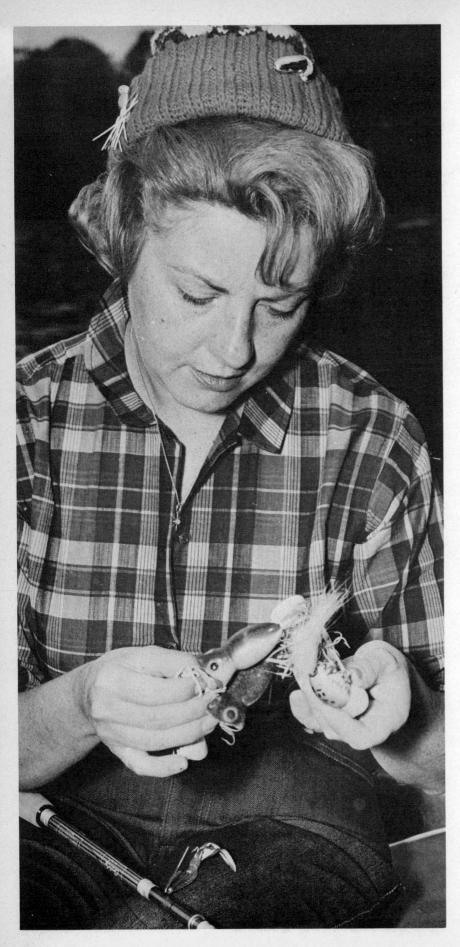

Treble hooks are great for hooking fish — and humans. It's a smart move to carry hook clipper to snip off barb, saving a trip to doctor's, and ruination of fine fishing trip.

It's the wise dad who takes the time to teach his children to understand the mysteries of different types of waters — where you can safely wade, types of waters to avoid and others.

lowing: Do not allow children under 12 years of age to wear chest-high waders of any type; if they fall while fishing, the weight of water in the waders might well pull them under. Hip boots, at the most, are all that should be used by a child in stream fishing until he has reached an age where he can handle himself in the water if a problem arises. Another thing: Children under 12 years of age should not be allowed to go stream fishing by themselves. If the child were to fall off the bank or sink in silt or become

involved in any of the accidents that do frequently occur in stream fishing, he would be in real trouble without a companion. But even a companion in this age group might not be too helpful. Personally, I feel that children of this age should be under adult supervision at all times when fishing in a stream or river. Just this past Summer, three young farm boys, all under 12, boys who by environmental opportunity are far better able to cope with certain emergency situations than their city cousins, found a silt concentration in an eddy that had been left by a flood stage of the water. Two of them were in the silt to their hips when the third, who had taken time to remove his sneakers, realized the seriousness of their predicament. He ran and found a long branch that the river had pushed onto shore. Then, without any outside help, he pulled both boys out and onto firm ground. That was lucky — and unusual. Too often the results are different and unpleasant.

There has been and still is a very real problem concerning fishing in lakes. The problem is not of the fisherman's making. The blame lies almost entirely with irresponsible young people who have been given a freedom of decision —

a responsibility for which they are often inadequately prepared. In the past eight years the number of small boats on lakes has grown to proportions that have caused safety officials to become increasingly alarmed. Their concern is not with the boats but rather with the careless, unskilled people who operate them. They are the hot-rodders, inconsiderate water skiers, and the rest of a reckless clan who can see only one use for their boats and high horsepower motors — speed and more speed! Too often, it is speed without caution; always for the hot-rodders it is speed without courtesy. (Please do not think that I am condemning all water skiers or boat enthusiasts. I speak of only fifteen

This narrow stream contains potentially dangerous white water, or riffles caused by the swiftly coursing stream. If you do fall in, keep your feet in front of you and try to ward off boulders with them, while working constantly toward shore. Don't try standing up — you can't.

percent of them — but fifteen percent is a high percentage in terms of the damage they do.)

Many ardent fishermen have become so fed up with having their boat or group buzzed by hot-rodders out for kicks that they have stopped going to certain stations on many lakes. Others have taken to evening and early morning hours rather than be swamped by a runabout cutting across their lines at high speed. These hours happen to be good fishing hours, so being forced into them has been of some value — though losing one's freedom to fish at will is not to be tolerated.

The first step in checking this new menace to safety was the issuance of license numbers to each boat equipped with a motor. It is now possible to report accurately those who violate the rules. Step number two, the training of all operators, is in the making — though far from a reality.

To correct what is becoming an increasingly intolerable situation, it is now also being suggested that the townships who patrol their lakes set aside specific areas for water skiing, racing, and fishing. Normally the fisherman fishes shorelines, coves, and drop-off areas. On the other side, the water skier and fast boats require deep, large areas of open water. Several lakes will be trying this arrangement of specialized areas, and we will be carefully evaluating the

In the surf, wear a safety belt around your chest-high waders to prevent large amounts of sea water from filling them if a big wave hits, or if you should happen to slip on rocks.

Opposite page: A good, sharp knife is a valuable asset on any fishing trip. Should the surface being cut offer resistance, turn the blade away from you to avoid the chance of stabbing or painfully cutting yourself.

Below: Always watch for unseen holes or crumbling banks. A sudden fall in strong water can be trouble. Look where you are placing your feet before you take each step.

results to determine its feasibility for wide-spread use.

But new plans and arrangements notwithstanding, the sensible fisherman, increasingly sensitive to the chance of swamping or capsizing on large lakes and impoundments, puts life jackets or approved floating cushions, one for each person, aboard his boat. Also, once again let it be said that common sense, plus some experience, is the byword when fishing in lakes, impoundments and very swift or wide rivers. Be advised of weather conditions, possible fog, and any other natural conditions that might be a possible hazard. Investigate and know your area before you attempt to fish it.

In deep sea fishing it must be understood immediately that when we fish in bays or open water we are contending with ocean conditions — conditions often subject to violent changes. Offshore fishing should never be attempted with inadequate boats, motors, or with inexperienced people in charge. All safety regulations deemed compulsory by the Coast Guard are minimum requirements for a careful fisherman. All fishermen with experience realize these rules and regulations are written for their protection and are not to be taken lightly.

Never attempt to stop the run of a big fish with your thumb on the spool; the drag was designed for this. The speed of the turning spool can take the skin off your thumb in nothing flat.

When boating big fish, never let the wire leader catch your hand against the boat's side. If the fish were to sound at this moment, it might well mean the loss of your fingers.

Never boat a dangerous fish — a shark, swordfish or ray — until it has been rendered senseless. A thrashing, snapping big game fish in a boat's cockpit is a dangerous companion.

Salt water fishing would be incomplete without mentioning the great interest in party boat fishing. Most accidents that take place on these boats are the direct result of haste, carelessness and lack of courtesy. Leaving hook rigs out in the open, allowing fish slime to collect on the deck, etc., contribute to the possibility of an imbedded hook or a sudden painful slip. Abide by the skipper's rules — he's a professional and has devised rules for the comfort and protection of his passengers.

In surf fishing be aware of rip tides; do not wade out past the point of no return. Respect the surf for the force it is. Keep in mind the possibility of undertow.

When not wearing a parka, wear a belt around your waist and over your waders. In case of a high wave it will save you from ending up with waders full of sea water.

When fishing the surf at night, carry a good flashlight. Such a light not only is a must for checking equipment, but is invaluable if you must perform the operation of gaffing and beaching your fish.

Do not venture far into the surf at night. There are holes and drop-offs that could prove extremely hazardous. You should familiarize yourself with terrain and contour problems during daylight hours, especially at low tide. A knowledge of the bottom contour, which is discernible at this period, makes for added safety at high tide or at night and certainly means more fish for you.

Big hooks can really hurt if not handled with the care they demand, such as this Louisiana youngster is applying. Also, keep on the lookout for sharp spines on fish, which get infected.

Jetties or breakwaters are to be treated with caution. They are excessively slippery. Those built of rocks are the worst, because of uneven spacing and large fissures. All contribute to the strong possibility of a painful accident for the inexperienced. If you are to fish in this type of area, there are several things you should keep in mind:

Wear special grips on your boots or waders. These will help grip slippery rocks and wood.

Wear one of the quickly inflatable life preservers that are hooked on your jacket with a safety clasp. They are widely used by skin divers, take up little space, and are inflated by a single squeeze of the hand if and when you are in need of it.

Many jetties are completely above water at low tide, but sections are under at high tide. Don't discover the truth

about your spot the hard way. I would like one dollar for every man that has had to be taken off a jetty by the Coast Guard or a helicopter. Remember: If this or any other accident should occur, you can be helped only by being seen or heard by others. Therefore, stay off jetties with which you are not familiar and which are not generally known to others.

When fishing at night, it is strongly recommended you do not fish alone. A companion can mean the difference between life and death. At the least it could mean the difference between spending a night alone with a broken leg on the end of a jetty, and having companionship and being helped.

In all phases of fishing you will be involved with hooks. Hooks, when treated with respect and care, are not apt to

A careful angler has no worries, even in a canoe. If your boat does tip over, though, remember that it will support you better than any life vest and can be righted in shallow water.

cause too great a share of injuries — not treated with respect they can cause real trouble. If through haste or carelessness you find that the worst has happened — someone has a hook and barb embedded in a finger or for that matter an ear lobe — what do you do, short of surgery? Normally you can push the hook on through until the barb emerges and then snip off the barb with a simple wire cutter bought in any hardware store. For the past ten years I have always carried an excellent little German cutter, the size of a set of very small pliers, in my tackle box. It has saved the day on three occasions for people who normally would have had to cancel the remainder of their outing to find a doctor to remove the hook. When you consider that I am outdoors on the average of 150 days out of each year, it becomes obvious that, although a possibility of becoming hooked is

there, it is not lurking around every corner. Yet, you should be careful and respect the hook.

Do not carry hooks, plugs, lures, or flies loose in your pockets at any time. All fishing tackle shops carry a selection of tackle boxes in all sizes and shapes that will provide a safe method of transporting and storing hooks and other implements of the art.

When walking with fishing rods on the trail — whether in the woods or just to the lake shore — never leave the hook or lure attached. It invites someone to bump into it. Wait until you are ready to fish before rigging up.

Let me conclude these brief notes on safe fishing in fresh and salt water by saying that fishing, with its millions of enthusiastic participants, has one of the best records for safety in the outdoor field. Through common sense and education let us strive to keep it that way.

GLOSSARY OF FISHING TERMS

ALGAE: Simple plants, most of which live submerged in water.

ANADROMOUS: Refers to fish which spend part of their lives in salt and part in fresh water.

ANCHOR: A weight or hook used to hold a boat in a fixed position when not under way.

ANNEAL: The subjection of metal to intense heat and gradual cooling, in order to increase the strength and reduce its brittleness.

ANTI-REVERSE: A mechanism which allows line to be pulled from a reel while the handle remains set.

AQUATIC INSECTS: The may flies, stone flies and caddis flies, to name a few. They are hatched in water, leave to mate — then return and deposit eggs. A cycle.

ARTIFACTS: Utensils used by early civilizations, relics.

AUTOMATICS: Reels that utilize a wind-up spring which in turn can be released to take up the fly line.

AWL: A long, needle-shaped instrument.

BACKLASH: A tangle of line caused by overrunning of the reel spool.

BAILER: A utensil for removing water from a boat manually.

BAIT-CASTING: A term used to describe the casting of plugs or lures which imitate baitfish.

BAIT-FISHING: Fishing with bait such as worms, minnows.

BALANCED TACKLE: Tackle that when carefully selected and correctly balanced will perform correctly, i.e., correct relationship between rod, reel and line.

BARBEL: Whisker-like feelers about the heads of some fish.

BARBULES: Tiny barbs which hold the rays of a feather together.

BASS-BUGGING ROD: A fairly stout fly rod of more than usual power to turn over the larger bass-bugs and poppers that are commonly used.

BILGE: The area along the keel inside a boat.

BILGE PUMP: A pump for removing water from the hull of a boat.

BILLFISH: An ocean fish having a long pointed bill.

BOAT NET: A landing net with a long handle for use from small boat or canoe.

BOBBER: A float tied to the line to keep the weighted bait at the correct water depth.

BRACKISH WATER: Fresh water that is mixed with salt water. Where a river joins a bay or ocean.

BUGGING TAPER: A fly line that has a short, heavy section in the forward area to turn over large bass-bugs during the cast.

BUNKER: Menhaden.

CABIN CRUISER: A large powerboat with living facilities for the occupants.

CARRYING RACK: A rack for carrying small boats on an automobile top.

CAUDAL PEDUNCLE: Body of a fish in front of the caudal fin.

CHARTER BOATS: Large, yacht-size boats available for private, day or longer charter fishing.

CHEAP TACKLE: Low-priced junk not worth buying.

CHENILLE: Fluffy, silky material used for bodies of flies.

CHINE STRIPS: Strips of wood at the base of the sides of a flat-bottomed boat to lend rigidity to the structure.

CHLOROPHYLL: The green coloring matter of plants.

CHUB: A baitfish.

CHUM LINES: A slick on the water caused by the dumping of ground-up fish. It is used to attract many school fish in salt water.

CLASPERS: Appendages on ventral side used to join fish during mating act, peculiar to sharks.

CLICK: The sound of the drag mechanism on reels to control line outgo.

CLINKER-BUILT: See Lapstrake.

CLOVE HITCH: A knot made by making two half-hitches around a post, useful for mooring boats.

COMBING: An upright, water-tight rail around a boat's cockpit to prevent spray from washing aboard.

CORK ARBOR: A cork filler to increase the diameter of reel spool.

CRANE FLY: An aquatic insect.

CRAYFISH: A crustacean resembling a small lobster.

CREEL: A willow basket or canvas bag that holds the caught fish.

CRUSTACEANS: Animals with hard exoskeletons.

CUTTYHUNK: Linen line.

DACE: A baitfish.

DEADFALLS: Spots that contain sunken trees, branches and the like. An excellent hideaway for fish.

DIATOMS: Any of a class of microscopic algae.

DINGHY: Usually a short, broad-beamed, round-bottomed boat of light construction, used as a tender on yachts.

DORSAL FIN: The top fin on the back of the fish.

DORY: A rowboat with a high prow, flaring sides and narrow bottom used chiefly for commercial fishing.

DRAG (or CLICK): Controls the tension under which a line goes off the reel.

DROP LINE: A handline used without a rod for still fishing.

DROP-OFF AREAS: Where the water suddenly goes from shallow to quite deep. A fast downhill plunge of the shoreline. Fish often lie off these spots and wait for baitfish to show.

DRY FLY: An artificial lure designed to imitate a floating insect.

DUGOUT: A canoe constructed from a single log.

EAGLE CLAW: A type of hook developed by Wright and McGill in which the point bends back toward the shank.

EELSKIN: The skin of an eel used for bait.

EPILIMNION: A thermal stratum in lakes above the thermocline.

FEATHERING: In rowing, bringing the blades of the oars back so that they are parallel with the surface of the water.

FEATHER JIG: A lure used in salt water having a metal head and a body of feathers to imitate a baitfish.

FEMALE FERRULE: The socket part of a ferrule.

FERRULE: A friction joint in a rod to permit it to be disassembled for transportation or storage.

FISHERMAN-SPORTSMAN: A fisherman is a man who fishes to catch fish. A sportsman is a man who fishes for the sport of fishing.

FISH LADDERS: Structures to permit fish to climb over or around dams.

FLASHER: A flashing spoon tied above the bait to attract fish to it.

FLIES, ARTIFICIAL: Those made to represent insects and baitfish on which the gamefish feed.

FLOAT FISHING: Angling while drifting down a stream.

FLUKE: The point of an anchor.

FULCRUM: The point around which a lever turns.

FUSIFORM FISH: A round-bodied fish, tapering toward the ends.

GALLEY: A boat's kitchen.

GAMEFISH: Designated fish species known for their fighting qualities and also those under conservation law protection.

GANG HOOKS: Fish hooks fastened together in series so that they are effective from all directions.

GEAR/TACKLE: Fishing equipment and accessories.

GILLS: Organs by which animals can breathe in water.

GORGE: A sliver of wood, metal or bone hung by its center on a line, forerunner of the fish hook.

GRAPNEL: A hook-shaped anchor with four or more tines.

GUIDES: Eyelets through which line is strung along a rod.

GUNWALE: The upper edge of a boat's side, or a wooden strip used to reinforce the upper side of a boat.

HABITAT: The environment in which fish find conditions satisfactory for existence.

HACKLE: A feather from the back or neck of a cock fowl. Used to simulate legs on flies for fishing.

HELLGRAMMITE: Larvae of the Dobson fly.

HERL: Single ray of a feather, used in fly tying.

HORSE (...a fish): To pull in the fish by sheer strength.

HUSHPUPPIES: A Southern dish consisting of batter with chopped onions, dropped in balls in hot deep fat.

HYPOLIMNION: A thermal stratum in lakes below the thermocline.

I.G.F.A.: International Game Fish Association.

IMPOUNDMENT: An artificial body of water.

JIG: An artificial bait for casting or trolling.

JOHN BOAT: A flat-bottomed, square-bowed boat developed for river fishing in the Ozarks.

JOLLY BOAT: A medium-sized boat used for rough work from a sailing vessel.

JUG FISHING: Fishing by tying baited lines to jugs which are allowed to drift on the surface as floats.

KEELSON: A strip of wood fastened along the keel inside a boat.

KEELSTRIP: A plank fastened along the line of the keel in a flat-bottomed boat as reinforcement and protection.

KYAK: A long, low, canoe-type, one-man boat with a full deck, developed by the Eskimos.

LAMINATED ROD: A rod built by cementing several strips of wood together with the grain parallel.

LAPSTRAKE: A type of construction in which the upper plank overlaps a portion of the lower plank, like clapboards on a house.

LARVA: The early stage through which certain animals pass, usually referring to those that effect a complete change of habits and food in adult life.

LEA: A measure of linen line, usually 300 yards.

LEADER: A strand of gut or nylon used between bait and line to minimize visibility. Also a strand of wire used to prevent fish with sharp teeth from cutting the line.

LEVEL-WIND MECHANISM: The mechanism which winds the line on the reel spool evenly without the aid of the guiding fingers of your hand.

LONGBOAT: A large boat carried by a merchant vessel.

LONG-ROD: Another name for the fly rod.

LUNATE TAIL: Moon-shaped tail.

LURE: A decoy or bait for fish.

MALE FERRULE: The insert part of a ferrule.

MEMBRANE: A thin sheet of tissue separating or supporting living organs.

MILT: In fish, the fluid bearing the sperm of the male.

MONOFILAMENT: Single-strand line.

MOSSBUNKER: A small, oily, salt water baitfish often used in chum.

MOTHER NATURE: The guiding force and knowledge of creation.

MUMMIES: Munnichogs, salt water baitfish.

NODE: A leaf scar or joint on a bamboo cane.

NON-MULTIPLYING REEL: Single-action; that is, one revolution of the spool to one of the handle.

NYMPHS: Any of certain insects in immature form.

OARS: Paddle-shaped levers for propelling a rowboat.

OFFSET HANDLE: A rod handle with the reel set offset for better positioning and ease in fishing.

OMNIVOROUS: Having a universal diet.

OUTRIGGER: Long pole used in trolling for big gamefish to carry the line to one side of the boat.

PALMER-TIED: A fly tying technique where the hackle extends the length of the body.

PANFISH: A small fish which is more fun eating than catching.

PARR: A young salmon.

PARTY BOATS: Very large boats, accommodating from twelve to near a hundred anglers in some cases.

PIROGUE: A small dugout canoe developed for swamp and marsh travel in Louisiana.

PLANKED: To cook and serve on a board.

PLANKTON: Minute plants and animals which live in the surface layers of salt or fresh water.

PLEISTOCENE: The epoch or age which followed the Tertiary Age; it preceded the present age.

PLUGS: Wooden or plastic lures designed in different shapes, colors and sizes.

POACH: (1) To fish on private property without the owner's permission. To fish illegally. (2) To cook in boiling water.

PORTAGE: Carrying of a boat or canoe and its duffel by hand, over or around a barrier in the water route.

PRACTICE PLUG: A rubber plug, similar in size and design to a fishing plug without hooks, for practice casting.

PRAM: In the United States, usually a short boat with a square bow used as a tender for a larger boat.

PREDACIOUS: Killing other animals for food.

PULPIT: A protective railing around the bowsprit of a boat or a platform at the bow from which fish may be harpooned.

PUNT: A flat-bottomed boat with square bow and stern built for use in rivers.

QUADRATE: Pertaining to a bony element on each side of the skull of a fish to which the lower jaw is jointed.
QUENELLE: A fish ball, fish chopped fine and highly seasoned.

RIFFLE: A slight disturbance in the surface current of a stream caused by a subsurface obstruction.
RIG: Equipment.
ROILED (water): Muddied or disturbed waters.
ROWLOCKS or OARLOCKS: Accessories fixed on the gunwale of a boat to serve as the fulcrum for an oar and to hold the oar in place.

SCHOOLS (of fish): Concentrations of fish of the same species.
SCHUSSES: Runs down rapids in a canoe.
SCUTE: Extremely bony or horny plate on a fish.
SEA SKIFF: A rowboat with a narrow, flat bottom, high prow and flaring sides.
SEINES: Nets.
SERRATED: Saw-toothed.
SHINERS: Minnows, baitfish.
SHOAL: A shallow area.
SILT: A fine, earthy sediment carried and deposited by water.
SILURIAN AGE: Pertaining to that part of the Paleozoic period, marked by coral-reef building and the appearance of the great crustaceans.
SINGLE-ACTION REEL: Non-multiplying.
SINKER: Weight for taking bait to deeper water.
SKEG: A small V-shaped strip fixed toward the stern of a rowboat to serve in place of a keel.
SKIFF: A small or medium-size rowboat.
SKITTERING: To draw the hook through or along the surface of the water with a quivering motion.
SNAGLINE: A line fitted with hooks for snagging fish.
SNAP SWIVEL: A swivel with a snap attached to it for attaching leaders, additional terminal tackle or lures.
SNELLED FLIES: Flies fastened to bits of gut.
SOLUNAR: A word coined by John Alden Knight to indicate his theory that living creatures have a tendency to become active during certain periods influenced by the sun and the moon.
SPAWN: The eggs of fish, oysters or other aquatic animals.
SPERRLING: A small salt water baitfish.
SPINNER: An artificial lure, the blade of which whirls continuously in a circular fashion around the axis of the line of traction.
SPLINE: A thin wooden strip.
SPONSON: A built-in flotation chamber along the gunwales of a canoe.
SPRAY RAILS: Strips along the side of a boat hull to repel spray.
STAR DRAG: A star-shaped adjustment on a reel to increase or decrease the rate at which fish may strip the line.
STEELYARD: A weighing device in which the fish is suspended from the shorter arm of a lever and its weight found by moving a counterweight along the longer arm.
STILL FISHING: Fishing without moving, generally from an anchored boat on a lake or quiet stream. The bait is cast and allowed to stay there awaiting the fish.
STINK BAIT: A malodorous bait formed usually of over-ripe cheese, chicken viscera and slaughterhouse wastes; used for catfishing.

STONE FLY: An aquatic insect.
STRIKING: A definite or quick tightening of the line in order to sink the barb of the hook into the mouth of the fish.
STRIP LINE: Draw line from the reel for casting (fly-fishing only).
STRIP PLANKED: A type of boat construction in which bottom and side planks are joined together smoothly and tightly. Patented joints usually are used and are sealed with marine glue.

TAGGING: Marking fish by affixing tags to them.
TAPERED LEADERS: Almost transparent leaders attached to the line and the end lure that taper from thick to thin in order to make the cast balance out in the air and float down on the water with a minimum of disturbance (fly-fishing only).
TAPERED LINES: Lines tapered from thick to thin to balance the line in the air for best casting (fly-fishing only).
TERMINAL TACKLE: That which is attached to the end of the line: leaders, spreaders, sinkers, hooks, bobbers, lures.
THERMOCLINE: A thermal stratum in a lake in which temperatures are static.
THOLE PINS: Hardwood pegs used in place of rowlocks.
THROW LINE: A line cast by hand for fishing without a rod.
THUMBING THE REEL: Controlling the outgo of the line by pressing on the spool during the cast (bait-casting only).
THWART: Cross bracing between the gunwales of a boat; the seats in a rowboat.
TIPPET: That section of the leader, nearest the fly, that is normally subject to greatest wear.
TRAILER: A wheeled vehicle towed behind an automobile for transporting boats or dunnage.
TRANSOM: The board forming the end of a square-sterned boat.
TRASH FISH: Fish which have neither game nor high food value.
TROLLING: Fishing by trailing bait and line behind a moving boat.
TROLLING PLATE: Plate fixed to an outboard motor to decrease its speed for trolling.
TROTLINE: Line, stretched across a stream or between buoys, having many baited hooks.
TUMP LINE: A band of soft leather about 2½ inches by eighteen inches to the ends of which are secured leather thongs or ropes about nine feet long; used in portaging.

ULTRA-LIGHT TACKLE: The lightest and sportiest tackle practical for the fishing conditions and fish species.
UMIAK: A large, skin-covered boat propelled by paddles; developed by the Eskimos.

WET FLY: An artificial lure tied to imitate a drowned insect or the larva of an aquatic insect.
WHALE BOAT: A round-bottomed, double-ended boat developed by the whalers of the Nineteenth Century for harpooning whales.
WOBBLER SPOON: An artificial lure attached to the leader at one end causing it to whip and wobble from side to side as it is drawn through the water.

X DESIGNATION: The diameter and pound test of leader material and monofilament lines for spinning and bait-casting.

FISHING TACKLE MANUFACTURERS DIRECTORY

Tony Accetta & Son
932 Ave. E, Riviera Beach, Fla. 33404
Lures & Baits, Fishing Accessories

Acme Tackle Company
69 Bucklin St., Providence, R.I. 02907
Lures & Baits, Fishing Accessories

Aero Precision Engineering
7117 Point Douglas Drive
Cottage Grove, Minn. 55016
Fishing Accessories

Airlite Plastics Company
914 N. 18th St., Omaha, Nebr. 68102
Fishing Accessories

Aitken-Warner Corporation
427 Beech St., Green Camp, Ohio 43322
Lures & Baits, Fishing Accessories

Al's Goldfish Lure Company
516 Main St., Indian Orchard, Mass. 01051
Lures & Baits, Fishing Accessories

Aladdin Laboratories, Inc.
620 S. 8th St., Minneapolis, Minn. 55404
Rods & Reels, Fishing Accessories

Allan Manufacturing Company
325 Duffy Ave., Hicksville, L.I., N.Y. 11801
Fishing Accessories

Alliance Manufacturing Company
3125 N. Milwaukee Ave., Chg., Ill. 60618
Fishing Accessories

American Sportsman Bait Company
21744 Dequindre Ave., Warren, Mich. 48091
Lures & Baits

Angler Products, Inc.
868 Mercer Rd., Butler, Pa. 16001
Lures & Baits

Angler Rod Company
1426 Oakland Ave., St. Clair, Mich. 48079
Rods & Reels

Anglers' Manufacturing Corp.
7729 N. Eastlake Ter., Chg., Ill. 60626
Fishing Accessories

Angling Products Company, Inc.
2704 Skyline Dr., Lorain, Ohio 44053
Lures & Baits, Fishing Accessories

Fred Arbogast Company, Inc.
313 West North St., Akron, Ohio 44303
Lures & Baits, Fishing Accessories

Axelson Fishing Tackle Mfg. Co.
1559 Placentia, Newport Beach, Calif. 92660
Fishing Accessories

B & B Tackle Company
P.O. Box 220, Lufkin, Texas 75901
Lures & Baits, Fishing Accessories

*Members of the American Fishing
Tackle Manufacturers Association*

B & M Company
P.O. Box 231, West Point, Miss. 39773
Rods & Reels, Lures & Baits, Fishing Accessories

B & T Manufacturing, Inc.
P.O. Box 249, Ryan, Okla. 73565
Rods & Reels, Fishing Accessories

Jim Bagley Bait Company
P.O. Box 110, Winter Haven, Fla. 33880
Lures & Baits

Bait-Saver
401 N. Main St., Thiensville, Wis. 53092
Fishing Accessories

Bass Buster, Inc.
P.O. Box 118, Amsterdam, Mo. 64723
Lures & Baits

Bay de Noc Lure Company
Box 71, Gladstone, Mich. 49837
Rods & Reels, Lures & Baits, Fishing Accessories

Bead Chain Mfg. Company
110 Mountain Grove St.
Bridgeport, Conn. 06605
Lures & Baits, Fishing Accessories

Bear Paw Tackle Company
P.O. Box 177, Farmington, Mich. 48024
Lures & Baits, Fishing Accessories

Berkley & Company, Inc.
1617 Hill Ave., Spirit Lake, Iowa 51360
Rods & Reels, Fishing Lines, Fishing Accessories

Best Tackle Mfg. Co.
P.O. Box 123, Unionville, Mich. 48767
Lures & Baits, Fishing Accessories

Betts Tackle, Ltd.
Box 57, Fuquay Varina, N.C. 27526
Lures & Baits, Fishing Accessories

Bevin Wilcox Line Company
Div. Brownell & Co., Inc.
Main St., Moodus, Conn. 06469
Fishing Lines

Big Jon, Inc.
14393 Peninsula Dr., Traverse City, Mich. 49684
Lures & Baits

Bluegrass Tackle Company
205 Robin Rd., Russell, Ky. 41169
Lures & Baits

Bohn Engineering Co.
1423 Walnut St., N.E.
Grand Rapids, Mich. 49503
Rods & Reels, Fishing Accessories

Boone Bait Company, Inc.
P.O. Box 571, Winter Park, Fla. 32789
Lures & Baits

Bow-Dilly Lure Co.
206 W. Ave. B—Suite 1 (Box 1210)
Killeen, Texas 76541
Lures & Baits, Fishing Accessories

Browning Arms Company
Route 1, Morgan, Utah 84050
Rods & Reels

Brunswick Corp., Sports Div.
69 W. Washington St., Chg., Ill. 60602
Rods & Reels, Lures & Baits, Fishing Accessories

Burke Flexo-Products Company
1969 S. Airport Rd., Traverse City, Mich. 49684
Lures & Baits

Bystrom Bros., Inc.
2200 Snelling Ave., Minneapolis, Minn. 55404
Fishing Accessories

California Tackle Company, Inc.
430 W. Redondo Beach Blvd.
Gardena, Calif. 90248
Rods & Reels

Carry-Lite, Inc.
3000 West Clarke St., Milwaukee, Wis. 53245
Fishing Accessories

Challanger Mfg. Corporation
118 Pearl St., Mt. Vernon, N.Y. 10550
Fishing Accessories

Championship Tackle, Inc.
3206 Hollywood Ave., Shreveport, La. 71108
Lures & Baits

Charley's Wonderworm Company
516 Market St., Mt. Carmel, Ill. 62863
Lures & Baits

H.C. Cook Company
28 Beaver St., Ansonia, Conn. 06401
Fishing Accessories

Cordell Tackle, Inc.
P.O. Box 2020, Hot Springs, Ark. 71901
Lures & Baits, Fishing Accessories

Cortland Line Company
P.O. Box 1362, Cortland, N.Y. 13045
Fishing Lines

Creek Chub Bait Company
E. Keyser St., Garrett, Indiana 46738
Lures & Baits

Creme Lure Company
P.O. Box 87, Tyler, Texas 75701
Lures & Baits

Cuba Specialty Mfg. Company
P.O. Box 38, Houghton, N.Y. 14744
Fishing Accessories

Ed Cumings, Inc.
Box 6186, Flint, Mich. 48508
Fishing Accessories

Daisy/Heddon Div. Victor Compt. Corp.
414 West St., Dowagiac, Mich. 49047
Rods & Reels, Lures & Baits

Daisy/Heddon
P.O. Box 220, Rogers, Ark. 72756

Daiwa Corporation
14011 S. Normandie, Gardena, Calif. 90247
Rods & Reels, Fishing Lines

Les Davis Fishing Tackle Company
1565 Center St., Tacoma, Wash. 98409
Fishing Lines, Lures & Baits, Fishing Accessories

Dayton Marine Products, Inc.
7565 E. McNichols Rd., Detroit, Mich. 48234
Fishing Accessories

DeLong Lures, Inc.
80 Compark Rd., Centerville, Ohio 45459
Lures & Baits

Dep, Inc.
1116 South J St., Fort Smith, Ark. 72901
Lures & Baits

Depew Manufacturing Company
359 Duffy Ave., Hicksville, L.I., N.Y. 11802
Rods & Reels, Fishing Accessories

DeWitt Plastics
P.O. Box 400, Auburn, N.Y. 13021
Rods & Reels, Lures & Baits, Fishing Accessories

Dr. Walker's Enterprises
224 New Hope Rd., Gastonia, N.C. 28052
Lures & Baits

Dragon Fly Company
P.O. Drawer 1349, Sumter, S.C. 29151
Lures & Baits, Fishing Accessories

E.I. du Pont de Nemours & Co., Inc.
1007 Market St., Wilmington, Del. 19898
Fishing Lines

Dynaflex Manufacturing Corporation
1075 W. 21st Place, Hialeah, Fla. 33010
Rods & Reels

Earlybird Company
P.O. Box 1485, Boise, Idaho 83701
Lures & Baits, Fishing Accessories

Lou J. Eppinger Mfg. Company
6340 Schaefer Hwy., Dearborn, Mich. 48126
Lures & Baits

F. B. Spinning Reels Div. Feurer Bros.
77 Lafayette Ave.
North White Plains, N.Y. 10603
Rods & Reels

Falls Bait Company
1440 Kennedy Rd., Chippewa Falls, Wis. 54729
Lures & Baits, Fishing Accessories

Famous Keystone Corporation
1344 W. 37th St., Chicago, Ill. 60609
Rods & Reels, Lures & Baits, Fishing Accessories

Featherweight Products
3454-58 Ocean View Blvd., Glendale, Calif. 91208
Rods & Reels, Fishing Accessories

Flambeau Plastics Corporation
801 Lynn St., Baraboo, Wis. 53913
Fishing Accessories

Fly Fish Kit Company, Inc.
612 N. Mantua St., Kent, Ohio 44240
Lures & Baits, Fishing Accessories

Fo-Mac, Inc.
Box 6217, Tulsa, Okla. 74106
Lures & Baits, Fishing Accessories

Frabill Manufacturing Company
2018 S. First St., Milwaukee, Wis. 53207
Fishing Accessories

Isaac Franklin Company, Inc.
620 N. Pulaski St., Baltimore, Md. 21217
Fishing Accessories

G & R Industries, Inc.
P.O. Box 18, Purdy, Mo. 65734
Lures & Baits

The Gaines Company
Box 35, Gaines, Pa. 16921
Lures & Baits

Gapen Tackle Company
Highway 10, Big Lake, Minn. 55309
Lures & Baits, Fishing Accessories

The Garcia Corporation
329 Alfred Ave., Teaneck, N.J. 07666
Rods & Reels, Fishing Lines,
Lures & Baits, Fishing Accessories

Generic Systems, Inc.
620 W. Main St., Rockaway, N.J. 07866
Fishing Accessories

Gladding Corporation
South Otselic, N.Y. 13155
Rods & Reels, Fishing Lines,
Lures & Baits, Fishing Accessories

Gladding Corp. (Executive offices)
P.O. Box 260, Syracuse, N.Y. 13201

Great Lakes Products, Inc.
312 Huron Blvd., Marysville, Mich. 48040
Rods & Reels

Gudebrod Bros. Silk Co., Inc.
12 South 12th St., Philadelphia, Pa. 19107
Fishing Lines, Lures & Baits, Fishing Accessories

H & H Development
909-A North Lake, Burbank, Calif. 91504
Lures & Baits

Harrison-Hoge Industries, Inc.
104 Arlington Ave., St. James, N.Y. 11780
Rods & Reels, Fishing Lines,
Lures & Baits, Fishing Accessories

Heb Manufacturing Company
Box 115, Chelsea, Vt. 05038
Fishing Accessories

John J. Hildebrandt Corporation
P.O. Box 50, Logansport, Indiana 46947
Lures & Baits, Fishing Accessories

The Hofschneider Corporation
848 Jay St., Rochester, N.Y. 14611
Lures & Baits

Hopkins Fishing Company
1130 Boissevain Ave., Norfolk, Va. 23507
Lures & Baits

Ideal Fishing Float Company, Inc.
2001 E. Franklin St., Richmond, Va. 23203
Fishing Accessories

Indian Head Sporting Goods, Inc.
Ripley, Miss. 38663
Rods & Reels, Fishing Accessories

Inventors Products Company
541 West 79th St., Minneapolis, Minn. 55420
Fishing Accessories

It, Inc.
693 N. Main St., Torrington, Conn. 06790
Lures & Baits, Fishing Accessories

Jamison Tackle Corporation
3654 W. Montrose Ave., Chicago, Ill. 60618
Lures & Baits, Fishing Accessories

Luhr Jensen & Sons, Inc.
P.O. Box 297, Hood River, Ore. 97031
Lures & Baits

Jeros Tackle Company, Inc.
111 16th St., Brooklyn, N.Y. 11215
Fishing Lines, Lures & Baits, Fishing Accessories

Louis Johnson Company
1547 Old Deerfield Rd., Highland Pk., Ill. 60035
Rods & Reels, Lures & Baits, Fishing Accessories

Johnson Reels Company
1231 Rhine St., Mankato, Minn. 56001
Rods & Reels

Kane Fiber Fisherman
1102 Bull St., Savannah, Ga. 31402
Rods & Reels

Keating Floating Sinker Company
3901 High St., Denver, Colo. 80216
Fishing Accessories

Kebek Industries, Inc.
Box 2381, Knoxville, Tenn. 37901
Fishing Accessories

Keel Guard Lures, Inc.
Box 181, Bowerston, Ohio 44695
Lures & Baits

Kent Sales & Mfg. Company
501 Dodge St., Kent, Ohio 44240
Fishing Accessories

Kinney Company
6448 Fireside Dr., Centerville, Ohio 45459
Fishing Accessories

Knotmaster Industries
Box 23201, San Diego, Calif. 92132
Fishing Accessories

Kodiak Corporation
Box 467, Ironwood, Mich. 49938
Rods & Reels

L & S Bait Company
148 S. Vasseur Ave., Bradley, Ill. 60915
Lures & Baits

La Push Lures, Inc.
P.O. Box 429, Ellensburg, Wash. 98926
Lures & Baits

Lake Products Company
Box 116, Utica, Mich. 48087
Lures & Baits, Fishing Accessories

Lakeland Industries
Isle, Minn. 56342
Fishing Accessories

Land-O-Tackle, Inc.
4650 N. Ronald St., Chicago, Ill. 60631
Fishing Accessories

Lazy Ike Corporation
512 Central Ave., Fort Dodge, Iowa 50501
Lures & Baits, Fishing Accessories

Leben Laboratories, Inc.
Suite 333, 100 Park Ave. Bldg.
Oklahoma City, Okla. 73102
Fishing Accessories

Lenjo Industries, Inc.
208 Market St., Philadelphia, Pa. 19106
Rods & Reels

H. L. Leonard Rod Company
P. O. Box 393, Central Valley, N.Y. 10917
Rods & Reels, Fishing Accessories

Lindy's Manufacturing Corporation
Route 7, Brainerd, Minn. 56401
Lures & Baits, Fishing Accessories

Little Beaver Manufacturing Co.
1244 Lafayette Ave., Terre Haute, Ind. 47804
Lures & Baits

Long Lure Company
P.O. Box 6, Savannah, Tenn. 38372
Lures & Baits, Fishing Accessories

Lure Corporation
20800 Chesley Dr., Farmington, Mich. 48024
Lures & Baits

Mac-Jac Manufacturing Co., Inc.
Box 116, Muskegon, Mich. 49443
Lures & Baits, Fishing Accessories

Major Rod Mfg. Co. (U.S.) Ltd.
Demars Blvd., Tupper Lake, N.Y. 12986
Rods & Reels

Marathon Bait Company
Rt. 2, Hwy. XX, Mosinee, Wis. 54455
Lures & Baits, Fishing Accessories

Marine Metal Products, Inc.
1222 Range Rd., Clearwater, Fla. 33515
Fishing Accessories

Marlynn Lure Company
Box 296, Blue Springs, Mo. 64015
Lures & Baits, Fishing Accessories

Martin Reel Company, Inc.
P.O. Drawer 8, Mohawk, N.Y. 13407
Rods & Reels

Mason Tackle Company
Otisville, Mich. 48463
Fishing Lines, Fishing Accessories

Master Fishing Tackle Corporation
13813 So. Main St., Los Angeles, Calif. 90061
Rods & Reels

Maxwell Manufacturing Company
P.O. Box 649, Vancouver, Wash. 98660
Rods & Reels, Fishing Lines
Lures & Baits, Fishing Accessories

Maybrun Manufacturing Company
2250 Clybourn Ave., Chicago, Ill. 60614
Fishing Accessories

Memphis Lure Company
208 N. Evergreen St., Memphis, Tenn. 38104
Lures & Baits

Men-Go Dot Line Mfg. Company
Box 364, Silver Lake, Wis. 53170
Fishing Accessories

Mercer Tackle Company, Inc.
2416 Gore Blvd., Lawton, Okla. 73501
Lures & Baits, Fishing Accessories

Mid-Lakes Manufacturing Company
3300 Rifle Range Rd., Knoxville, Tenn. 37918
Lures & Baits, Fishing Accessories

Mildrum Manufacturing Company
230 Berlin St., East Berlin, Conn. 06023
Fishing Accessories

Mill Run Products Company
1360 W. 9th St., Cleveland, Ohio 44113
Lures & Baits, Fishing Accessories

Mille Lacs Manufacturing Company
P.O. Box 27, Isle, Minn. 56342
Lures & Baits, Fishing Accessories

Minno-Matic Sales Company
23539 Aviva, Mt. Clemens, Mich. 48043
Fishing Accessories

Mit-Shel Company
640 South Fifth, Quincy, Ill. 62301
Fishing Accessories

National Expert, Inc.
2928 Stevens Ave., South
Minneapolis, Minn. 55408
Lures & Baits

National Fiber Glass Products, Inc.
52 St. Casimir Ave., Yonkers, N.Y. 10701
Rods & Reels

Nature Faker Lures, Inc.
108 Benton St., Windsor, Mo. 65360
Lures & Baits, Fishing Accessories

Nickelure Line, Inc.
1526 S. Dixie Ave., Vero Beach, Fla. 32960
Lures & Baits

Nicki Rig Co.
3409 S. Whitnall Ave., Milwaukee, Wis. 53207
Lures & Baits

Nor-Mor, Inc.
P.O. Box 893, Lewisville, Texas 75067
Lures & Baits, Fishing Accessories

North American Sports Products, Inc.
18320 John R., Detroit, Mich. 48203
Fishing Accessories

Nutron Plastic Company
7975 W. 20th Ave., Hialeah, Fla. 33014
Fishing Accessories

The Oberlin Canteen Company
P.O. Box 208, Oberlin, Ohio 44074
Fishing Accessories

The Orvis Company
Union St., Manchester, Vt. 05254
Rods & Reels, Lures & Baits, Fishing Accessories

P.C. Fishing Tackle, Inc.
2974 Cheyenne Dr., Owensboro, Ky. 42301
Lures & Baits

Padre Island Company, Inc.
Box 5310, San Antonio, Texas 78201
Lures & Baits

Palmer's Manufacturing Company
R.D. #1—P.O. Box 222, West Newton, Pa. 15089
Fishing Accessories

Parrish Industries
1312 W. Lee St., Greensboro, N.C. 27403
Lures & Baits, Fishing Accessories

E. H. Peckinpaugh Company
P.O. Box 15044, Baton Rouge, La. 70815
Lures & Baits

Pedigo Pork Rind Co., Inc.
500 W. 10th St., Bowling Green, Ky. 42101
Lures & Baits

Penn Dart Lure & Equipment Co., Inc.
5223 E. Simpson Ferry Rd.
Mechanicsburg, Pa. 17055
Lures & Baits

Penn Fishing Tackle Mfg. Company
3028 W. Hunting Park Ave.
Philadelphia, Pa. 19132
Rods & Reels

J. F. Pepper Company
Box 445, Rome, N.Y. 13440
Fishing Accessories

Pequea Fishing Tackle, Inc.
19 Miller St., Strasburg, Pa. 17579
Rods & Reels, Lures & Baits, Fishing Accessories

Perfection Tip Company
3020 E. 43rd Ave., Denver, Colo. 80216
Fishing Accessories

Peterson Manufacturing Company
P.O. Box 3709, Sarasota, Fla. 33578
Fishing Accessories

Phillips Fly & Tackle Company
P.O. Box 188, Alexandria, Pa. 16611
Lures & Baits, Fishing Accessories

Phillipson Rod Company
2705 High St., Denver, Colo. 80205
Rods & Reels

Plano Molding Company
P.O. Box 189, Plano, Ill. 60545
Fishing Accessories

Plas/Steel Products, Inc.
P.O. Box 176, Walkerton, Indiana 46574
Rods & Reels

Plastilite Corporation
Box 12235, Omaha, Neb. 68112
Fishing Accessories

Play-mor Products, Inc.
P.O. Drawer 740, Cape Girardeau, Mo. 63701
Rods & Reels, Lures & Baits, Fishing Accessories

Point Jude Lures, Inc.
451 Main St., East Greenwich, R.I. 02818
Lures & Baits

Eddie Pope & Company, Inc.
25572 Stanford Ave., Valencia, Calif. 91355
Lures & Baits, Fishing Accessories

Praid, Ltd.
1121 University Blvd., Silver Spring, Md. 20902
Lures & Baits

REB Manufacturing Company
P.O. Box 179, Pontiac, Mich. 48056
Lures & Baits

Recreational Development, Inc.
Box 4029, Tallahassee, Fla. 32303
Rods & Reels, Lures & Baits

Reel-Assist Corporation
430 E. First St., Casper, Wyo. 82601
Fishing Accessories

Reel Power Equipment, Inc.
3530 First Avenue, North
St. Petersburg, Fla. 33713
Rods & Reels, Lures & Baits

Ribbon Lure Company
53 Leitch Ave., Skaneateles, N.Y. 13152
Lures & Baits

The Don Rich Company
372 Franklin Ave., Redlands, Calif. 92373
Lures & Baits

Riley Company
Box 1108, Grand Rapids, Mich. 49501
Fishing Accessories

Riviera Die & Tool Mfg. Company
2819 West 28th St., Grand Rapids, Mich. 49509
Rods & Reels, Fishing Accessories

Robfin Industries
7000 E. Camelback Rd., Suite 20
Scottsdale, Ariz. 85251
Lures & Baits

Romeek Devices, Ltd.
3104 Tyre Neck Rd., Portsmouth, Va. 23703
Fishing Accessories

RTC Industries, Inc.
920 W. Cullerton St., Chicago, Ill. 60608
Fishing Accessories

J. A. Runge Company
415 "A" St., Seminole, Okla. 74868
Fishing Accessories

St. Croix Corporation
9909 South Shore Dr., Minneapolis, Minn. 55441
Rods & Reels

Sampo, Inc.
North St., Barneveld, N.Y. 13304
Lures & Baits, Fishing Accessories

Sanford's Float-a-Lite Kit, Inc.
1215 S. Central Ave., Fairborn, Ohio 45324
Fishing Accessories

Santee Lure & Tackle Company, Inc.
730 East Trade St., Charlotte, N.C. 28202
Lures & Baits, Fishing Accessories

Scientific Anglers, Inc.
Box 2001, Midland, Mich. 48640
Rods & Reels, Fishing Lines

Seneca Tackle Company
P.O. Box 2841, Providence, R.I. 02907
Lures & Baits

Sevenstrand Tackle Mfg. Company
14799 Chestnut St., Westminster, Cailf. 92683
Rods & Reels, Fishing Lines,
Lures & Baits, Fishing Accessories

Shakespeare Company
241 E. Kalamazoo Ave., Kalamazoo, Mich. 49001
Rods & Reels, Fishing Lines,
Lures & Baits, Fishing Accessories

Shakespeare Co. (Executive Offices)
P.O. Box 246, Columbia, S.C. 29202

Shellee Industries, Inc.
2516 Atlantic Ave., Brooklyn, N.Y. 11207
Fishing Accessories

Siberian Salmon Egg Company
4660 E. Marginal Way South
Seattle, Wash. 98134
Lures & Baits

Space Age Plastics
P.O. Box 9188, Knoxville, Tenn. 37920
Fishing Accessories

Sportsman's Products, Inc.
841 E. 38th St., Marion, Indiana 46952
Lures & Baits

Steffey Manufacturing Company
404 Martin Dr., Irwin, Pa. 15642
Lures & Baits

Stembridge Products, Inc.
Box 90756, East Point, Ga. 30344
Lures & Baits, Fishing Accessories

Still Fish Reel Company
4006 Vermaas Ave., Toledo, Ohio 43612
Rods & Reels

Stratton & Terstegge Company
1520 Rowan St., Louisville, Ky. 40201
Fishing Accessories

Strike Master, Inc.
411 N. Washington Ave.
Minneapolis, Minn. 55401
Lures & Baits, Fishing Accessories

Subria Corporation
P.O. Box 113, Montclair, N.J. 07042
Lures & Baits, Fishing Accessories

Sunset Line & Twine Company
Box 691, Petaluma, Calif. 94952
Fishing Lines, Fishing Accessories

Symonds & Company
1414 S. Michigan Ave., Chicago, Ill. 60605
Fishing Accessories

T.M.T., Inc.
P.O. Box 92, Birmingham, Mich. 48012
Rods & Reels, Fishing Accessories

Tack-L-Tyers
939 Chicago Ave., Evanston, Ill. 60202
Lures & Baits, Fishing Accessories

Thompson Fishing Tackle Co., Inc.
P.O. Box 275, Knoxville, Tenn. 37901
Lures & Baits

Tiki Lures, Inc.
1805 E. Eleven Mile Rd.
Madison Heights, Mich. 48071
Lures & Baits

Titan Corporation
3620 N. Central, Indianapolis, Ind. 46205
Lures & Baits

Tri Mi Lures, Inc.
711 East 16th St., Cheyenne, Wyo. 82001
Lures & Baits, Fishing Accessories

Trophy Products
9712 Old Katy Rd., Houston, Texas 77055
Fishing Accessories

True Temper Corporation American Tackle Division
1623 Euclid Ave., Cleveland, Ohio 44115
Rods & Reels, Fishing Accessories

U.S. Line Company
22 Main St., Westfield, Mass. 01085
Fishing Lines

Uncle Josh Bait Company
P.O. Box 130, Fort Atkinson, Wis. 53538
Lures & Baits

Union Manufacturing, Inc.
54 Church St., LeRoy, N.Y. 14482
Fishing Accessories

Universal Freeze Dried Products, Ltd.
41 Decker St., Copaigue, N.Y. 11726
Lures & Baits

Vari-Lure, Inc.
1605 Cedar Ridge, N.E.
Albuquerque, N.M. 87112
Fishing Accessories

Varmac Manufacturing, Inc.
4201 Redwood Ave., Los Angeles, Calif. 90066
Fishing Accessories

Vlchek Plastics Company
P.O. Box 97, Middlefield, Ohio 44062
Fishing Accessories

Walton Products, Inc.
P.O. Box 456, Atlantic, Iowa 50022
Fishing Accessories

Water Gremlin Company
4370 Otter Lake Rd.
White Bear Lake, Minn. 55110
Fishing Accessories

Weber Tackle Company
1039 Ellis St., Stevens Point, Wis. 54481
Rods & Reels, Fishing Lines,
Lures & Baits, Fishing Accessories

Erwin Weller Company
2105 Clark St., Sioux City, Iowa 51104
Lures & Baits, Fishing Accessories

Western Cutlery Company
5311 Western Ave., Boulder, Colo. 80302
Fishing Accessories

Whale Enterprises, Inc.
204 Dailey St., Piedmont, Ala. 36272
Fishing Accessories

Wood Manufacturing Company
Box 486, Conway, Ark. 72032
Lures & Baits

Woodstock Line Company
83 Canal St., Putnam, Conn. 06260
Fishing Lines

Woodstream Corporation
P.O. Box 327, Lititz, Pa. 17543
Rods & Reels, Fishing Lines,
Lures & Baits, Fishing Accessories

The Worth Company
P.O. Box 88, Stevens Point, Wis. 54481
Lures & Baits, Fishing Accessories

Wright & McGill Company
Box 16011, Denver, Colo. 80216
Rods & Reels, Fishing Lines,
Lures & Baits, Fishing Accessories

Yakima Bait Company
Box 310, Granger, Wash. 98932
Lures & Baits, Fishing Accessories

Zebco Division—Brunswick Corp.
Box 270, Tulsa, Okla. 74115
Rods & Reels, Lures & Baits, Fishing Accessories